Commemorative Events

Commemorative events emphasise remembering. They are held on the anniversaries of significant past events, either annually or after significant time periods. Commemorative events provide fascinating insight into how societies see themselves, their heritage and their identity. These events however carry high propensity for controversy as memory and identity are highly subjective and other stakeholders hold different views of what should be commemorated and why.

This is the first book to provide an in-depth critical examination of commemorative events, particularly what they mean to societies and how they are used by governments as well as the impacts on other stakeholders. The book fully explores these issues by reviewing all the major types of commemorative events, including nationhood or independence, wars, battles, famous people and cultural milestones from varying geographical regions and stakeholder perspectives. By doing so the book furthers understanding of these types of events in society as well as knowledge of social and political uses and impacts of events.

This thought provoking volume will be valuable reading for students, researchers and academics interested in events.

Warwick Frost is an Associate Professor and Co-ordinator of the Events Program at La Trobe University, Australia.

Jennifer Laing is a Senior Lecturer in the Department of Marketing and Tourism and Hospitality at La Trobe University, Australia.

Routledge Advances in Event Research Series

Edited by Warwick Frost, School of Marketing and Tourism and Hospitality, La Trobe University, Australia

Jennifer Laing, School of Marketing and Tourism and Hospitality, La Trobe University, Australia

Events, Society and Sustainability
Edited by Tomas Pernecky and
Michael Lück

Exploring the Social Impacts of Events
Edited by Greg Richards, Marisa de Bito
and Linda Wilks

Commemorative Events
Memories, identities, conflict
Warwick Frost and Jennifer Laing

Forthcoming:

Power, Politics and International Events
Edited by Udo Merkel

Event Audiences and Expectations
Jo Mackellar

Event Portfolio Planning and Management
A holistic approach
Vassilios Ziakas

Fashion, Design and Events
Edited by Kim Williams,
Jennifer Laing and Warwick Frost

Conferences and Conventions
A research perspective
Judith Mair

Commemorative Events
Memory, identities, conflict

Warwick Frost and Jennifer Laing

Routledge
Taylor & Francis Group

LONDON AND NEW YORK

First published 2013
by Routledge
2 Park Square, Milton Park, Abingdon, Oxon OX14 4RN

Simultaneously published in the USA and Canada
by Routledge
711 Third Avenue, New York, NY 10017

Routledge is an imprint of the Taylor & Francis Group, an informa business

British Library Cataloguing in Publication Data
A catalogue record for this book is available from the British Library

Library of Congress Cataloging in Publication Data
Frost, Warwick.
Commemorative events : memory, identities, conflict / Warwick Frost and
Jennifer Laing. – 1st ed.
    p. cm.
Includes bibliographical references and index.
1. Special events. 2. Anniversaries. 3. Memorials. I. Laing, Jennifer.
II. Title.
GT3405.F76 2013
394.2–dc23   2012035801

ISBN: 978-0-415-69060-7 (hbk)
ISBN: 978-0-203-37461-0 (ebk)

Typeset in Times New Roman
by HWA Text and Data Management, London

Printed and bound by CPI Group (UK) Ltd, Croydon, CR0 4YY

For Graeme Laing

Contents

List of figures   viii
List of tables   ix

1 Understanding commemorative events   1

2 Imagining national identities   15

3 Dark, disturbing and difficult commemorative events   31

4 The tourism paradox   46

5 It happened at the world's fair   62

6 The re-enactors' world   78

7 A day at Battle   97

8 Cultural commemorations   108

9 Commercial commemorations   124

10 The legacy of commemorative events   141

11 Why we need commemorative events   159

References   171
Index   184

Figures

1.1	Bonfire Society banner, Hastings	4
1.2	Bonfire Night, 2011 in Hastings	5
2.1	Soldiers on parade on Bastille Day 2010, in Bordeaux	17
2.2	Delhi Gate, India, site of a parade and ceremony on Republic Day	19
2.3	Eiffel Tower, Paris	23
3.1	Grave of Elvis Presley at Gracelands, Memphis	33
4.1	Titanic inflatable slide at the Yakkerboo Festival in Pakenham, Australia	59
5.1	Interpretive panel at Eugene Mercier, showing the giant barrel en route to the 1889 Exhibition	68
5.2	Interpretive panel at Eugene Mercier, showing restoration of the giant barrel for its centenary and the bicentenary of the French Revolution	68
6.1	Re-enactors at the Monster Meeting, 2010	83
6.2	Meeting the re-enactor playing Banjo Paterson at the Man from Snowy River Festival	85
7.1	Mock battles at the re-enactment of the Battle of Hastings, 2011	102
7.2	Meeting the re-enactors at the medieval encampment, 2011	104
8.1	Charles Dickens Museum, London	117
9.1	Promotional poster in London for the fiftieth anniversary of the E-type Jag	135
9.2	Perrier-Jouët headquarters in Épernay, France	138
10.1	Hand-made sign placed in the Place de l'Alma, Paris	145
10.2	Diana Memorial Fountain, Kensington Gardens	148
10.3	Louvre Pyramid in Paris	150
10.4	Replica of the *Endeavour* docked in Melbourne	153

Tables

1.1	Studies of commemorative events	13
2.1	Examples of national days	18
2.2	Significant anniversaries of nationhood	23
2.3	Historical commemorative events contributing to national identity	25
4.1	Examples of rural commemorative festivals with a strong tourism focus	54
4.2	Film and television productions for the centenary of the sinking of the *Titanic*, 2012	61
5.1	Commemorative exhibitions	64
5.2	Cancelled commemorative exhibitions	66
11.1	Selected commemorative events in 2011 and 2012	162

1 Understanding commemorative events

To the Dolphin, where he and I and Captain Cocke sat late and drank much, seeing the boys in the streets flying their crackers, this day being kept all the day very strictly in the City.

(Diary of Samuel Pepys, 5 November 1661, www.pepysdiary.com)

Some events are specifically staged so that society may remember and reflect upon past occurrences and their relationship to today. These commemorative events are held on anniversary dates, either annually, or after significant time periods, such as 50 or 100. In form and organisation, they usually share similarities with a wide range of other types of planned events and festivals. However, it is this focus on remembering which distinguishes commemorative events.

It is important from the beginning to understand that remembering is a process. There is a subtle difference between the related concepts of memory and remembering. A memory is something that we have (or have lost or never had). Our memories may be individual or shared amongst communities, groups, even nations. Remembering is a process which includes the construction and retention of that memory. The process may incorporate solemn reflection, or celebration, or both. It may invoke sadness, happiness, pride, humility, anger or compassion. It may be an individual and solitary process, or one that is shared with others.

Commemorative events are typically planned with intentions of affirming and reinforcing memories that provide a sense of heritage and identity. Heritage is what we value and wish to preserve for future generations. The related concept of identity refers to what we perceive as defining and distinguishing us, including what makes us similar to some, but also distinct from others. Accordingly, the objectives of organisers and stakeholders for commemorative events tend to be couched in terms of the positives that will be achieved in helping society to remember and better understand its heritage and have a greater sense of its identity. However, not all stakeholders will agree on what heritage and identity is important, appropriate, or worthy of commemoration. The meanings of events are often contested and for commemorative events the level of contestation may be very high and difficult to resolve. This is one of our key themes throughout this book.

The process of remembering benefits from having a focal point, a symbol that draws attention and triggers the desire for ritual and ceremony. For commemorative events, a date provides that centrepiece (Connerton 1989); arguably a talisman imbued with special transforming power. For annual commemorations that date is often widely known, for example 4 July *is* Independence Day in the USA. It commemorates the signing of the Declaration of Independence in 1776, but is far more than just remembering that single historical incident. For Americans, it is a date and a commemorative event that they see as defining themselves and their national spirit.

For anniversary commemorative events, the date provides a form of authenticity and justifies the organisation of the event. Focussing on the date in these cases makes a strong statement that it is a special day when something important happened in the past and is *worthy* of being remembered in the present.

Emphasising a key date and a significant number of years fits well with the way popular media are constructed. It provides an easily digested news event, a minute or two in the nightly news or a good photo in a newspaper. This suitability makes it easier to gain important media coverage. The media may even initiate or be co-opted into the commemorative event. For example, in 1936 the French writer Jean Cocteau commemorated the centenary of the birth of Jules Verne by re-enacting the journey which is the subject of Verne's most famous novel, *Around the World in Eighty Days*. Cocteau secured funding from the Paris newspaper *Paris Soir* for this event. In return, he provided regular articles on his progress (Cocteau, 1936). In this case, his re-enactment could have been done at any time, but the media interest and funding was only forthcoming as it was tied to the special (one-hundredth) anniversary of Verne. Some organisations view commemorative events and the attendant media publicity as the best opportunity for fund-raising appeals. For example, the Talyllyn Heritage Railway in Wales was established in 1951 and is argued to be the oldest volunteer-run steam train in the world. It used its fiftieth (in 2001) and sixtieth (in 2011) anniversaries to successfully run appeals for major capital works.

Generally, more attention is given to anniversaries of certain key numbers. For example, a hundredth anniversary is more important than a ninetieth or ninety-ninth. Years in groups of tens and hundreds capture our imagination, a practice that dates back to the Romans and the ways they organised numbers (Feeney, 2008). Shorter anniversaries, for example a twentieth, have significance if they are of events that are widely remembered and valued. Such commemorative events typically involve the still living participants of the original incident. Accordingly, they are expressions of *personal memory*. In contrast, centenaries and longer commemorations cannot utilise the actual memories of participants. Instead, they draw on the construction or imagination of *collective* or *social memories* to determine their importance and meanings (Anderson 1983; Lane Fox 2009).

In most cases, we count off anniversaries in blocks of continuous years – 50, 100, 200 and so on. There are exceptions. The Tour de France, for example, was first held in 1903 and its hundredth anniversary was celebrated in 2003. However, this sporting event has not taken place every year. There have been breaks for both world wars. As a result, the 2013 Tour de France will be commemorated as the hundredth instance of its staging.

In summary, commemorative events combine two key features: remembering something important and a special date. It is the combination of these two features which distinguishes them from other types of events. This combination is well illustrated by the case of Guy Fawkes Night, held annually in England.

Guy Fawkes Night

This event, also known as Bonfire Night, commemorates the foiling of the Gunpowder Plot. On 5 November 1605 a group of conspirators tried to blow up the Houses of Parliament in London. They hoped the explosion would kill King James I and his government, paving the way for the restoration of a Catholic monarch. Guy Fawkes had the job of lighting the fuse and is popularly identified as the hapless ringleader. The plot was discovered and all concerned tried and executed.

Introduced as an official holiday, Guy Fawkes Night reinforced the legitimacy of a Protestant regime while simultaneously denigrating the alternative of a return to Catholicism. As has happened before and since, the ruling authorities absorbed and changed the meanings of traditional events to suit their purposes:

> An unequivocally Protestant celebration on 5 November therefore provided a handy replacement for what was now regarded as a redundant Catholic holy day, and also filled All Saints' Day's role as a festival marking the onset of winter, with celebratory bonfires defying the November darkness just as the holy candles had done. In modern parlance, Bonfire Night had replaced Hallowe'een.
>
> (Sharpe 2005: 85)

Guy Fawkes Night has been commemorated annually for over 400 years. It is characterised by the lighting of bonfires and fireworks. This is a good example of what Falassi (1987) termed *ritual inversion*, re-creating the explosion and destruction which the attendees are celebrating did *not* occur. Furthermore, it is curiously named after the villain of the piece. It is a traditional grassroots event, with activities organised by local bonfire societies (see Figure 1.1) in towns and villages, rather than the national government. Even today, it remains very popular. In 2011, for example, we attended a Guy Fawkes Night at Hastings in south-east England, which attracted over 20,000 people (see Figure 1.2. and Chapter 7).

Part of the ritual of Guy Fawkes Night is the communal recital of the traditional rhyme:

> Remember, Remember, the Fifth of November
> Gunpowder Treason and Plot
> I Know of No Reason
> Why the Gunpowder Treason
> Should Ever be Forgot

Figure 1.1 Bonfire Society banner, Hastings. Photo by J. Laing.

This chanting of this simple rhyme emphasises the key elements of all commemorative events. It is an exhortation for the community to remember and this is reinforced through the shared community recital of a rhyme. It begins with the instruction to remember and ends with the reminder that the community must never forget. Coming straight after the instruction to remember, is the exact date to commemorate. That November rhymes with remember reinforces this. Repeated twice is what is being remembered – the Gunpowder Plot is treason – and this is reinforced with the rhyme with reason.

Guy Fawkes Night also illustrates three common features of commemorative events. First, beyond the spectacle of bonfires and fireworks, its underlying message is sectarian and divisive. It is a Protestant event, commemorating the defeat of an attempt to overthrow not just the government but the state religion. It reinforces an identity which values loyalty to the state and one's religion. That identity is also defined in terms of anti-Catholicism and adherents of that faith are both excluded and denigrated. This religious hatred was made especially tangible in the seventeenth through to nineteenth centuries, with the effigy of the Pope being burnt and local variants on chanted rhymes identifying Catholics as treasonous (Sharpe 2005). Commemorative events are often distinguished by such conflict or dissonance between stakeholders and we examine this in depth in Chapters 2 and 3.

Second, Guy Fawkes Night follows a strong ritual pattern based on tradition and repetition. The bonfire, the fireworks, the burning of an effigy of Guy Fawkes and the communal chanting are all integral to the event. The pattern of ceremonies is repeated year after year. Falassi (1987) argues that most events follow a similar

Figure 1.2 Bonfire Night, 2011 in Hastings. Photo by J. Laing.

ritual structure and this is very apparent in commemorative events. The ritual of inversion is particularly apparent at Guy Fawkes Night.

Third, while the rituals are firmly in place, their social meanings may change over time. In England, Guy Fawkes Night has remained popular, though religious intolerance has decreased markedly. Instead, it is embraced as a signifier of local identity and traditions. Even though the emphasis is now on spectacle rather than its original meaning, there are relics of popular protest. The Guy burnt in effigy is often modelled on contemporary politicians, rather than the Pope. At the 2011 Hastings Guy Fawkes Night, 'Hoodies' were symbolically burnt, representing community anger at those held responsible earlier that year for riots and the looting of shops.

Outside England, Guy Fawkes Night is celebrated in former colonies. In Australia during the 1950s and 1960s, Guy Fawkes Night was particularly popular, reflecting religious divisions within society. In the 1970s and 1980s, it was celebrated less, partly as it was too sectarian for modern societies and partly due to the limitations on the sale of fireworks. In the 1990s, it was revived somewhat, catering for baby-boomer nostalgia. However, nowadays it seems to have disappeared again, replaced by the increasingly popular Halloween. In North America, it survives in various towns along the Atlantic coast, such as Brigus in Newfoundland (Schwoeffermann 1994).

Most strangely, in recent years Guy Fawkes has been embraced by Generations Y and Z. He features strongly as a meme in computer chat rooms and other social media. He has starred as the avenging hero in graphic novels, movies (*V for Vendetta*) and computer games (*Fallout 3*). At a wide range of recent protest events, the Guy Fawkes mask is now the costume of choice for many young activists. Nor is the new use of Guy Fawkes confined to England. The masked protesters have featured in media reports of demonstrations in the USA, Germany, France, Greece and Russia. This new cyber Guy Fawkes is stripped of his sectarian and religious meanings. He is now reimagined as a lone voice of justice, acting against oppressive authority, akin to the fictional Zorro or Batman. Perhaps surprisingly, part of his new appeal is that historically he was a failure. His new symbolism is that he *tried* to change society.

Finally, it is worth noting that Guy Fawkes Night has limited tourism engagement. It is staged by local communities purely for their own purposes. It is not commercial, nor is it even associated with a particular place. Many commemorative events are similar in having little or no objective of encouraging tourism. In contrast, others are staged with that as a major purpose. This varying nexus between tourism and commemorative events is explored in Chapter 4.

A typology of commemorative events

A wide variety of events have these common characteristics of a primary objective of remembering and utilising a significant date or year as a focal point. At this stage, it is worth considering a range of examples and trying to distinguish patterns and categories. In our work on the strategic management of events (Frost and Laing 2011), we proposed a basic typology for commemorative events. Below is an extended version, recognising a wider range of types:

National days and anniversaries. These include dates commemorating independence, republics and founding of countries. For the USA it is 4 July commemorating the Declaration of Independence in 1776. India commemorates its 1947 Declaration of Independence on 15 August. For Singapore, National Day on 9 August marks its separation from Malaysia in 1965. In France, the key day is Bastille Day on 14 July, which commemorates the French Revolution in 1789. England has no specific national day and recent consideration of creating one has led to widespread criticism and derision.

Major anniversaries of independence or nationhood. The USA staged a major series of commemorative events for both the centenary of the Declaration of Independence (1876) and the bicentenary (1976). Australia staged a bicentenary in 1988 – commemorating the first European settlement – and a Centenary of Federation in 2001. Italy celebrated the hundred and fiftieth anniversary of its reunification or *Risorgimento* in 2011.

Foundation days. Similar to national days and commemorations of nationhood, these focus on the foundation of cities. Rome has a festival called the Natale di Roma, which celebrates that the city was founded on 2 April, 753 BC. However, that festival only dates back to the first century BC. For Constantinople – the 'New Rome' – there was a formal inauguration as the capital on 11 May 330 AD. This subsequently became celebrated annually as its foundation day. More recently, Dublin staged a major commemoration of its thousandth anniversary in 1988 and Amsterdam its seven-hundredth anniversary in 1975.

Religious anniversaries. Many religious festivals have a commemorative element. These may be attached to symbolic rather than precise dates, as in the cases of Christmas and Easter. Each saint has a day devoted to their festival. Some are linked with local, regional or national identity, as in the case of St Patrick's Day (17 March) celebrated both in Ireland and by the Irish diaspora around the world. In Pamplona (Spain) the festival of San Fermin (6–14 July) has become famous for its running of the bulls, which attracts large numbers of tourists. Important dates in religious history may be the subject of commemorative events. For example, in 1996, Reims in France commemorated the one-thousand-five-hundredth anniversary of King Clovis converting to Christianity. Marked with a papal visit to its cathedral, this commemorative event attracted 200,000 people.

Protest or oppositional events. In contrast to official commemorations, some events are staged on significant dates to oppose or protest against government policies and have the specific objectives of changing government policy. Examples include Hiroshima Day (6 August) and Australia's Sorry Day (26 May), which remembers the 'Stolen Generation' of indigenous children (the date commemorated is of the release of the *Report of the National Inquiry into the Separation of Aboriginal and Torres Strait Islander Children from their Families*).

War remembrance days. Many countries observe Armistice or Remembrance Day on 11 November, commemorating the end of World War One in 1918. Australia and New Zealand stage ANZAC (Australia and New Zealand Army Corps) Day on 25 April, the date when troops landed at Gallipoli (Turkey) in 1915.

Battles. A number of major battles are commemorated by re-enactment events, sometimes involving thousands of people dressed in period costumes. Examples include the battles of Hastings (England 1066), Waterloo (Belgium 1815), Gettysburg (USA 1864) and Little Bighorn (USA 1876). In 1961, the centenary re-enactment of the Battle of Bull Run attracted 25,000 uniformed participants and 50,000 spectators (Elliott 2007). It is expected that re-enactment events for the hundred and fiftieth anniversary of the American Civil War, which will be staged between 2011 and 2015, will attract much greater numbers than this.

Other historical events. A wide variety of commemorations are staged, often with historical re-enactments. In 1998, California commemorated the hundred and fiftieth (sesquicentenary) of the discovery of gold, as Australia also did in 2001 (Frost 2001). The UFO Festival at Roswell started with a fiftieth anniversary in 1997, which was so successful it became an annual event (Paradis 2002).

Cultural anniversaries. Denmark marked the bicentenary of writer Hans Christian Andersen in 2005 (Liburd 2008). 2009 was both the two-hundredth anniversary of the birth of Charles Darwin and the sesquicentenary of the publication of his *On the Origin of Species*. Commemoration events included museum exhibitions, competitions, re-enactments and conferences. In 2009, Hobart (Australia) staged a festival to commemorate the hundredth anniversary of the birth of Errol Flynn, who achieved fame as an action star in Hollywood, playing Robin Hood and the pirate Captain Blood. Dublin (Ireland) hosts an event called Bloomsday on 16 June each year, this being the day on which the

James Joyce novel *Ulysses* is set. In 2007, events were staged to mark the thirtieth anniversary of the death of Elvis Presley, the centenaries of the births of actors John Wayne and Gene Autry and the fortieth anniversary of the release of the Beatles' *Sergeant Pepper's Lonely Hearts Club Band*.

Buildings and constructions. This is a form of cultural anniversary, specifically linked to the construction or completion of buildings and other structures. Recent examples are the three-hundredth anniversary of the completion of St Paul's Cathedral in London (2011), the hundredth anniversary of the building and the launching of the *Titanic* in Belfast (2011–2), the eight-hundredth anniversary of the beginning of the construction of Reims Cathedral in France (2012) and the seventy-fifth anniversary of the construction of the Golden Gate Bridge in San Francisco (2012).

Corporate and product anniversaries. Businesses are increasingly using anniversaries to promote themselves, anchor marketing campaigns and relaunch products. Examples include the fortieth anniversary relaunch of *Sergeant Pepper's Lonely Hearts Club Band* (2007) and the 1998 cinema re-release of the film *Grease* to mark its twentieth anniversary. In 2009, there were celebrations to mark the fiftieth birthday of the Barbie doll and in 2007, Kraft staged the fiftieth anniversary of its iconic Vegemite advertisement and jingle.

The structure of commemorative events

A diverse range of activities may be included in these commemorative events. Some are directly connected to the ceremonial process of remembering, honouring and reflecting upon the past. These include speeches, parades, performances, the dedication of monuments and statues, religious ceremonies, flag raisings, street parties and dinners. Two activities which have become particularly associated with commemorative events are major trade exhibitions (often tied to demonstrating national achievement and progress) and historic re-enactments. These are considered in detail in Chapters 5, 6 and 7.

While commemorative events may have some distinct features, in many ways they are quite similar to other festivals and events. In organisational structure, they typically follow a common events model of an organising committee of stakeholders who develop a concept and who then hire an event organiser to stage the event (Frost and Laing 2011). Logistically, the elements that comprise the staging of a solemn remembrance ceremony are no different from that of a celebratory and joyful party. Both may require the construction of a stage and provision of appropriate audio technology. Both may require ticketing, security, parking, waste disposal and so on. Furthermore, quite serious commemorative events may include elements that are celebratory and could easily be transferred to a completely different type of event. It is notable that there is a trend for commemorative events to include component events including concerts, art exhibitions, dinners and even fashion shows. All of these, for example, were included in the seventieth anniversary of the bombing of Darwin, staged in 2012 (see Chapter 11).

Authenticity and contestation

As they are based on the past, organising commemorative events requires close attention to historical detail. This might seem a simple matter of checking the history books. However, history is not that simple. There may be disputes over what happened in the past, even over when it exactly happened. In using the past to satisfy present goals, organisers may find that their interpretation of history is contested by other stakeholders who hold a different view. The following examples illustrate these arguments over the authenticity of commemorative events.

In 1988, England commemorated the four-hundredth anniversary of the defeat of the Spanish Armada in 1588. As the Spanish invasion fleet had sailed up the English Channel, a series of beacons was lit along the English coast to warn of their approach. As part of the commemoration, the National Trust organised a spectacular re-enactment of the lighting of these fires, entitled 'Fire over England'. This was staged on 19 July 1988, as the fires were lit on 19 July 1588. However, dates in 1988 follow the Gregorian calendar, whereas 1588 dates are based on the older Julian calendar. Britain only adopted the Gregorian calendar in 1752. The fires were actually lit on 29 July 1588 according to the modern dating system. If the organisers wanted to be absolutely historically exact, their re-enactment needed to be ten days later (Hewison 1988). Of course, some dates have particular resonance and we may not wish to adjust them. Guy Fawkes Day, for example, is the fifth of November, not the fifteenth of November. Nonetheless, key anniversaries, such as the birth of George Washington and the Battle of the Boyne have been altered in accordance with the new calendar (Feeney, 2008).

Coincidentally, 1988 also saw the commemoration of the thousandth anniversary of the founding of Dublin in Ireland. Commemorative events based on such a large timescale are very rare. It is also rare to have anniversaries of the founding of cities, as we usually do not know exactly when they were established. Most examples of foundation days are for nineteenth-century cities in North America and Australia, where there are clearer historical records. For example, Chicago commemorates 1832 as its founding and Melbourne 1834. In the case of Dublin's anniversary, organisers chose 988 as there were documents demonstrating that Dublin existed by that date. However, it was also clear that a settlement had existed at Dublin for at least 100 years earlier. In this case, the organisers made a strategic decision to choose one date, in full awareness that they might attract some debate and criticism over its veracity. Similarly, Amsterdam chose to stage its seven-hundredth anniversary in 1975. The rationale was that the first official document referring to the city was from 1275. However, as with Dublin, there were other sources indicating its existence well before this.

A similar issue underlies the 2012 three-hundred-and-fiftieth anniversary of Punch and Judy. Who created these beloved puppet characters is not known. What is known is that there is a reference in the Diary of Samuel Pepys to him seeing them perform at Covent Garden in London on 9 May 1662. Accordingly, this has been taken as the date of their 'birth' and the three-hundred-and-fiftieth anniversary was staged in 2012. Of course, it is always possible that an earlier date may be uncovered in the future.

Getting dates right is one thing, what about if there are doubts over whether the event being commemorated ever actually occurred? On the evening of 19 September 1870, a group of adventurers sat around a campfire in the Yellowstone region of western USA. In the last few days they had encountered an impressive array of waterfalls, canyons, thermal springs and geysers. Some people around the campfire suggested they could make their fortune by buying the land and developing it for tourism. One of them, a young lawyer named Cornelius Hedges, introduced a quite different idea, that 'there ought to be no private ownership of any portion of that region, but that the whole of it ought to be set apart as a great National Park' (Langford 1905: 117–118). The others agreed and successfully lobbied for the creation of the world's first national park (Frost and Hall 2009).

Between 1957 and 1964, the US National Parks Service staged a re-enactment of this campfire discussion each 19 September. It was staged at the exact location within Yellowstone National Park, with actors in costume and character, following a script based on the 1905 account of the expedition by one of the adventurers, Nathaniel Langford (Schullery and Whittlesey 2003). While this was very popular with tourists, some staff of the National Parks Service began to question its authenticity. Clearly some sort of discussion had taken place somewhere, for some of the group did lead the campaign for Yellowstone's protection. However, there were doubts about the accuracy of Langford's version, especially as it was published 35 years later (see Schullery and Whittlesey 2003 and Frost and Hall 2009 for a more detailed debate). Accordingly, as the authorities felt they could not justify the truthfulness of the re-enactment, after 1964 it was decided not to stage it again.

While historical accuracy throws up some intriguing cases, most commemorative events get it right enough to satisfy the great majority. The main sources of controversy and contestation are differences over the meaning of what is being remembered. Guy Fawkes Night has already been referred to and two more introductory cases are useful to illustrate this problem.

In 1988, Australia commemorated its bicentenary, based on the landing of the First Fleet of European settlers in 1788. Different stakeholder groups took up different positions as to what should be remembered and reflected upon. Many felt there was a need to recognise that this was essentially an invasion, resulting in the dispossession and poor treatment of indigenous Australians. Others, particularly those who could trace their ancestry back to the First Fleet, wanted an emphasis on historical re-enactments.

The Australian government established the Australian Bicentennial Authority to coordinate the event. That body was concerned that the commemorations could be ruined by protest and controversy. Their strategic position to what they perceived as a potential problem was to strip the event of its historical elements. While there was a spectacular re-creation of the voyage (the tall ships), there was no official focus or re-enactment on the landing of that First Fleet. Ironically, only indigenous protesters re-created the arrival of the Europeans. Instead the authorities created the theme of 'Celebration of the Nation', with the marketing exhorting people that this was the opportunity for a great, once in a lifetime, birthday party.

The resulting event was widely viewed as bland, unfocussed and unsatisfying (Bennett *et al.* 1992; Frost and Laing 2011; Spillman 1997; White 2004). Many stakeholder groups were disappointed that all meaning had been stripped from this important commemoration. The bicentenary powerfully illustrated that sometimes commemorative events could be constructed to forget or ignore, as well as remember. In the 1990s, governments and the tourism and events sectors saw the bicentenary as a byword for excessive expenditure with little purpose and the spectre of this wastage hung over the funding requests of subsequent commemorative events. However, out of the disaster came change. The organisers of the Sydney Olympics in 2000 were very careful not to make the same mistakes. In their opening ceremony they emphasised the issues of White/indigenous interactions, stimulating a great deal of discussion and reflection upon Australian history.

Australia's bicentenary is widely known as a controversial commemorative event. Co-incidentally, another commemorative event in another country in the same year raised similar issues of relationships between Whites and indigenous peoples. In 1988, the apartheid regime in South Africa staged the five-hundredth anniversary of its 'discovery' by the Portuguese navigator Bartolomeu Dias. As with Australia, the authorities tried to use the event to promote unity through emphasising multiculturalism. Also as with Australia, there was a re-enactment of the voyage from Europe, utilising a replica vessel. And, very much the same as with Australia, the event provoked discussion and debate about the modern meanings of European 'discovery' which organisers engaged in futile attempts to manage (Witz 2009).

Meanings

Commemorative events are important for their meanings. In events studies there is often a strong interest in goals and objectives. These are the outcomes that the organisers are trying to achieve. Meanings are subtly different. Meanings are how people see an event, what it tells them about themselves and society. Such insights might differ from person to person and may change over time. Most importantly, they are not necessarily the same outcomes that the organisers have planned for (Frost and Laing 2011). This variance is particularly distinct with commemorative events. Organisers want people to reflect upon the past to reinforce a specific interpretation of what that means to the modern world. However, that process may stimulate debate and discussion, even dissonance. Commemorative events, planned with a strategic outcome, often provoke multiple, contested meanings.

1988 was a special year for the range of commemorative events which were staged across the world. Twenty-five years later, it is worth looking back, remembering and reflecting upon how meanings change, both dependent on perspectives and over the course of time. The Australian bicentenary has become a model of how not to plan a commemorative event, the objectives of its organisers lost in a storm of criticism and controversy. The range of commemorative events in 1988 led heritage researcher Robert Hewison to write in a 'viewpoint' article in

Tourism Management of 'our obsession with anniversaries', noting that 'this year the UK is celebrating 1588, 1688, 1788, and even 1968' (1988: 239). Pondering what it all meant, Hewison argued that the Glorious Revolution of 1688 seemed to have little relevance in modern Britain. In contrast, he thought that the massive social and economic changes which distinguished the 1980s had led people to embrace the images of national emergency and determined resistance incorporated in the defeat of the Spanish Armada. Mischievously, Hewison concluded by wondering why no one in 1988 was commemorating the fiftieth anniversary of the *Anschluss* (Hitler annexing Austria to Germany) in Austria.

What is interesting in looking back on Hewison's viewpoint article is how meanings have evolved since then in line with changes in how we see the world. What stands out are the commemorative events that Hewison had little or nothing to say about. He dismisses it as scarcely credible that 1968 is worth thinking about and perhaps in 1988 it did seem to have decreasing relevance. Twenty-five years later, we look forward to 2017 and 2018 as potentially a massive series of 50-year anniversaries. 1967 saw the Summer of Love and death of Che Guevara. 1968 included the Prague Spring, student riots in France, Mexico and the USA, the Tet Offensive and My Lai Massacre in Vietnam and the assassinations of Martin Luther King Jr and Robert F. Kennedy. Our prediction might be wrong, but these occurrences seem to have increased in relevance in recent years and we expect them to be prominently commemorated in the future. Finally, Hewison made no mention of 1988 as the hundred-and-twenty-fifth anniversary of the Battle of Gettysburg. Yet, all indications are that the sesquicentenary in 2013 will be a huge event, with massive media coverage around the world.

The importance of varying meanings is the main theme of much of the research on commemorative events. In Table 1.1, we have set out a list of studies of commemorative events in the tourism and events literature. It is a small and limited body of work. Nearly all are either individual case studies or comparisons between two or three case studies. In addition (but not shown), are incidental references and cases in broader studies, particularly of cultural heritage (see for example Lowenthal 1998). Even allowing for these, this listing reveals a disconnection between the widespread staging of commemorative events and academic analysis of the phenomena.

Table 1.1 also reveals some interesting trends. It is noticeable that the earlier studies tended to be mainly concerned with the link between these events and nation-building and national identity. In recent years, the trend has been more towards anniversaries of conflicts. Cultural and commercial commemorative events have attracted little attention from researchers.

Our approach

While this literature is increasingly focussed on the meanings and contestations evident in commemorative events, it is very much concerned with individual case studies. What is lacking is a more thematic approach, drawing out patterns and issues. Our aim in this volume is to fill that gap. By concentrating on themes

Table 1.1 Studies of commemorative events

Authors	Countries	Event
Hewison (1988)	England	400th Anniversary of Defeat of the Spanish Armada
Cressy (1989 and 1994)	England	Guy Fawkes Day and other sixteenth- and seventeenth-century commemorative events
St Onge (1991)	Canada	125th Anniversary
Linenthal (1991)	USA	Commemorative events for five US battles
Bennett et al. (1992). Edited book.	Australia. Comparisons with USA, Canada and France.	Bicentenary of European settlement
Spillman (1997)	USA Australia	Bicentenary of Declaration of Independence Bicentenary of European settlement
Weiermair (1998)	Austria	700th Anniversary of the Tyrol
Frost (2001)	Australia and USA	150th Anniversaries of the Gold Rushes in California and Victoria
Paradis (2002)	USA	50th Anniversary of Roswell incident
Fuller (2004). Edited book.	19 case studies of various countries	National Days
Sharpe (2005)	England	Guy Fawkes Day (book written to commemorate 400th Anniversary)
Ray et al. (2006)	USA	Bicentenary of Lewis and Clark expedition
McDonald and Méthot (2006)	USA, Canada and Western Europe	Historical overview of various nationalist commemorations
Elliott (2007)	USA	Annual re-creations of the Battle of Little Big Horn
Ryan and Cave (2007)	New Zealand	Armistice Day
Frost (2007)	Australia	150th Anniversary of Eureka Stockade
Frost, Wheeler and Harvey (2008)	Australia	150th Anniversary of Eureka Stockade, Ned Kelly Weekend and ANZAC Day
Liburd (2008)	Denmark	Bicentenary of Hans Christian Andersen
Witz (2009)	South Africa	500th Anniversary of Bartolmeu Dias rounding the Cape of Good Hope
Gapps (2009)	Australia	Commonwealth Jubilee celebration (50th Anniversary of Federation)
Gapps (2010)	Australia	Bicentenary of Battle of Vinegar Hill (convict rebellion)
Walvin (2010)	UK	Bicentenary of abolition of slavery by the British
Laws and Ferguson (2011)	Canada	Canada Day
Frost (2012)	Australia	Centenary of Federation

rather than case studies, we hope to encourage a deeper understanding of the role and importance of commemorative events.

Our primary interest in commemorative events is what they mean for individuals and societies. The concept for this volume arose from two main sources. The first was an exploratory section using commemorative events to illustrate meanings in our book on the strategic management of events and festivals (Frost and Laing 2011). As we worked on that book, it became increasingly apparent that there was a need for a research-focussed work delving deeper into this phenomenon.

A second source of inspiration was the importance of commemorative events in our personal lives. As we compared notes on our experiences, we were surprised to find that as primary school children we had both been taken to view royal tours as part of commemorative events. As young adults, we had excitedly experienced special commemorations, including the Centenary Test and the Tall Ships. Later, as university lecturers, we taught students about commemorations as part of events units we had developed, engaged in research studies and one of us was on the organising committee of a major commemorative event. Writing this book was stimulated by these experiences and allowed us to reflect upon what they meant to us and others.

This book is structured around a number of key themes. The first chapter introduces the concept of commemorative events, setting out the key elements and issues and providing a basic typology. Chapter 2 examines how commemorative events are used by governments to build and reinforce notions of national identity. Such nation-building events often provoke protests from those who object to being disenfranchised or marginalised by such a process. Chapter 3 considers commemorative events that deal with issues that are dark, disturbing and difficult. While many in society would want to forget, others use these events to proclaim the importance of remembering. Chapter 4 looks at the tension between commemorative events having objectives of altering or reinforcing identities, while often purporting to have a tourism element. Both successful and unsuccessful examples of this link to tourism are considered. Chapter 5 examines international expos, a major feature of many anniversaries of nationhood. Chapter 6 explores the role of re-enactments of commemorative events. Chapter 7 extends this discussion by presenting a detailed case study of the annual re-enactment of the Battle of Hastings in England. Chapter 8 considers cultural anniversaries, while Chapter 9 looks at the increasing emphasis on commemorative events of commercial products and brands. Chapter 10 examines the legacy of commemorative events, particularly permanent physical structures and monuments. In Chapter 11, we return to the issue of the role of commemorative events in society and we argue strongly that there is an inherent and powerful need for people to remember and reflect and ultimately reconcile themselves to past incidents through structured and communal events. This final chapter also concludes with a brief examination of future trends and proposes an ongoing research agenda.

2 Imagining national identities

To preserve the memory of the French Revolution, to maintain fraternity among the citizens, to strengthen their loyalty to the fatherland and its laws.
(Rationale for national commemorative festivals, added as supplementary articles to the revolutionary constitution, quoted in Ozouf 1976: 61)

In his seminal work on nationalism, Benedict Anderson (1983) argued that modern nations are imagined communities. In traditional societies, people tended to only feel connected to the few hundred other people they worked with, lived closed to, or saw occasionally. These communities were tight-knit, parochial and geographically limited. Everyone else was an outsider; to be regarded with suspicion, even avoided. However, with the growth of nation states in the eighteenth and nineteenth centuries, Anderson argued that it was now no longer possible to personally know, recognise, or interact with all members of these new larger, national communities. To function as a coherent and unified nation, people had to imagine that they were connected. Accordingly, a host of institutions, symbols and ceremonies were developed, often promoted, funded and operated by governments, to convince people that they were included within the nation and that the national identity they now belonged to was special and valuable. These ranged from the tangible (national galleries, museums and cultural institutions, statues and monuments), to the less tangible (national stories, attributes, heroes and myths). Though diverse, they shared a common role, 'communicating the tenets of an abstract ideology in palpable, concrete terms that evoke instant emotional responses from all strata of the community' (Smith 1991: 77).

Much of the discourse about the shaping of national identities has tended to focus on political and intellectual elites (see for example the influential works by Anderson 1983 and Smith 1991). However, in recent years, there has been an increasing focus on the greater population. This includes the part that tourism plays in this imagining of national identity (see for example, the collection edited by Frew and White 2011). When domestic tourists visit sites of national significance, the experience and interpretation reinforces their sense of inclusion within the nation. Visits by international tourists to national sites validate that these places are truly important and worthy in the eyes of others. Commemorative events work in a similar way. They are a mechanism to encourage remembering and reflection on the national story. National commemorative events are particularly effective promoters of national unity and loyalty. They are often large-scale, officially authorised and funded events, deliberately designed to reach and involve very large numbers across a broad geographical area. For the people of a country, they provide a sense of belonging. They are a powerful force for the creation and maintenance of a collective national memory. Furthermore, if people from other countries take part or acknowledge the importance of these ceremonies, this reinforces the international standing of the country.

In this chapter, we aim to explore national commemorative events and how they are used to promote national unity and identity. We consider three main types of national commemorative events: national days, anniversaries of nationhood and other commemorative events which have a strong national flavour. A wide range of examples are provided to demonstrate that these phenomena occur around the globe and cannot be just seen as the product of a particular political system or region. In the last part of this chapter, we consider the problem that in certain circumstances, national commemorative events may highlight or encourage disunity and conflict. Again we provide a range of case studies to demonstrate that this is a regular occurrence. Arguably, all national commemorative events have this discordant element and event organisers have to incorporate this into their strategic planning.

National days

The concept of a particular day to annually commemorate the establishment of a state or regime dates back to antiquity and ancient Rome. Unlike the Greeks, the Romans developed a calendar with the same dates for each year. This allowed, for the first time, the celebration of specific dates as individual birthdays. This concept was then applied to dates of national significance. Most important was the marking of the founding of their city by Romulus and Remus. The resulting festival was the Parilia, commemorated every 21 April. Both the founding and its date were shrouded in the mystery of mythology. Roman scholars initially fixed the year as around what we now see as 750 BC. This placed it well after the semi-mythical Golden Age (including the fall of Troy). Instead it was somewhere at the beginning of recordable history, roughly at the same time as the Olympic Games were thought to have started. Further scholastic refinement established the foundation date as 753 BC. Commemorating it as an annual holiday gave the legend an official imprimatur, reinforcing Rome's antiquity. Fixing an official date allowed for major commemorations. The eight-hundredth anniversary of the city was commemorated in 47 AD and the nine-hundredth in 147 AD. In 248 AD, the Emperor Philip the Arab (he was from the Roman province of Arabia) staged elaborate festivities and games in the Colosseum to mark 'Rome's thousand years'. For Philip, this commemoration was intended to define his reign and affirm his sovereignty. In a move repeated many times since, he commissioned the historian Asinius Quadratus for a definitive confirmation of 753 BC as the foundation date (Feeney 2008).

In 1925, Rome's anniversary was revived as an official holiday by Mussolini. The Natale di Roma (Birth of Rome) is still a carnivalesque event commemorating ancient Rome. Now stripped of its political meanings, it is more an excuse to dress up in costume. Constantinople – the New Rome – celebrated its foundation by the Emperor Constantine on 11 May 330 AD. Here there was no myth, the actual date documented and verifiable as the day the emperor presided over the consecration of his creation. In both cases, there was a distinction between honouring the anniversary of the accession of the ruling emperor, which changed for each one, and the absolutely set date of foundation of their continuing state and culture.

In the modern world, two late eighteenth-century revolutions set the pattern for national days. For the USA, it was the signing of the Declaration of Independence on 4 July 1776. For France, it was the storming of the Bastille on 14 July 1789, officially known as la fête nationale or the national celebration (see Figure 2.1). The choices of these dates are interesting, as they are raised above others in these conflicts. The USA could have chosen the Boston Tea Party or the surrender of the British. The French could have opted for the date of the Tennis Court Oath or the execution of their king. Instead, these two were selected almost immediately by the revolutionaries as symbolically worthy of representing their aspirations. Indeed, they were part of the revolution, recognised for their symbolism and commemorated to encourage people to engage in the revolutionary struggle.

Other countries have followed their leads in declaring national days (Fuller 2004). Table 2.1 lists a range of examples. Most typically, they remember constitutions rather than conflicts, following the model of Independence Day rather than Bastille Day. This suggests that governments use them to promote their legitimacy, disseminating

Figure 2.1 Soldiers on parade on Bastille Day 2010, in Bordeaux. Photo by K. Williams.

Table 2.1 Examples of national days

Date	Country	Event remembered
1 January	Cuba	Revolution of 1959
26 January	Australia	Arrival of First Fleet in 1788
26 January	India	Constitution of India comes into force
6 February	New Zealand	Treaty of Waitangi 1840
17 March	Ireland	St Patrick's Day
27 April	South Africa	First democratic elections 1994
20 May	East Timor	Independence 2002
2 June	Italy	Vote to establish the republic 1946
1 July	Canada	Federation 1867
4 July	USA	Signing of Declaration of Independence 1776
4 July	South Sudan	Independence 2011
14 July	France	Storming of the Bastille during the French Revolution 1789
9 August	Singapore	Independence from Malaysia in 1965
15 August	India	Declaration of Independence in 1947
2 September	Vietnam	Liberation from the Japanese and independence from France 1945
7 September	Brazil	Declaration of Independence 1822
3 October	Germany	Re-unification 1990
25 October	Kazakhstan	Break-up of Soviet Union and creation as independent country 1990
26 October	Austria	Adoption of neutral constitution 1955
12 December	Kenya	Independence 1963

the message that they came to power through a lawful and just process. In contrast, a focus on revolutionary struggle raises the uncomfortable paradox of mixing violence and dissent with peace, unity and sovereignty (Ozouf 1976).

There are a number of interesting waves (or groupings) of dates of independence. Most of the South American countries commemorate the Bolivarian revolutions of the early nineteenth century. For Asia and Africa, most remember the end of European colonialism after World War Two. The end of the Soviet Union, the reunification of Germany and the break-up of Yugoslavia form the basis of national days for the countries created out of these changes. Continuing regime changes lead to new commemorations, reminding us that these are political constructs. As we write, the fallout from the Arab Spring of 2011 continues and we expect that the new governments will mark their birth and legitimacy through appropriate national days.

There are some curious anomalies. Austria marks its neutrality, an independence of sorts. Whereas Canada remembers its federation through its national holiday, Australia does not. Australia is alone among the 'new world settler nations' in

Figure 2.2 Delhi Gate, India, site of a parade and ceremony on Republic Day. Photo by J. Laing.

focussing on the date of the first arrival of Europeans. This is even more curious when it is remembered that this was a convict settlement. New Zealand stands alone with a national day marking a treaty between European settlers and the indigenous peoples. Most striking is the case of the United Kingdom. Three of its four constituent countries – Scotland, Wales and Northern Ireland – have national days commemorating their patron saints. England, however, does not have a national day at all. Furthermore, recent government proposals to consider creating one led to a storm of incredulous criticism and the idea was quickly dropped.

National days typically have a strong official imprint. They are declared public holidays. There are major formal ceremonies in capitals involving political leaders and government dignitaries. Often there will be postage stamps issued to commemorate the national day, even the issue of commemorative medals, coins or souvenir flags to schoolchildren. National heroes and institutions are honoured. Juxtaposed with iconic national figures, ordinary citizens may be singled out and formally honoured for having made a contribution to the development, security or prosperity of the nation. In many cases there are military parades, ceremonies and religious services (see Figure 2.2). In their inclusiveness, there may be elements of compulsion, the sense that while these are for everybody in the nation, everybody must take part (Ozouf 1976). Accordingly, public holidays compel businesses and schools to close and it is often expected that people will be enthusiastically involved. Strongly symbolic, these events are intended to engender national identity and unity. The marking of the national day is repeated on a smaller scale by communities throughout the country, so that all citizens have the opportunity to be involved and gain a sense of belonging (see the example of small towns staging Canada Day events in Laws and Ferguson 2011).

Balancing the official ceremonies may be festive and celebratory events. These include concerts, parties, parades and fireworks. In some cases this may lead to disquiet. Are these not meant to be solemn and dignified occasions? If people are enjoying themselves, perhaps getting drunk or dancing, are they likely to be reflecting on the importance and achievements of their country? On the other hand, such public and communal events are bringing people together and enforcing a sense that they are connected with a common national purpose.

While national days are primarily about imagining identity, they may have a tourism role. The provision of a public holiday provides an opportunity to travel, often to visit friends and relatives. Spectacle and ceremony in capital cities attract tourists (for a good discussion of this phenomenon see the edited volume by Maitland and Ritchie 2009). Smaller places may also use the national day to leverage tourism benefits. For example, Bridgeport in California (USA) is a small town in the Sierra Nevada with an attractive main street of historic wooden buildings. It stages an annual 'old fashioned fourth of July' festival (www. bridgeportcalifornia.com/fourth.php). The 2012 festival is claimed to be the town's hundred and fiftieth. Such a festival provides an appealing mix of nostalgia and small-town authenticity, reinforcing community spirit and drawing tourists.

The intensity of engagement with national days is variable. It is influenced by both the level of official commitment and the enthusiasm of the general populace. The latter reflects broad views on the state of the nation and the impact of messages of national unity. For Nigeria, independence on 1 October 1960 was initially commemorated with euphoria and optimism. However, recent national problems have diminished this enthusiasm. As Musa and Oyeleye argue,

> the annual pomp and pageantry that surrounds the celebration of Nigeria's nationhood has long ceased being the symbol of hope and opportunity for millions of disaffected and disenchanted Nigerians; instead, it has become a farcical road show, put on only for the benefit of the political elite ... and the diplomatic community.
>
> (2004: 161)

To take another example, in Romania:

> Despite the fact that December 1 is for many Romanians their country's 'finest hour', each post-Communist attempt at making the new holiday truly popular has failed. Each year the official celebration is an object of political infighting; all major political parties try to use it for scoring the most propaganda points possible. Local and individual involvement is sporadic or nonexistent. Most Romanians take advantage of the day off to tend to their private affairs.
>
> (Matei 2004: 183)

Anniversaries of nationhood

In contrast to the routine commemoration of annual national days, far greater emphasis and resources are allocated to significant anniversaries of nationhood. As discussed in Chapter 1, there is something about the special groupings of certain cardinal numbers, such as the fiftieth, hundredth and two-hundredth, which captures our collective imagination. Their significance may be seen in two ways. First, they represent an achievement. The nation has established itself. It was born, often out of a struggle. There have been trials and conflicts, but the nation has *endured* and *proven itself*. Second, this is essentially a once-in-a-lifetime opportunity for individual people to engage in this special celebration and reflection.

Again, the historical template for these events came from the USA and France. In the late nineteenth century, they successfully staged centennial commemorations of their revolutions. Both held large and long events, which captured worldwide attention and established formats which were taken up by other countries. Both had major international exhibitions as centrepieces, ostensibly promoting global trade and commerce, but really demonstrating their advancements (these commemorative exhibitions are considered in greater detail in Chapter 5). Most importantly, the US and French centennials demonstrated that such events, properly staged, were highly effective in encouraging national pride and unity. For the governments of other nations, that was (and continues to be) a very attractive formula and outcome.

The US centennial took place only 11 years after the end of its bloody and divisive Civil War. The President – Ulysses S. Grant – had come out of the war as the victorious commander of the Union forces. He was accordingly both admired and hated by many. The South had fought for the primacy of the states in a federal system. Strange as it may seem to us today, many identified with their home state rather than the nation. They saw themselves as Virginians or from Massachusetts. Up to the Civil War, national spirit had seemingly been diminishing. In this period, even the annual commemoration of 4 July had declined across the divided nation (Spillman 1997).

The centennial came at a time of reconstruction and growing confidence and was accordingly warmly embraced (Lowenthal 1985; McDonald and Méthot 2006; Spillman 1997). It was the culmination of a series of symbolic achievements and national institutions. In 1867, the Atlantic and Pacific coasts of the continent were linked through the opening of the Union-Pacific Railway. In 1872, Yellowstone was preserved as a national park. Its urban equivalent – New York's Central Park – was completed in 1873 and was envisaged by its designers as 'the big art work of the Republic' (Vaux 1865: 385). A long economic boom stimulated a growing national sense of confidence and achievement. In turn, the national reflection engendered by the centennial dampened disquiet about the consequences of rapid industrialisation and population growth (Lowenthal 1985). Following the success of the centennial, Americans warmly embraced the concept of nationalist commemorative events, particularly focussed around important national figures, such as explorers (McDonald and Méthot 2006).

Right at the highpoint of the US centennial, the nation was shocked by news from its Western frontier. On 25 June, General George Custer had led his Seventh Cavalry in an attack on a large Sioux encampment at Little Bighorn in Montana. Custer's command of 225 soldiers were all killed. News of the defeat reached Washington on 7 July. For the remainder of the centennial year, US military policy would be focussed on vengeance and demonstrating to a shaken nation that they were once again in control of the frontier (Philbrick 2010).

Similarly, the centennial in France came just over a decade after a divisive and bloody civil war. France had been soundly defeated in the Franco-Prussian War (1870–1), leading to the deposition of the ambitious Emperor Napoleon III. The new Third Republic faced an immediate crisis with the declaration of the radical Paris Commune. The capital was the scene of major fighting and many of the communards were executed or imprisoned. The regime continued to be dogged by indecision about possible restoration of the monarchy and/or military dictatorship. Growing militarism in the 1880s led to the appropriation of the virtually moribund Bastille Day as a celebration of the armed forces rather than democracy. Even in 1889, the centennial year, the Boulanger Affair demonstrated French political instability.

The centennial functioned as a counterpoint to this political turmoil. Its main feature was the Paris Exhibition, which was dominated by the construction of the modernist Eiffel Tower, intentionally the largest structure in the city. The centennial emphasised commercial success, colonial power and technological advancement. The Eiffel Tower, in particular, became a symbol of national achievement (see Figure 2.3). Co-incidentally, another symbol of French status and skill – the Statue of Liberty – also neared completion. Originally this had been conceived as France's centennial gift to the USA, honouring the revolutionary link between the two countries. However, the Franco-Prussian War and ongoing French instability had greatly delayed it.

Both centennials symbolised the power of national commemorative events in aiding reconstruction and reconciliation. In their successful commercial exhibitions they also demonstrated economic achievement. Other countries, in staging their anniversaries of nationhood, aimed to emulate these successes. Table 2.2 lists some examples.

Much of the literature on nationhood commemorative events focusses on New World countries, such as the USA, Canada and Australia (McDonald and Méthot 2006; Spillman 1997). This is in line with the argument that these were early adopters (or imaginers) of national identity, taking their national form in the eighteenth and early nineteenth centuries, a period when the Old World was either fragmented or imperial (Anderson 1983). However, recent examples of anniversaries of nationhood suggest a distinct change in this pattern. The Asian superpowers of China and India have enthusiastically marked their breaking away from colonial domination just after World War Two. In 2010 and 2011 respectively, Germany and Italy have commemorated their unification. In contrast, at the same time, the former Soviet Union republics have been commemorating their independence. While historically, anniversaries of nationhood seemed to be centred on the richer New World countries, they are now a more broadly global phenomenon.

Figure 2.3 Eiffel Tower, Paris. Photo by J. Laing.

Table 2.2 Significant anniversaries of nationhood

Date	Country	Commemoration
1876	USA	Centennial of Declaration of Independence
1889	France	Centenary of French Revolution
1967	Canada	Centenary of Confederation
1976	USA	Bicentennial of Declaration of Independence
1997	India	50th Anniversary of Independence
1998	Turkey	75th Anniversary of the Republic
1999	China	50th Anniversary of Declaration of the Peoples' Republic
2001	Australia	Centenary of Federation
2010	Germany	20th Anniversary of re-unification
2010	Mexico	Bicentenary of Independence (similar for other former Spanish colonies in the Americas)
2010–11	Former Soviet Union countries	20th Anniversaries of their independence
2011	Italy	150th Anniversary of proclamation of the kingdom of Italy

As with national days, there are variations in the popular enthusiasm for these anniversaries of nationhood. In Turkey, for example, there was great enthusiasm for the tenth anniversary of the republic in 1933. This is hardly surprising, given how it was still in recent memory, the battle had only just been won and the future seemed bright. In contrast, the fiftieth anniversary was a lesser event, reflecting doubts about national progress. The seventy-fifth was more commodified and superficial, though with increasing media penetration there seemed to be greater enthusiasm. These widely different approaches reflect a nation still searching for its national identity and place in an increasingly globalised world (Nalçaoglu 2004).

Other national commemorative events

National stories and identities are built upon a wide range of historical occurrences that are held to be important and deserving of commemoration. Indeed, some of these are so deeply ingrained in the national imagination that they are viewed as more significant than the dates of independence or nationhood. Amongst this group are commemorations of battles, wars, arrival of settlers, 'discovery' by explorers and the births or deaths of national figures such as writers, poets and political leaders (see Table 2.3 for some examples). Some of these are already observed annually as National Days, but significant anniversaries allows for larger-scale commemorative events.

The interpretation and national significance of the commemorative events may be highly subjective and even open to debate and contestation. Meanings may change dramatically over time. For example, for a long time the building of the Berlin Wall hardly seemed a matter worthy of positive commemoration. The twentieth anniversary of its fall was a major event. Most surprisingly, the fiftieth anniversary of its construction was also commemorated in 2011. With the new reunified Germany just over 20 years old, it was then something worth marking and reflecting upon. When France commemorated the bicentenary of its revolution in 1989, Jacques Chirac the conservative Mayor of Paris downplayed its radicalism. Instead, he concentrated the city's resources on the centenary of the Eiffel Tower. External events also came into play. The fall of the Berlin Wall in 1989 became linked with the fall of the Bastille 200 years before. Tiananmen Square, and the looming reunification of Germany entwined the current and the historic (Crisp 1992).

Battles, in particular, evoke a wide range of interpretations. Some are major commemorative events, with major government involvement and funding, such as the anniversaries of the Spanish Armada, the Battle of Britain and Gallipoli. These are staged to reinforce notions of national spirit and pride. In contrast, some battles are commemorated, but without these nationalist overtones. The Battle of Waterloo is an example of such a case. It is perhaps surprising that the two-hundredth anniversaries of Napoleon and many of his victories have not been prominently commemorated in France. This seems to reflect that the French are still uncertain of what Napoleon means to them. Finally, there are battles in which issues of national identity have still not been fully resolved and their meanings are a source of contemporary conflict. In the last section of this chapter, we consider this issue of contested national commemorative events in greater detail.

Table 2.3 Historical commemorative events contributing to national identity

Date	Countries	Commemorative event*
1970	Australia	Bicentenary of 'discovery' of Australia by James Cook
1988	England	400th Anniversary of defeat of the Spanish Armada
1988	Australia	Bicentenary of First Fleet (arrival of European settlers/ convict fleet at Sydney)
1988	South Africa	500th Anniversary of 'discovery' of South Africa by Bartolomeu Dias (rounding Cape of Good Hope)
1990	Australia and New Zealand	75th Anniversary of landing of troops at Gallipoli
1992	USA, Spain	500th Anniversary of 'discovery' of the Americas by Christopher Columbus
2001	Australia	150th Anniversary of discovery of Gold
2006	Denmark	200th Anniversary of writer Hans Christian Andersen's birthday
2009	Germany	20th Anniversary of the fall of the Berlin Wall
2010	England	70th Anniversary of the Battle of Britain
2011	Germany	50th Anniversary of the building of the Berlin Wall
2011–2012	Northern Ireland	100th Anniversary of the building, launch and sinking of the *Titanic*
2011–2015	USA	150th Anniversary of Civil War
2012	South Africa	100th Anniversary of the founding of the African National Congress
2012	England	200th Anniversary of the birth of writer Charles Dickens

* Many of these events are commemorated regularly at appropriate intervals. We have listed the most recent major commemorative event.

Contested national commemorative events

National commemorative events are a form of heritage and like all heritage are often subject to contested meanings and conflict between stakeholders. In their seminal work, Tunbridge and Ashworth coined the term *heritage dissonance* to describe situations where there was a 'discordance or a lack of agreement and consistency' amongst communities as to the meanings and significance of heritage (1996: 20). Such disagreements could range from different emphases to downright hostility. Being unsettling and disruptive, such dissonance often leads to event organisers strategically planning to resolve, cover up or prevent contrary interpretations (Frost and Laing 2011).

For national commemorative events, the temptation for organisers is often to present a single, incontestable view. After all, the primary objective of most national commemorative events is to promote national unity and loyalty. It therefore seems logical that such events need to get everyone in the nation imagining the same national bonding and vision. Such an approach is reinforced when, as typically happens, national commemorative events are centrally organised by government agencies.

Accordingly, national commemorative events are often characterised by the following elements:

1   Organisation of the events is influenced by official views of what is being remembered and what it 'truly' means. Such an approach is termed *official nationalism*.
2   How the event is organised also follows an official government line. This includes which national symbols and stories are included, or excluded; the rituals to be followed and the official protocols.
3   The nature and form of the commemorative event are functions of the current political climate and concerns about key issues. Accordingly, there may be varying emphases on patriotic fervour, militarism, jingoism, imperialism and xenophobia. The degree to which this occurs may vary according to political structure. For example, a single party state may use commemorative events to reinforce a view that the leader is a national paternal figure selflessly guiding (even chastising) the citizens as if they were his own children.
4   The meaning of the event may be *appropriated* by various elite stakeholder groups who aim to convey the persuasive message that their interests are entwined with those of the nation. Such elites include ruling dynasties, political parties, businesses and industry groups, the military, religious bodies and dominant ethnic groups.
5   A growing form of this appropriation is *commercial nationalism*, where national symbols are linked or utilised by businesses to promote their products and brand. Using commercial nationalism, such businesses promote the imagining that they, too, are part of the same national community. While promoting their national connections, this may also entail identifying other brands and products as foreign and therefore tainted.
6   In contrast to the privileged position of the elites, marginalised and dispossessed groups in society will find that they are excluded from the decision-making process and that their views and stories are not represented.

To close this chapter, we examine two of these elements in greater detail. The first is that commemorative events are a product of current political pressures and issues. The second is the exclusion or marginalisation of certain groups within the nation, who may in turn stage their own commemorative events.

The nation under siege

The political pressures which governments face determine the form and function of commemorative events. As discussed above, the centenaries of the US Declaration of Independence and the French Revolution came during periods of great change in society and after two bloody and divisive wars. Accordingly, these commemorative events were partly constructed as reconciliatory. Another good example is to consider England in the sixteenth and seventeenth centuries. Cressy has argued that that this is one of the first examples of a society which strongly engaged with commemorative events. As he puts it, 'in many ways the calendar of seventeenth-century England had less in common with Renaissance France or Spain, and more with twentieth-century America or Australia' (Cressy 1989: xi).

The government of Early Modern England was besieged by internal and external threats. Foremost was the Reformation – the decision by Henry VIII to break with Catholicism and establish the Church of England. For the next 150 years there was the constant threat of this being reversed, either through pro-Catholic rulers such as Mary or James II; or invasions such as the Spanish Armada. The Tudors had come to power through the War of the Roses and their legitimacy was open to question. When their bloodline ran out, they were replaced by the Stuarts, whose disputes with Parliament led to the Civil War.

In such an environment, there were conscious and sustained efforts to create and reinforce national identity and unity through commemorative events. As Cressy argued, 'by the seventeenth century, when politics and religion became dangerously fraught and fractured, much of England's political discourse ... revolved around the interpretation, celebration, and control of remembered historical events' (1994: 61). As early as the 1530s, there were proposals to create an annual triumph with bonfires, feasts and ceremonies. Such a celebratory remembrance was intended to focus popular support for the policies of Henry VIII.

With the accession of the staunchly Protestant Queen Elizabeth in 1558, an annual commemoration began to be staged each 17 November. Known as *Crownation* (later evolving into Coronation) *Day*, it celebrated both the popularity of the monarch and the successful establishment of a Protestant state. Across England, the day was marked with bonfires, bell-ringing, beer and banquets. Such celebratory markers were not unique to England, but were common throughout Europe during religious festivals. What was distinctive was that they had now been 'harnessed to the needs of the state' (Cressy 1989: 67). Crownation Day continued after the death of Elizabeth, simply moved to appropriate dates for different rulers. Nonetheless, Elizabeth's Crownation continued to be commemorated on 17 November, particularly in strongly Protestant towns. Indeed, it was widely revived during the reign of Charles 1, often outshining his Crownation Day (Cressy 1989).

After the defeat of the Spanish Armada in 1588, annual commemorative events were staged to remind the nation of how close they had come to invasion and to reinforce, even imagine, the role of Elizabeth in its defence. In 1606, a year after the Gunpowder Plot, 5 November was legislated as an official commemorative day. Again, the defeat of the enemies of the state was ritualised and sanctioned by the state (Cressy 1989 and 1994).

Throughout the seventeenth century, Guy Fawkes Night – commemorating an incident still within living memory – went through multiple changes in meaning depending on the political climate, particularly the position of the monarch (Sharpe 2005). Under James I, it gave thanks for his deliverance from assassination. When his son, Charles I, became embroiled in political struggles with parliament, 5 November changed to being a celebration of the constitution and a reminder of the need for constant vigilance. With mounting concerns that Charles was sympathetic to Catholicism, the event became more stridently anti-Catholic. It was at this time that the first effigies were created for the bonfires. However, they were not of Guy Fawkes, but rather the Pope. In 1640, the Long Parliament was recalled on 3 November and the closeness of the dates consequently led to Guy Fawkes Night being linked to reform.

With the Restoration of Charles II in 1660, Guy Fawkes was recaptured by royalists. The new ruler purposefully championed reconciliation and this event was refashioned to symbolise unity. In 1688, William of Orange displaced James II as ruler. A key symbolic part of this Glorious Revolution was William's laying claim to the heritage and meanings of Guy Fawkes Night. This claim was manifest by his landing in England on 5 November, linking his accession to the now established national day (Sharpe 2005).

Marginalising the conquered

This reinforcement of identity through commemorative events is often at the expense of others. The dominant narrative behind commemorative events often exposes a power imbalance. Ethnic, religious and regional minorities may be excluded and further marginalised. The decision to exclude any consideration of the plight of the Aborigines from the 1988 Australian bicentenary of European settlement is often cited as an example of this (see Chapter 1 for a fuller discussion). Similarly, the 1976 US bicentenary and the five-hundredth anniversary of Columbus in 1992 were criticised for inadequate recognition of the impact of the historical events commemorated on indigenous peoples. In this chapter, we consider two further examples of how organisers of national commemorative events may forget or ignore some aspects rather than remember.

In 1913, the Netherlands staged the centenary of its independence from Napoleonic France. Officials in their colony of the Dutch East Indies (now Indonesia) were keen to encourage the Indonesians to take part in the commemorations, thereby demonstrating that they were loyal members of the Dutch Empire. Nationalist leaders quickly pointed out that this was an absurd situation. Why would Indonesians want to celebrate Dutch independence when they were really far more concerned about achieving their own independence? Furthermore, if independence was a worthy goal valued by the Netherlands, then they should immediately grant it to their colony (Anderson 1983). This is an important example, for in this case, the dispossessed were not the minority. Numerically, the Indonesians were easily the majority, but they had little power in making decisions.

In 1996, the hundred and fiftieth anniversary of the Bear Flag Revolt was staged at Sonoma, in rural California. The revolt occurred at the beginning of the Mexican-American War of 1846–8. An American army survey team under John Fremont had arrived in California seeking supplies. Knowing war to be imminent, they persuaded American settlers to declare an independent republic. Their flag featured a grizzly bear and is still the state flag of California. Defeating Mexican forces, they linked up with invading American troops. The end result of this war was that Texas, Colorado, New Mexico, Arizona and California were ceded by Mexico to the USA. Celebrating the victory of the Bear Flag Revolt was therefore celebrating the triumph of the USA over Mexico (Frost 2001). In a state with a high proportion of people of Hispanic origin, this was going to cause controversy. As reported by an historian at the event:

> Public attendance at the Sesquicentennial was smaller than anticipated, possibly caused by advance knowledge that Mexican-American student protesters would be there in an attempt to disrupt the celebration. Nearly 50 protesters did show up with banners and signs and they shouted and screamed and blew horns during the opening ceremonies ... Sonoma police officers told this writer that violence might break out between the protesters and the celebrants. A police helicopter flew overhead ... The protesters became loudest during Governor Wilson's address ... To the dismay of the celebrants, most media coverage focussed on the protesters rather than the Sesquicentennial activities.
>
> (Anderson 1996: 10)

40,000 years doesn't make a bicentenary

In contrast to a 'top-down' approach of controlled and official nationalism, some commemorative events are planned to provide alternative or subversive memories and identities, even protesting against nationalist agendas. The commemoration of the anniversary of the Bear Flag Revolt was matched, even overshadowed, by a protest event remembering the same historical incident. In the case of Australia's bicentenary of European settlement, indigenous groups staged a number of protest events. The most powerful of these inverted official versions of the national story. These included the only re-enactment of the arrival of the First Fleet and activist Burnim Burnim standing on the White Cliffs of Dover in traditional clothing and claiming England for the Aboriginal people. The marketing of the event was also inverted, the official slogan of 'Let's celebrate 88' became 'Don't celebrate 88'. Most powerful was the attack on the fundamental absurdity of selective memory with the number of years, as in the protest slogan '40,000 Years Doesn't Make a Bicentenary'.

While some subversive national commemorative events are reactions against the official versions, others are staged to publicise that the authorities are hoping that people will forget dark and disturbing incidents from the past (and this will be explored in greater detail in Chapter 3). Examples of these are:

• Hiroshima Day – 6 August. Staged to commemorate the dropping of the Atomic Bomb on Hiroshima, Japan and to more generally protest against nuclear weapons. 2011 was the first year that the USA sent an official representative.

- Sorry Day – 26 May. Focuses on government inaction regarding Australia's stolen generation – indigenous children forcibly removed from their parents. It commemorates the release of the *Report of the National Inquiry into the Separation of Aboriginal and Torres Strait Islander Children from their Families*. Again, inversion is at play. This protest event remembers a government action, in order to press the point that further government policy has not gone far enough.
- Annual march to commemorate 'Bloody Sunday' in Londonderry, Northern Ireland. The march commemorates the killing of 14 protesters on 30 January 1972. The purpose of the march has been to call for a full independent enquiry, which was finally achieved in 2011.

While dissonance and subversion may seem frightening and undesirable to event organisers, they may also be good for society. Acceptance of the mistakes of the Australian Bicentenary of European Settlement, led the organisers of the 2000 Sydney Olympics and the 2001 Centenary of Federation to adopt a far more inclusive approach. Rather than ignore the problems of indigenous Australians, these events directly addressed them, demonstrating that events may be a valuable tool in dealing with social issues. These two examples illustrate a major change in how national identity is imagined through events. They point to a trend for greater inclusion and recognition that dissonance and debate are integral to the development of a nation.

3 Dark, disturbing and difficult commemorative events

> Suppose a society is divided over the very event it selects for commemoration. Suppose that event constitutes a painful moment for society, such as a military defeat or an era of domestic oppression ... How is commemoration without consensus, or without pride, possible?
>
> (Wagner-Pacifici and Schwartz 1991: 379)

The practice of commemorating dark, disturbing or difficult episodes in our lives has a long history. It has been observed that 'collective memories have a tendency to coalesce around violent traumas' (King 2010: 2). *Dark tourism* – 'the packaging and consumption of death or distress as a tourist experience' (Strange and Kempa 2003: 387), is an increasingly popular focus for academic study (see also Lennon and Foley 2000; Logan and Reeves 2009; Stone 2006). However, this literature primarily deals with tourist attractions and cultural heritage sites. In contrast, there is a paucity of research on *dark events*. This is particularly surprising given that many of the elements of interpreting and reconciliation with darkness are played out in the context of events. It is definitely time that both events and dark tourism researchers focussed their attention on this field. In this chapter, we aim to stimulate this discussion by examining dark commemorative events. We define these as events that commemorate or mark the anniversaries of incidents that are distressing, macabre or involve death or suffering.

While there is some crossover between the concepts of dark tourism and dark commemorative events, the latter may not necessarily be aimed at or attractive to tourists. The lack of research on dark commemorative events reflects the dearth of work on commemorative events more broadly. Our aim in this chapter is to start to fill this gap, by considering dark commemorative events as a social phenomenon, developing a typology and exploring the reasons why we feel the need to mark dark anniversaries through the staging of events.

Even the labelling of these commemorative events as dark might be somewhat problematic. Organisers and participants might view them as uplifting and inspirational, rather than depressing or morbid. For example, even war may be seen as having some positive social outcomes, such as the safeguarding or reintroduction of political freedoms, the defeat of tyranny and the building of a nation. Other commemorative events remember the ending of dark periods, as in, for example, the two-hundredth anniversary of the abolition of slavery in the British Empire. The act of commemoration of sad or distressing events of the past might be understood as a necessary step in moving forward, seeking closure rather than continuing to be mired in the past.

It should also be recognised that dark heritage generally follows a *spectrum of intensity* (Stone 2006) and there will be debates about whether some commemorative events should be categorised as dark, given differing stakeholders' views on the historical episodes on which they are based. In this chapter, we attempt to provide examples from both ends of the spectrum (darkest to lightest), as well as those in between. We also note that events can alter over time in terms of their level of perceived darkness, although we do not subscribe to the view that time must inevitably lead to a *lightening* of these events. While Lennon and Foley (2000) argue that dark tourism focuses on living memories of recent history, it is also important to recognise that history *beyond memory* may take on a resonance which has become intensified with the passage of time (Knox 2006; Willard *et al.* 2013).

The most obvious examples of dark commemorative events are associated with warfare, usually linked with victories. Many countries label them *remembrance days* or *victory days* and make them an annual event. Other events commemorate defeats, massacres, civilian casualties and war crimes. Hiroshima Day is held in Japan on 6 August, the anniversary of the dropping of the atomic bomb on the city in 1945. Opinions are divided about the morality and political necessity of the bombing; whether this was instrumental in the cessation of hostilities and what (if any) moral justification there was for such an act (Goldberg 1999). Such is the level and diversity of this debate, that it is noteworthy that Hiroshima Day is also marked by events in places around the world.

Aside from warfare, events may also commemorate difficult times in history, such as the end of the slave trade, indenture or imprisonment, or heinous crimes. At present, 39 American states celebrate Juneteenth (also known as Freedom Day or Emancipation Day) on 19 June, some with a state holiday, marking the date when the last black slaves discovered they were to be freed after the American Civil War on 19 June 1865 in Galveston Texas (Donovan and DeBres 2006). Many states stage festivals on this date. In some cases, it has been adopted as an alternative to other commemorative events. In 1976, for example, the people of Buffalo in New York State decided to mark Juneteenth annually with a festival 'as a culturally relevant alternative to the country's Bicentennial Celebration' (www.juneteenthofbuffalo.com).

Dark pasts or anniversaries might also be commemorated through a variety of different events, including exhibitions; memorial concerts, services and ceremonies; parades and marches; or festivals. These are generally linked with a particular date, such as the 2011 ceremony at the World Trade Centre in New York to mark the tenth anniversary of the 9/11 bombings. Sometimes they are recurrent, such as the annual candlelight vigil at Gracelands in Memphis, Tennessee (see Figure 3.1), held on the anniversary of Elvis Presley's death (Rojek 1993).

Figure 3.1 Grave of Elvis Presley at Gracelands, Memphis. Photo by J. Laing.

There are variations in the resilience and ongoing meanings of dark commemorative events. There is a life-cycle for some events. Initially, they assist with dealing with grief, but in time there may be a need for closure and the withdrawal of the event. This is seen in the decision to discontinue the formal commemorative services at the formal penal colony of Port Arthur in Tasmania, Australia, the site of the killing of 35 people by a lone gunman, Martin Bryant, in 1996. The role of the event in assisting community healing is now taken up by the establishment of a memorial garden, where the visitor can sit and quietly contemplate the tragedy, and two plaques, one of which provides the names of the victims and the other a short overview of what occurred that day (Frew 2012).

Sometimes we simply have no wish, either personally or collectively, to remember the dark past. We conclude this chapter with a discussion of why dark commemorations might not be welcomed or countenanced in some instances. Lowenthal (2003) observes that commemoration is only one of five different strategies of dealing with 'heritage that hurts' (the others being to ignore, to erase, to celebrate or to transmute). This is a variation on Foote's (1997) four-fold categorisation of responses to tragedy – sanctification, designation, rectification and obliteration (see also Logan and Reeves 2009). Ignoring difficult pasts might be seen as a way to help communities deal with their grim pasts, or facilitate economic development, including tourism, through focusing on more positive narratives (Rivera 2008). Some communities or governments go further than this – they may actively seek to conceal or wipe difficult histories from our collective memory. Hewison (1988) provides the example of Austria's decision to not mark the fiftieth anniversary of the *Anschluss* in 1988.

Purpose and role of dark commemorative events

Dark commemorative events have an important place in society. They allow us to move on from terrible moments in history, to cope with distressing issues or circumstances, or make sense of human tragedy. They provide a liminal space within which to process emotions associated with the fear of death and suffering, and, in turn, experience a beneficial emotional release or closure. As a result of staging or attending the event, we gain a sense of control over these dark episodes in our lives. Seaton (1996) contends that a *thanatoptic tradition*, exemplified by a fascination with places of death and suffering, can be traced back far beyond the modern era. Marking these occasions symbolically through an event helps us to come to terms with the inevitable; which arguably contributes to our health and wellbeing (Stone and Sharpley 2008). In this way, dark commemorative events might have more to do with 'life and the living, rather than the dead and dying' (Stone and Sharpley 2008: 590).

Festivals like the Mexican Day of the Dead, Halloween and Salem's Festival of the Dead make light of mortality, through festive rituals such as the wearing of costumes, often with ghoulish or macabre themes, parades, dancing, music, eating special food and celebrating with friends and family. Dark commemorative events sometimes perform the same function, and may have an element of black humour through them. The use of bonfires and the burning of effigies may be seen as playful and carnivalesque, but it may also be interpreted as a symbolic purging or vengeful ritual. This practice is most associated with Guy Fawkes Night. In the seventeenth century the effigy was usually the Pope, but from the nineteenth century it has tended to be Guy Fawkes himself, though sometimes named as some contemporary villain such as an unpopular politician. How bonfires and effigies may be used in multiple ways is illustrated in Patrick Leigh Fermor's account of Peace Day in 1919:

> A throng of villagers had assembled around an enormous bonfire all ready for kindling, and on top of it, ready for burning, were dummies of the Kaiser and Crown Prince. The Kaiser wore a real German spiked-helmet and a cloth mask with huge whiskers ... At last someone set fire to the dry furze at the bottom and up went the flames in a great blaze. Everybody joined hands and danced round it, singing *Mademoiselle from Armentières* and *Pack up Your Troubles in Your Old Kitbag*. The whole field was lit up and when the flames reached the two dummies, irregular volleys of bangs and cracks broke out; they must have been stuffed with fireworks ... Everyone clapped and cheered, shouting: 'There goes Kaiser Bill!'
>
> (Leigh Fermor 1977: 47–8)

Generally, however, these playful elements are less prevalent within dark commemorative events. That they are focussed on remembering an anniversary, perhaps gives them a *gravitas* and an authenticity that makes us take them too seriously to engage in Halloween style play.

The celebration of anniversaries of victory in war is a social mechanism for expressing relief or gratitude, making sure the memory of this event is kept alive, perhaps as a warning for future generations, or remembering the sacrifices made by those who died. However, some are uncomfortable with these commemorations, arguing that they may be adapted to glorify or conversely sanitise war and warfare (Whitmarsh 2001) or ritualise what should be done freely; namely the act of remembering and expressing gratitude. Nicolson (2009: 177–8) recounts the diary entries made by the then schoolboy Evelyn Waugh in relation to the two-minute silence on Remembrance Day: 'A disgraceful day of national hysteria. No one thought of the dead last year. Why should they now?' In Australia, ANZAC Day's decline in the 1960s and 1970s was a reaction to the jingoistic reminiscing of veterans, this dissatisfaction best exemplified by the success of Alan Seymour's satirical play *The One Day of the Year* (1960) (Seal 2004). The ways in which such commemorative events have the potential to polarise, sheds light on the vastly different meanings that can be attributed to the same episode in history.

War remembrance days are promoted or staged as a cathartic way for communities to express collective or personal grief, which is otherwise bottled up or has no outlet for expression. After World War One, the idea of a two-minute silence was put forward by Edward Honey as a mechanism to give people time for reflection and a focus for a conscious and collective act of memory (Nicolson 2009). The passing of time also provides different meanings for war remembrances. In the years immediately following conflicts, they tend to be dominated by reunions of veterans (Linenthal 1991; Seal 2004). In later years, they change their emphasis, as societies realise the war generation is passing on. The seventieth anniversary of the bombing of Coventry in 2012, for example, had special significance due to the thinning of the ranks of survivors. There may be a symbolic passing of the flame to a new generation; as exemplified by the surge of participation by young people in ANZAC Day, following the seventy-fifth anniversary in 1990 (Frost *et al.* 2008; Scates 2006).

Occasionally, dark commemorative events are seen as tasteless, maudlin or inappropriate. Their timing might have an important influence on how they are perceived and this influences organisers in structuring the staging of the event. The 2009 Sound Relief concert, held at the Myer Music Bowl in Melbourne in the wake of the catastrophic Black Saturday bushfires in Australia, gave survivors a sense that others empathised, not just in terms of willingness to raise funds but also sharing their desolation at the tragedy. However, no concert was planned for the later anniversaries of the fires, perhaps in recognition that such an event might be seen as irreverent or disrespectful to the survivors, who were engaged in rebuilding their communities. Instead, the 2010 anniversary of Black Saturday was marked with more low-key and sober events, such as small services in individual townships, and a memorial service in Melbourne's Federation Square, attended by the Prime Minister of Australia.

A typology of dark commemorative events

These fall into seven basic categories:

Dark exhibitions involve the viewing of material evidence or symbolic representations of particular deaths or dark events (Seaton 1999). These exhibitions might be typically staged in conventional galleries or museums. There may be purpose-built museums and interpretive centres, with changing exhibitions. In 2004, the UNESCO headquarters in Paris was used to house the exhibition 'The Slave Route: Africa's Connections with Jamaica', as part of the international year for the commemoration of the struggle against slavery and its abolition. Travelling exhibitions were also used to mark this year, which was also the bicentenary of the independence of Haiti.

There is often dissonance and controversy with respect to the types of artefacts selected and how they are interpreted to visitors. Stone (2006) refers to the example of 'September 11: Bearing Witness to History', an exhibition at the Smithsonian Museum of American History, which included artefacts and images about the terrorist attacks, including the collapse of the Twin Towers in New York. He argues that it was sanitised to safeguard against the 'emotional baggage' that visitors brought to the event, but it could also be argued that the curators wished to avoid the political fallout that might result from one particular narrative being presented to the public. The prior controversy over plans for an *Enola Gay* exhibition at the Smithsonian in 1995, 50 years after the dropping of the atomic bomb on Japan, might have led curators to take a more cautious approach to interpretation.

The 1995 *Enola Gay* exhibition was cancelled due to the inability to reconcile competing memories and narratives. Goldberg (1999) argues that the museum governors bowed to political pressure, particularly from veterans, who felt that their war record was being criticised and the Japanese were being treated too sympathetically in the planned interpretation. There is conjecture over the meanings placed on the dropping of the atomic bomb, and attempts were made to present this complexity, which were met with disapproval and complaints that history was being distorted (Goldberg 1999; Whitmarsh 2001). The potential for dissonance with respect to dark commemorative events is discussed later in this chapter.

Dark re-enactments are simulations or re-creations of dark events in history, including battles or grisly deaths. Those who take part can 'relive history' and there is often a great nostalgia for the past, even where war and suffering were involved (Ray *et al.* 2006; Turner 1989). These events also have a role in identity-building, as 'they most often aim to celebrate and reaffirm some aspect of a culture's (local, regional or national) history and sense of place in the world' (Carnegie and McCabe 2008: 352). The dark elements may facilitate this, by giving people a sense of a shared tragedy or trauma. It might be difficult for individuals to engage in an open dialogue on some of these painful episodes, whereas involvement in the re-enacted event could allow some of the difficult aspects to be explored in a less threatening or confrontational manner. The level of performance or role-play involved does however mean that these elements cannot be too dark or realistic, or they would be unbearable, either to re-create as a participant or to witness by an audience.

There are re-enactments of seminal historical moments such as the Battle of Hastings, the Battle of Little Bighorn, the Alamo, the Gunfight at the OK Corral in Tombstone, and American Civil War battles (see Chapter 6). The darkness of the subject matter should not be overlooked as a result of their ubiquity and commodification. Re-enactments can also be an element of peaceful anniversary celebrations, such as the 2007 bicentenary of the Abolition of the Slave Trade Act in the British Empire. The speech in the British Parliament by William Wilberforce, supporting the abolition of slavery, was re-created in central London.

National days of mourning or remembrance are another type of dark commemorative event. Many countries mark the end of wars with remembrance days or victory days, where the variation in name denotes a different philosophical approach to the same episode in history. It can be viewed as a sobering occurrence that should never be forgotten, or simply as something to be celebrated and rejoiced over. The eleventh day of the eleventh month is Armistice Day for the Allies in World War One (known as Remembrance Day in Great Britain and Australia and Veterans Day in the United States), in recognition of the Armistice signed in 1918 with Germany. The change of name reflects the feeling that the day should commemorate all the war dead, not just the historical act of signing the armistice. Some countries further mark this event with a period of silence at 11:00 am, to mark the anniversary of the cessation of hostilities and as a mark of respect for the fallen.

Gillis (1994: 8) argues that there is nothing 'automatic about commemorative activity' and national days are no exception. Some are contested, particularly where they involve difficult anniversaries or dark pasts. In France, new anniversaries after the fall of the Bourbons such as Bastille Day were problematic for conservatives, who preferred the old anniversaries connected with the former monarchy (Gillis 1994). Independence Day in Philadelphia, until the mid-nineteenth century, was marked by riots between different groups, who held conflicting interpretations of the struggle for independence from the British (Gillis 1994).

Hiroshima Day was neglected by the Japanese, until nuclear fallout was generated by atomic testing near Bikini Atoll in 1954. Until that time, the Japanese were trying to forget the events of the war, partly the result of trauma, but also from a desire to embrace the narrative of deliverance by the Americans and focus on reconstruction and recovery. The contamination of Japanese tuna after Bikini Atoll created a new sense of solidarity and identification with the victims of nuclear weapons. This led to large numbers of anti-nuclear rallies and a surge in attendance at the Peace Memorial Ceremony in 1954 (Saito 2006).

Memorial services and concerts might be one-offs, or become an annual event, depending on the role they play within a community and the resilience of the memories involved. Services are often held in connection with the death of public figures or for the dead from natural disasters or war, and are generally held in a place of worship or a *site of memory* (Nora 1989), such as a battlefield or grave site. The commemoration of International Holocaust Remembrance Day on 27 January was observed in 2011 by a candle-lighting ceremony in the Hall of Remembrance at the US Holocaust Memorial Museum in Washington. In this instance, the memorial ceremony was staged at a site in a different country to where the history being remembered occurred.

Greater access to cheaper travel has opened up greater possibilities for participants to journey to actual sites. A dawn service is held at Gallipoli in Turkey each year on ANZAC Day to commemorate sacrifices associated with that battle, with increasing numbers of people, particularly the young, travelling there. The large numbers have raised concerns about the site's carrying capacity and the centenary in 2015 is already sold-out. The Australian government has developed ANZAC services at other battle sites, such as Villers-Bretonneux in France, to spread the load (Frost *et al.* 2008; Scates 2006). In 2012, the seventieth anniversary of the Kokoda campaign in Papua New Guinea was marked by a series of on-site commemoration services to coincide with the dates of various battles. Tour companies such as Back Track Adventures (www.trekkokoda.com. au) offered anniversary treks incorporating attendance at some of these services.

Memorial concerts may have an aim of raising funds for charity, in addition to acting as the focus for public grief or mourning. The Diana Memorial Concert raised £1.2 million for eight charities, including the Diana Princess of Wales Memorial Fund. The presence of the Princess' two sons, William and Harry, gave concert-goers and those watching the event on television a sense of the next generation taking up her philanthropic mantle, and perhaps a modicum of closure with respect to the shock of her premature death in a car accident in Paris.

Another concert commemorating a premature death was the *Strummer of Love*, staged in Somerset, UK in 2012 (www.strummeroflove.com). This weekend music festival honoured the tenth anniversary of the death of Joe Strummer, lead singer of *The Clash*. Strummer died suddenly from an undiagnosed heart condition at the age of 49. The memorial concert was organised by his two daughters. It attracted 5,000 people, with profits going to charity.

Significant anniversaries are either one-off commemorations, or annual events given far greater emphasis. As discussed in Chapter 1, we tend to relate to anniversaries of significant numbers, such as centenaries. Key examples include the seventieth anniversary of the bombing of Coventry in 2011, the 2004 international year for the commemoration of the struggle against slavery and its abolition and the 2012 centenary of the sinking of the *Titanic*.

In some cases, these represent a one-off opportunity to remember a dark event that has not been marked previously. The talismanic qualities of a significant anniversary date act as a catalyst for bringing people together and help to generate funding and media coverage. In 2007, we attended a weekend event to mark the hundred-and-fiftieth anniversary of the Buckland Riots on the Australian goldfields. These were race riots in which Chinese miners were violently expelled from the diggings, with at least three deaths. This one-off event was staged in Bright, the town the Chinese fled to. The festivities included a parade with Chinese dragons, musicians and descendants of the survivors. Significantly, the event focussed on the positive stories of survival.

Dark parades, marches and processions are often a subset of commemorations, but deserve their own category due to their high-profile and ubiquity. Gillis (1994) observes that memorial days connected to death often have a parade or procession at their heart, which replaces pilgrimages to graves and cemeteries.

Marching may be deliberately provocative, reaffirming identity at the expense of others. An example of this are the marches connected with the Glorious Twelfth (of July), or Orangeman's Day, which marks the Battle of the Boyne on the Irish east coast between King James II of England and VII of Scotland and Prince William of Orange (Hill 1984). The Protestant Prince of Orange was victorious and ascended the British throne alongside his English wife Princess Mary. These marches organised by Protestants in Northern Ireland, carrying flags and banners, often resulted in violence with Catholic groups. Clothing plays a symbolic part, with marchers wearing black suits and bowler hats, matched with a draped collar, often in orange. These are simultaneously markers of identity and inflammatory symbols.

The device of a parade or march might be seen as unduly ostentatious or tasteless in some contexts, or an attempt to sway public opinion or make a political statement. The procession of the body of the Unknown Warrior through the streets of London and its subsequent burial on Remembrance Day 1920 struck the writer and journalist Winifred Holtby as 'hypocritical' and 'an appeal to sentiment to carry England away from the realisation of a practical evil' (quoted in Nicolson 2009: 344). More festive was how the 2007 bicentenary of the abolition of the Slave Trade Act in the British Empire was commemorated by the 'march of the abolitionists' from Hull to Greenwich, but is hard to visualise parades or marches for more recent anniversaries of tragedies such as the Holocaust.

A key issue is who has the right to parade and who decides this. Descendants figure prominently, as in the hundred-and-fiftieth anniversary of the Buckland Riot. In some cases this is highly contentious, leading to a refighting of old battles. The hundred-and-fiftieth anniversary of the Eureka Stockade, an armed rebellion of disgruntled gold miners, was commemorated in 2004. Two stakeholder groups grappled for prominence of their memorial walks. One was organised by Eureka's Children, a group open only to descendants of the miners, which argued it should be in charge of all the heritage of Eureka. The other, a cemetery walk, was criticised for starting in the soldiers' camp. It also gained massive media coverage for inviting as a speaker the father of David Hicks, an Australian, who was at that time incarcerated in Guantanamo Bay (Frost 2007).

Dark festivals are a less common way to mark troubled pasts. Perhaps this is the result of the meanings the word festival bestows, as something light-hearted, anarchic or carnivalesque, which is an inappropriate association in many dark contexts. Rather than labelling them festivals, neutral terms like days or weekends might be used. Exceptions include the Juneteenth festivals in the United States, held on the anniversary of the emancipation of slaves, and the Mt Kembla Mining Heritage Festival in Australia.

Mt Kembla on the NSW coast of Australia was the scene of a mining disaster in 1902, where 96 men and boys died in an explosion, attributed to a gas leak. This led to the closure of the mine (Eklund 2002). The festival grew out of the 2002 centenary of the Mt Kembla Mine disaster. Past festivals have involved a ceremony of lighting 96 candles, in memory of those who died in 1902, as well as heritage displays, poetry readings, football matches, a parade, coal shovelling and roof-bolting competitions, and a memorial service in the local church. The festival has focused on building community through commemorating its mining legacy, including raising interest in the creation of a mining heritage interpretive centre in Mt Kembla, which was opened in 2008. Festival organisers tend to concentrate on a positive story – the recognition and marking of the mine site as a heritage 'hard won by the founders of the local area' (quoted in Hoctor 2008) – rather than highlighting what is said to be Australia's worst industrial accident.

The *whitening* of commemorative events

It has been argued that dark events lose their dark edge, becoming sanitized or *whitened* over time (Lennon and Foley 2000). In some cases, death, rather than being feared, becomes a figure of fun, as in Halloween. Time also heals the grieving process, and there may be a desire to stop living in the past, continually evoking memories that are painful or divisive. In some cases, this is not a planned process; it just occurs naturally with the passing of time. Even for modern commemorations of tragedies, there is a sense that they have a finite life, and the memory must be eventually laid to rest.

In 2009, it was announced that the annual 'Bloody Sunday' marches in Northern Ireland would be discontinued. These were held as protest events on the anniversary of the shootings of demonstrators in 1972. An official apology from the British Prime Minister David Cameron and the handing down of the Saville Report seemed to have provided the closure that the families and supporters needed in their campaign for justice (Conway 2009). However, continuing concerns about delays in taking action on the Saville Report's findings mean that the event may be staged again.

The Juneteenth festival, which marks the anniversary of the proclamation of the end of slavery in the United States on 19 June 1865, has over time lost its strong emancipatory focus. These days, instead of being a political rite, it is more about 'community building, civic contributions and a sort of homecoming celebration' (Donovan and DeBres 2006: 380). Atmosphere is created by the serving of traditional food, such as barbecue, which is a gentler introduction to African-American culture than re-enactments of past injustice and more fitting in a festival context.

Remembering the American Civil War seems to have lost some of its dark edge. Re-enactments of battles from the American Civil War are labelled 'fun' (Turner 1990) and gain a 'play identity [which] transforms the re-enactor into someone else – a Civil War-period personage – and at the same time someone more fully himself: a creative individual freely engaging in a personally meaningful activity' (Turner 1990: 126). The re-enactor learns about what it is like to be in a war situation, but in a largely safe and controlled environment. While some may continue to see the Civil War in political terms, and campaign to prevent the 'horrors of slavery' being forgotten (Blight 1989: 1161), through the lens of the re-enactment, this is a 'bloodless war' where 'the pain, violence and misery … have been extracted, leaving camaraderie, exhilaration, and a certain beauty' (Turner 1990: 134).

That a re-enactment is felt to be appropriate, even enjoyable, by large numbers of people in the community is significant and marks the lightening of the way we view the original episode in history. Nonetheless, some re-enactments would be met with strong condemnation and political heat, such as, for argument's sake, re-creating the Nuremberg rallies in Germany, the Battle of Culloden in Scotland or the activities of Pol Pot and the Khmer Rouge in Cambodia. The scars are still raw and likely to remain so – over 300 years in the case of Culloden (Willard *et al.* 2013). In other cases, politics or squeamishness do not seem to be a barrier. Lowenthal (2003: 5) refers to plans to hold mock auctions of slaves at Colonial Williamsburg, which were criticised by black activist groups as 'demeaning, insulting, pornographic'. These went ahead, and despite being more 'decorous' than their historical antecedents, were found to have helped raise awareness of slavery. There have been re-enactments of the Warsaw uprising by Polish groups (Carnegie and McCabe 2008). The latter might be more palatable as it involves enthusiasts re-creating 'other people's wars', while maintaining a distance from their own dark history.

Commemorations linked to horrific acts or episodes that the world can never forget or that have a deep emotional resonance for a culture or nation, such as the Holocaust, arguably maintain their dark edge, although there is still dissonance surrounding these events. Domansky (1992) analyses the fiftieth anniversary of *Kristallnacht*, where the Nazis staged a series of riots or pogroms against Jews in Germany, smashing windows and looting and burning their synagogues, businesses and homes. Domansky argues that Germany simultaneously remembers and forgets the Holocaust – while remembrance is the price paid for being accepted as a player on the international stage, there is also a 'wall of silence' and a desire 'to repress the past'. There might also be fears in some quarters that commemorations could fuel a surge in neo-Nazi activities.

A public outcry greeted the speech made in the West German Bundestag by the then Chairman, Phillip Jenninger to mark the anniversary. This speech emphasised the perspective of the *perpetrators* rather than the victims and provided concrete examples of what occurred. There were also concerns that Jewish people were not part of the official program of commemoration. Jenninger subsequently resigned. Domansky suggests that focussing on the perpetrators and their activities made people uncomfortable, as it heightened their feelings of guilt and responsibility for the crimes. Contrition for the victims was a less threatening option, along with the more traditional narrative of the Holocaust as inexplicable and puzzling and thus best to be ignored (Domansky 1992). This event still has a strong emotional resonance, as evidenced by the debates over its meaning and the way in which it should be commemorated. This is 'a heritage that unsettles' (Macdonald 2006: 23).

Dissonance and power struggles

The multiplicity of meanings attached to dark commemorative events can lead to contestation, with various stakeholders having different expectations about the type of event that is appropriate, who should be the custodian of the event and the interpretation of the past that should be presented (Frost 2007; Frost *et al.* 2008). Tunbridge and Ashworth (1996: 95) have noted that dissonance is particularly likely, long-lasting and extreme where 'atrocity tourism' is concerned. This is because it is very significant to a large proportion of people, involving complex reactions and 'highly charged controversy' and may have important political consequences. Dark commemorative events fall within this aegis and thus involve considerable dissonance. Blight (1989: 1159) discusses this in the context of the American Civil War, noting that there were 'rival versions of the past', resulting in a struggle to see one's preferred version become accepted wisdom: 'The historical memory of any transforming or controversial event emerges from cultural and political competition, from the choice to confront the past and to debate and manipulate its meaning'.

While Goldberg (1999: 184) argues that there is a place for exhibits to be both 'commemorative and analytical', this might be unrealistic. Domansky (1992) suggests in her work on the anniversary of *Kristallnacht* that controversy over the speech made in the West German Bundestag highlights the priority the public gave to 'the rituals of commemoration' over analysis. People wanted 'publicly created memory' with respect to the Holocaust, not the bald facts and 'professionally produced history' (Domansky 1992: 69). In line with this sentiment, exhibits in war museums, such as the displays in the Flanders Fields Museum in Ypres, Belgium, are moving towards interpretations of war that focus on the effects on individuals. For example, visitors to the exhibits are given a token bearing the name of someone on the museum database, who was involved in the war, which helps them to empathise with personal narratives (Whitmarsh 2001). This trend can be seen in other dark commemorative exhibitions, such as the recent one in Melbourne on the *Titanic*, where visitors were given the name of a passenger on the ship when they entered the exhibition, and then found out their fate at the end. While such a trend in interpretation might be engaging for visitors, there is a danger that the larger narratives and meanings may be lost.

The *Kristallnacht* example also illustrates how power struggles over memory can sometimes be wielded by governments, who use memory 'as an instrument of rule' (Hoelscher and Alderman 2004: 349). The tight control over the way the anniversary was commemorated in the West German Bundestag, with no Jewish person taking part in the speeches, was ultimately thwarted, as the commemoration was greeted with widespread public derision and condemnation (Domansky 1992). This illustrates Cesarani's contention that 'commemoration of the Holocaust may well act as a social "glue" in the widest sense, extending the embrace of community beyond the tribal limits usually marked out by commemorative events' (2000: 64).

Power over memory does not necessarily reside in the government of the day. Other stakeholders can also be very effective in shaping or even controlling the dominant narrative of commemorations. American World War Two veterans, for example, played a key role in the decision to cancel the Enola Gay exhibition. They saw themselves as custodians of the legacy left behind by the events of 1945 and were keen to ensure that this was not sullied by alternative or revisionist versions of history (Goldberg 1999). Eureka Day in Australia is another dark commemorative event involving stakeholders who have appointed themselves *custodians* over a historical episode. The group known as Eureka's Children claim that they have the right to manage the legacy that is Eureka. They set up their own commemorative procession at dawn, as a rival to the walk organised by the municipal art gallery, as the latter follows the route of the soldiers, rather than the miners. They have also lobbied to have the Eureka flag – *the Southern Cross* – moved from the art gallery, which is on the site of the soldiers' camp. They considered this an improper location, given the way the flag was treated by the authorities at the time of the uprising. All of these disputes came to a head in the 2004 hundred-and-fiftieth anniversary and still remain unresolved (Frost 2007).

In an attempt to avoid friction, some commemorations are deliberately skewed towards neutral ground, to allow all stakeholders the opportunity 'to share the same commemorative space' (Rivera 2008: 614). This may lead to accusations that the anniversary has been sanitised or whitewashed, as in the case of the 9/11 Exhibition in New York. Similarly, the black activist Frederick Douglass was concerned that commemorations of the American Civil War had forgotten its ideological roots in the movement against slavery, and were instead emphasising the valour of both sides (Blight 1989). Douglass felt this was a message that conveniently overlooked the guilt of slavery in the South. He saw it as his mission to alter the meaning of the Civil War in the eyes of the public, often through various speeches he made on anniversaries associated with the war, and thus to reassert power over the creation of cultural mythology (Blight 1989).

Authenticity and the dark past

While all commemorative events involve issues of authenticity, this is particularly challenging with respect to the dark variety. There are questions of taste with respect to re-enactments – how far can the event organisers go in trying to re-create the past, particularly where it is troubled, terrifying or tragic? Where dark commemorative events aim for strict historical accuracy, they can sometimes veer towards the macabre. Allred (2004: 5) refers to a commemoration of the American Civil War with 'surgeons' re-enacting 'with ghastly realism (and a roast of beef) a limb amputation'.

Authenticity is a challenging goal. Changes in the meanings of an event might result in the narrative being changed or transmuted. The concept of memory is elastic, and 'remembrance, as a collective memory, is continually revised' (King 2010: 3). Lowenthal (2003: 5) waspishly refers to the way that 'righteous victimhood today remakes sites of glorious victory into sepulchres of contrition chic', providing the example of Custer's Last Stand at Little Bighorn. The emphasis in recent re-enactments is more balanced. Historical inaccuracies are tolerated and even expected, such as ceremonies where combatants are reconciled and forgiving (Linenthal 1983). Other elements add to the fantasy, but do not impinge on the overall sense of realism. For example, the event-goer may meet figures from history. The annual Gettysburg re-enactment includes a session to 'discuss Gettysburg' with General Robert E. Lee in its schedule of events, while the Bosworth battlefield anniversary re-enactment in 2011, organised by English Heritage, allowed event-goers to 'meet' King Richard at lunch and 'ask him questions you may have about the impending battle' (www.bosworthbattlefield.com).

Authenticity might be understood in terms of the way in which the event has meaning for its participants. Carnegie and McCabe (2008) refer to the importance of existential authenticity in re-enactments, where the individual feels a more authentic form of *themselves* through their involvement in the event. The level of objective authenticity is not the issue here. Reenactors try to get it right as much as possible, but realise that they are not truly living in the past (Allred, 2004; Carnegie and McCabe 2008; Elliott 2007; Gapps 2010; Linenthal 1991; Turner, 1990). As Turner (1989: 56) remarks: 'reenactors do not use real bullets nor do they live for years in hard conditions'. Numbers involved are generally less than would have been the case for the original event (Turner 1989). The reenactors also acknowledge the existence of an audience and a sense of 'self-consciousness' (Turner 1989, see also Chapter 6).

The site of the commemorative event is also pertinent in this context. Holding the event at the actual site where something dark occurred might be unsettling, but bestows a sense of authenticity. The site itself might take on the character of a *sacred place*, such as Little Bighorn (Linenthal 1983) or Waterloo (Seaton 1999). There is a difference between re-enactment events staged at the site of the Battle of Little Bighorn, and those re-creations which took place as part of Buffalo Bill's Wild West Show at various sites throughout the USA and Europe (Linenthal 1983). The former have a haunting quality, bestowed on them by their setting in *lieux de mémoire* (sites of memory) (Nora 1989). American Civil War re-enactments sometimes take place on the actual battlefield, but due to National Parks Service prohibitions, more often at 'a nearby location with similarities in terrain which has been made available' (Turner 1989: 54). This does not seem to affect their authenticity for participants, perhaps because of the proximity.

Avoiding remembrance and dark commemorations

Lowenthal (1985: 347) observes in the context of museums that 'nothing seems too horrendous to commemorate'. Some commemorations are however too painful to be marked by an event. For example, 2011 marked the fiftieth anniversary of the withdrawal of the morning sickness drug thalidomide, responsible for many birth defects. Should that have been commemorated with an event? Other anniversaries will not be publicly acknowledged, due to feelings of embarrassment or deep shame, high levels of contestation or the level of emotional distress that the event will bring in its wake (Rivera 2008). The mere idea of staging an event to mark a dark past may strike some as crass. A memorial statue, plaque or marker might be considered as far as some places will go to commemorate what has happened, while others will not even take that step.

The case of Croatia brings these issues to the fore. According to Rivera (2008), in an attempt to manage their image on the international stage, including destination image for tourism purposes, the Croatian government has either downplayed or omitted any reference to the war in the 1990s, which transmuted into episodes of 'ethnic cleansing'. She argues that their failure to commemorate the war in any way, including memorials, monuments, or museum exhibits, is an attempt to limit the damage to their reputation, despite the fact that some countries have developed tourism products acknowledging a difficult past and marketed them successfully to visitors. Hungary for example has the House of Terror in Budapest, a museum which provides exhibits on Hungary's fascist and communist dictatorships 'as a fitting memorial to the victims' according to its official website (www.terrorhaza.hu).

This type of cover-up might prevent Croatia from using this episode as the cornerstone of a new national identity, based on recognising mistakes of the past, and making reparation in the future. Australia's refusal to formally apologise for the forced removal of indigenous children from their families became an open sore that was partially healed by the act of contrition led by the then Prime Minister Kevin Rudd on 13 February 2008. The anniversary of the apology is celebrated by many schools in a government-led program, reflecting the change of heart and realisation of the important symbolism of the apology in national reconciliation efforts. This was an example of a commemoration that would not be denied, however difficult its subject-matter and the temptation to forget.

4   The tourism paradox

What do I believe in? I believe in tourism.

(Deon Crosby, Roswell UFO Festival organiser, quoted in Paradis 2002: 38)

Events equate with tourism. This is a common public policy view, that sees the main rationale for supporting and planning events as the tourism and economic benefits they create. This is reinforced by organisational structures and processes. In most countries and cities, event planning falls under the control of government tourism departments and destination marketing organisations (DMOs). Strategic plans for event portfolios are typically included as part of broader destination tourism strategies with the objective of generating tourism benefits. Well-known terms, like mega events and hallmark events are defined in terms of their relationship to tourism. And, of course, events units and programs at tertiary level are nearly always taught by tourism departments and staff.

Public funding for staging commemorative events is often provided on the basis that it will stimulate tourism, creating a tangible (and measurable) economic legacy, which justifies the expense. However, this may be a high-risk strategy, as commemorative events may have limited tourist appeal. While some commemorative events strongly engage with communities, this connection is often very personal and the impact may be focussed on particular local, ethnic or national groups. The appeal to outsiders may be quite limited. Yet, it is these outside groups that governments and other stakeholders expect to provide flows of tourists and economic benefits. Commemorative events are often distinguished by this paradox of tourism expectations. In encouraging locals to reflect upon their identities and remember historical incidents, commemorative events have an important role in society. They may also attract tourists, but they may not. The common trap is believing that their significance to local and national identities will translate to interest amongst groups that do not share these identities. Falling for that trap, organisers and funding bodies may find there is a financial hangover and disappointment that the promised tourism benefits did not materialise.

Beyond the economic benefits, attracting tourists to commemorative events serves to validate the importance of identities. Outsiders showing interest and attending events demonstrates that what is being commemorated is worthy and valued. Both tourists and external media coverage function to justify that the organisers did a good job and that the resources (particularly public funding) were well spent. This often leads to a type of *cultural cringe*, where success is dependent on what outsiders thought and said. A good example of this occurred during the two-hundredth anniversary of explorers Lewis and Clark journeying from the Mississippi to the Pacific. At Bismarck, North Dakota, 50,000 people attended, commemorating what is arguably the most important historical event to occur in that town. However, what made front page news in the local *Bismarck Tribune* newspaper was that several British tourists were present, thereby lending international significance to the event (Ray *et al.* 2006).

In this chapter, we examine this paradox of expecting and planning for commercial tourism benefits for commemorative events. We begin with examining the common model of destination events tourism planning and how that structure links funding to tourism. We then consider the three main ways in which commemorative events generate tourism benefits. A range of tourism-focussed commemorative events are used as illustrative examples, including two salutary case studies which did not deliver the expected tourism flows or revenue. We conclude with a detailed examination of the 2012 centenary of the *Titanic*, particularly considering how that was used to generate tourism and how that tied in with other meanings generated by the commemoration.

Destination events tourism planning

In developing and staging events to promote tourism, destinations follow a common model or pattern. Tourism and hospitality operators (the 'tourism industry') tend to see events as one of its subsidiary 'products', which can be 'leveraged off' to attract tourists and revenue for their businesses. Adopting an organisational structure based on geographic destinations, such as countries, cities or regions, private tourism and hospitality businesses co-operate with each other and government agencies. These formal DMO structures are characterised by their emphasis on the combination of competing and co-operating (*co-opition*), networking and government-industry 'partnerships'. As part of their tourism strategy, DMOs seek to build a suite of attractive events through partnering with existing event organisers, networking with other stakeholders, providing assistance with marketing, funding, bidding processes and working as an advocate of specific events through liaison with governments (Frost and Laing 2011; Getz 2008; Richards and Palmer 2010; Stokes 2007; Ziakas 2010). These relationships are usually quite formal, either with key tourism representatives joining event organising committees or event sub-committees functioning under the umbrella of the DMO structure. In some cases, DMOs may even take the lead in creating new events specifically to target specific market segments or attract tourists during traditional low seasons.

As events become more important to destinations a, recent trend has been towards the development of an *events portfolio strategy*. This is an alternative to the risks of investing in individual and opportunistic bids for mega-events. Instead, DMOs choose to focus on a group of hallmark events tied to the destination. Under an events portfolio strategy, DMOs:

Assess the value of different events to be hosted, seeking to appeal to a wide range of market segments and placing events at different times of the year according to regional, market or environmental conditions … This means that rather than capitalizing on single events, each event needs to be cross-leveraged with others in the host community's portfolio in order to maximise intended outcomes.

(Ziakas 2010: 146–7)

This widely-adopted strategic approach emphasises co-operative planning and networking with a goal of leveraging events for tourism benefits. However, to effectively implement it, certain types of events need to be privileged over others. Clearly, repeated events appealing to tourists will be favoured. In turn, irregular events without a strong tourism focus hold lesser appeal. Commemorative events, in particular, may be difficult to include in such an approach.

Some annual commemorative events may be developed as hallmark events within an events portfolio strategy. An example of this is the Hastings Week festival, in south-east England. It includes two annual commemorative events – the re-enactment of the Battle of Hastings and Bonfire (Guy Fawkes) Night – as anchors of a week of cultural, heritage and community events.

However, planning for commemorative events of major anniversaries, such as centenaries, is usually well outside the events portfolio strategy. Irregular, perhaps once in a lifetime, commemorative events of major anniversaries are square pegs in a world of round holes. Accordingly, they either struggle for support, or are treated as special cases, which in turn creates a range of problems. Most commemorative events simply do not fit the organisational structures for destination events tourism. Nor do bodies organising commemorative events necessarily understand tourism policy or structures. In a study of the 2005 Hans Christian Andersen bicentenary in Denmark, Liburd noted this was 'virgin territory' for the Danish tourism industry and 'there was a mutual lack of knowledge and respect between the culture and tourism sectors' (2008: 48).

Anniversary commemorative events tend to have purpose-created organisational structures, separate from governments and DMOs. Unlike DMOs, these are usually temporary, limited to a very specific purpose and bound by sunset provisions. Their expertise in tourism may be quite limited, though there is an expectation that like other events they will aim to generate tourism. Indeed, they may be competing against DMOs and their events portfolio for government funding. There are three common scenarios for these organisational structures; these are a *top-down, bottom-up* and what we term *sideways*, approaches to their establishment and governance.

Top-down planning structure

In this instance, the government establishes a separate body to plan and manage the commemorative event. This is a QANGO, or quasi-autonomous non-government organisation. Nominally independent, with its own board, staff and budget, it is partially controlled by the government which has created it, funded it, set up its aims and approved its board. The nominal independence is important, as it avoids complaints of too much government interference and promotes a sense of bi-partisanship. Nonetheless, such QANGOs are still subject to criticism, usually for being overly bureaucratic and lacking sensitivity towards community concerns. Such structures are typically created for anniversaries which governments view as being of major importance, particularly those connected with national identity. Examples of top-down planning organisations include the Australian Bicentenary Authority and the Australian Centenary of Federation Authority.

Bottom-up planning structure

The contrasting scenario is an organisational structure which is created by community groups and then lobbies the government and other stakeholders for funding and other support. Such a structure has the advantage of greater community engagement, but the disadvantage of expending much of its energy in chasing funding. An example is the hundred-and-fiftieth anniversary of the gold rushes, held in Australia in 2001. Its planning involved over 40 groups coming together and forming Gold 150 as an umbrella company. Even with strong government support, it took four years before funding was approved (Frost 2001).

Sideways planning structure

This third approach may not fit the usual perspectives of public policy, but is fairly common for events planning. Under this scenario, an organisational structure is created to develop and stage the commemorative event. This may either be top-down or bottom-up. Parallel to this is an existing DMO interested in using events to leverage increased tourism. The DMO creates a sub-committee or organisation to use the commemorative event for destination marketing and tourism opportunities. It liaises with the commemorative event organisers, but remains structurally quite separate. Indeed, it may be a *free rider*, benefiting from the event, but not contributing any funding. An example of this scenario occurred with the 2005 Hans Christian Andersen bicentenary in Denmark. There was a Hans Christian Andersen 2005 Foundation staging the event and a separate tourism task force established by the Danish Tourist Board. Whilst there was liaison between the two bodies, they had quite different operating styles and objectives (Liburd 2008). A variation occurred with the 1938 hundred-and-fiftieth anniversary of British settlement in Australia. A hundred-and-fiftieth Anniversary Celebrations Council was established, which engaged the semi-official DMO, the Australian National Travel Association, to market the event overseas. This marketing was funded by a third party, in the form of the Australian government (Wells 2011). The result was seemingly successful and might have become a template for future arrangements, except for disruption due to World War Two.

Tourism benefits

The relationship between commemorative events and tourism is shaped by a series of frustrating paradoxes, misconceptions and disconnections. Organising committees of commemorative events often sit outside the structure and vision of destination event tourism strategies, particularly the recent trend towards event portfolios. As argued above, organisers may lack expertise in understanding and promoting tourism and there may be communication blockages between them and DMOs. To gain funding, commemorative event organisers are hurried into promises of tangible economic benefits, even though their event has limited appeal to tourists. Indeed, it is important to recognise that some commemorative events will have almost no appeal to tourists at all. As with many different types of events (not just commemorative ones), there has been a tendency to assume tourists will be attracted, often with unfortunate consequences (McKercher *et al.* 2006).

Faced with these difficulties, the organisers of commemorative events have three main strategies for attracting tourists. The first (and most obvious) is through tourists attending the event itself. In addition, there are two ways of having a longer term influence on tourism. Publicity about the event may promote the desire to travel to a destination after the event and there may be a legacy of permanent tourism attractions and infrastructure resulting from the event.

The commemorative event as a tourist attraction

The ideal scenario is that a commemorative event will have such broad appeal that it will attract significant numbers of tourists as well as locals. These tourists will then spend money not only on the event, but also on accommodation, meals, transport, tours and shopping. Their expenditure is viewed as a measurable economic benefit, revenue gained by the economy through the event that would not otherwise have been generated. In contrast, money spent by locals is not regarded as an increase in economic benefit; rather it is simply seen as a reallocation of expenditure from one leisure activity to another (Crompton 2006; Frost and Laing 2011).

What type of tourist is attracted to a commemorative event? What motivates them? Unfortunately, there has been very little research on tourists and commemorative events. This is partly due to the one-off nature of many major anniversary events. We are not aware of any academic research studies into the motivations of tourists at commemorative events. Such studies are widely conducted for a range of events, generally using the concept of a scale of motivational factors, including for example, having fun, meeting others and learning new skills. Survey respondents are asked to numerically rate the importance of these factors. Through factor analysis, the key motivations are identified. It is intriguing to speculate how such an analysis would play out for a commemorative event. One scenario would be that the theme of the commemorative event would dominate, out-polling the more generic motivational factors. An alternative is that the standard factors would still rate highly, signifying the attraction of the event was not really connected to the theme. In this case, participants would be indicating that they were primarily motivated by spectacle, fun, music, a party atmosphere and socialisation; rather than the deeper meanings. Such a research outcome would be highly unpalatable to organisers and other stakeholders. Perhaps, given the inherent limitations of factor analysis, a qualitative approach is needed, with in-depth semi-structured interviews to tease out what exactly attendees expect from commemorative events.

Before a commemorative event, there may be enthusiastic and exaggerated projections of tourism numbers and economic impact based on wishful thinking. Once over, there seems to be little motivation for undertaking an evaluation of an event that may not occur again for decades. For example, while the bicentenary of explorers Lewis and Clark (USA, 2003–2006) was hailed as generating tourism for towns along their route, there were no formal economic impact studies undertaken, nor did satisfied stakeholders see any need for them (Ray *et al*. 2006). It is also partly that commissioned research, such as feasibility studies, does not delve too deeply into such matters. Such studies are typically concerned in boosting the claims and decisions of the commissioning stakeholder, rather than providing a fully independent analysis (Crompton 2006).

Accordingly, our analysis of tourists to commemorative events is only exploratory and speculative. With these limitations in mind, we identify six main possible elements of commemorative events which may attract tourists:

1   *International exhibitions.* A number of very large international exhibitions (or world expos) have been staged as part of national commemorative events. In scale and scope, these are intended to attract international tourists. A major element in national commemorative events strategies, these are considered in detail in Chapter 5.
2   *Museum and gallery special exhibitions.* Specially staged for commemorative events, they are an opportunity to experience collections that might not always be on show. Examples include special museum exhibits for the two-hundredth anniversaries of Charles Darwin, Charles Dickens, and Hans Christian Andersen and major travelling museum exhibits for the hundred-and-fiftieth anniversaries of the gold rushes in California and Australia.
3   *Historical re-enactments.* Visitors are attracted by the spectacle and novelty of costumed re-enactments of historical events. This is particularly the case with battle re-enactments. These are discussed in greater detail in Chapters 6 and 7.
4   *National pageants, parades and ceremonies.* National capitals attract tourists, partly for their history and partly as centres of power where resources have been directed towards monuments, national galleries and national museums (Maitland and Ritchie 2009). The role of events in encouraging tourists to national capitals also needs greater consideration (Frost 2012). National commemorative events, with pageants, parades, ceremonies, concerts, fireworks and appearances by world leaders, have the spectacle, drama and splendour to attract visitors, particularly domestic tourists.
5   *Diaspora events.* Commemorative events have the power to attract members of diaspora communities, providing a reason for them to 'return home' and be reunited with relatives.

6   *Participatory events.* Examples include the World Gold Panning Champion-
ships which were staged in California and Australia as part of their hundred-
and-fiftieth anniversaries of their respective gold rushes and Bloomsday in
Dublin, where fans follow the path through the city of the main character in
Ulysses by James Joyce.

In addition, some visitation is always *incidental*, tourists attending an event
purely because they just happen to be in the destination at the time (Frost and
Laing 2011). Incidental tourist attendance will tend to be higher in destinations
which already generate strong flows of visitors.

Measuring tourism numbers and benefits

Measuring the numbers of tourists who visit an event is often difficult. The ideal
scenario is the capturing of this data through ticket sales linked to postcodes and
country of origin. However, this may be affected through tickets being purchased
by locals for visiting friends and on-selling via agents, tours, accommodation and
electronic media. It also sometimes occurs that origin data are collected, but not
analysed nor shared with DMOs. Furthermore, many commemorative events are
staged across multiple venues with a mix of different managers. While some of
these events will have paid admission, others will have no ticketing, as in the
case of a street parade or free concert. The problems this causes are illustrated
in an annual commemorative event for which we recently undertook a research
consultancy. With multiple sites organised by various sub-groups, including some
with free entry in public spaces, the event committee did not know how many
people attended each year. Even though they were under pressure from their local
council for trend data and the proportion of attendees who were tourists, they had
no process in place to systematically collect that data. Instead, they relied on best
estimates, really 'guesstimates', that were hotly debated and disbelieved both by
committee members and external stakeholders.

The calculation of economic benefits from tourists attending events is
highly controversial. It has been the subject of much debate, both within local
communities and amongst academic researchers. As Crompton (2006) argues,
those conducting economic evaluations are rarely independent. They are usually
paid by organisers or governments to provide an analysis that will justify the
decision to fund and stage the event.

Successful commemorative events with a tourism focus

It is difficult, nearly impossible, to point to a commemorative event that has
objectively succeeded in meeting its aims of attracting tourists. We are certain
such events exist, just as it is clear that many have failed. The lack of empirical
evidence that will withstand independent scrutiny leads us to be quite cautious.
Accordingly, we are taking a different approach. The following examples are of
commemorative events which have adopted a tourism focus. That is, their design

and theme have been fashioned with a primary aim of attracting tourists. Most importantly, their organisers have not simply hoped or assumed they will attract tourists; rather they have actively and realistically planned for that outcome. We start this section with what we consider the best example of a commemorative event that has a strong tourism focus.

The fiftieth anniversary of the Roswell UFO landing

Roswell is a medium-sized regional town in New Mexico, USA. It is in a remote and arid area, not on an interstate highway and is approximately 300 kilometres from Albuquerque and Santa Fe. Its notoriety comes from an alleged crash landing of a UFO in 1947. That incident has become one of the staples of popular culture and online folklore and the subject of films such as *Independence Day* (1996) and *Men in Black* (1997) and television series *Roswell* (1999–2002) and *Taken* (2002). Ongoing interest in the incident is tied to place, the town's special place in popular culture, ensuring that 'few small places outside of Roswell can claim national and international name recognition without spending a single promotional dollar' (Paradis 2002: 24). Through its annual commemorative festival, Roswell has succeeded in capturing the economic benefits of that reputation and recognition. In this analysis of the development of that event, we have drawn heavily on the excellent qualitative study of that event by Paradis (2002).

The first festival was staged in 1996. It was small, attracting about 1,000 people, but served to demonstrate its tourism potential, particularly as many were from overseas. The second festival in 1997 was conceived on a larger scale, primarily as it was to commemorate the fiftieth anniversary. Here was a chance to capture global attention for this small-town event. With the assistance of the New Mexico Department of Tourism, domestic and international media were targeted. The results were that 450 journalists attended, generating over 1,000 articles in 450 magazines, free publicity which was valued at US$ 4.4 million. The expectation was that it would attract up to 60,000 tourists. Though this was not achieved, attendance was 48,000 (co-incidentally the same as the population of the town) and organisers and stakeholders were satisfied (Paradis 2002: 30–1). Roswell was now on the tourist map.

The organisers were fully aware that there was no firm evidence that the UFO incident actually took place and that there was intense local scepticism about pandering to popular culture. However, they understood the power of the myth that had grown up about it. They also understood that it was intrinsically tied in with the name of the town and was easily the most famous thing associated with it. The initial newspaper report of the UFO crash had been on July 8 1947, so the festival could be conveniently scheduled for the July 4 holiday weekend.

The success of the fiftieth anniversary festival established that it should be staged annually. These continued to be successful, gaining international media coverage (images of participants dressed as aliens, mutants and avatars constantly make the news) and attracting large flows of domestic and international tourists.

Dusty Huckabee, one of the festival organisers, explained how the festival had changed tourism within the town:

> It put Roswell on the map, it's really made an impact. We've built four new motels because of it ... [the town levies] a five per cent lodgers tax ... The lodgers tax also built this [convention centre]. Now we get $30,000 a year for festivals. Most of the festivals I get right in the heart of downtown and that's what keeps people coming into downtown.
>
> (interviewed in Paradis 2002: 33)

In addition, the impact of the festival on tourism extended beyond Roswell:

> The newly discovered UFO theme became an important component not just of Roswell's local economy, but of the entire state of New Mexico. The theme had fused with state and local tourism development initiatives. By 1999 the UFO theme had invaded nearly all [tourism] promotional materials and informational products.
>
> (Paradis 2002: 34)

Rural commemorative festivals with a tourism focus

Many of the best examples of commemorative events which have become tourism focussed festivals are from rural areas (see Table 4.1). Those listed are all annual festivals, held on weekends closest to the dates of the historical incidents being commemorated. Most started as one-off commemorative events. Roswell was a fiftieth anniversary, the Man From Snowy River a centenary, Ned Kelly a hundredth-and-twenty-fifth and Little Bighorn was first staged for the centenary of Montana. When local stakeholders realised that these commemorative events drew in good numbers of tourists, they decided to stage them as annual festivals.

Table 4.1 Examples of rural commemorative festivals with a strong tourism focus

Name	Town	Region, country	Event commemorated
Roswell UFO Festival	Roswell	New Mexico, USA	1947 crash of UFO
Helldorado Days	Tombstone	Arizona, USA	1881 gunfight at OK Corral
Battle of Little Bighorn Days	Hardin	Montana, USA	1876 battle
Battle of Hastings re-enactment	Battle	Sussex, UK	1066 battle
Ned Kelly Weekend	Beechworth	Victoria, Australia	1882 capture and trial of bushranger
Man From Snowy River Weekend	Corryong	Victoria, Australia	1897 publication of poem

The success and importance of these commemorative festivals is related to the special qualities and limitations of rural events. Country towns use festivals based on local heritage icons to attract tourists (Frost and Laing 2011). In many cases, historical incidents and people are the main medium for gaining notice and attracting tourists. Indeed, they may be the only reason that most potential tourists have ever heard of the town. In the cases listed in Table 4.1, the historical incidents are easily the main – even sole – claim to fame of the towns. Accordingly, it makes sense to construct a tourist-focussed festival around these markers and their relationship to the towns. This results in a strong sense of place at the heart of each of these festivals.

The style of these commemorative festivals is intriguing. There is a mix of history and popular culture. There are iconic personalities and tragic defeats. Flawed heroes (Custer, Wyatt Earp, Ned Kelly, King Harold) are popular. Re-enactments are a common element, as are street parades and performances. Most, though not all, have a playful attitude. Visitors can slip into the past, dressing up and playing historical characters. Balancing this are elements that are nostalgic and elegiac, recognising that while these times have passed they are still partly maintained in rural towns. Though based on real events, these festivals rely heavily on fantasy. Their popularity leaves them open to criticism for fakery and bad taste (Paradis 2002; Walsh 1992).

Larger cities do not have this same tendency to construct commemorative events as tourist festivals. While they often aim to attract tourists, it is more often a by-product. This may be due to their larger populations, providing a constituency that needs to be reassured about its identity. In such cases, reinforcing or reimagining identities may be more of a priority for policy makers than tourism. It may also be that large cities see other opportunities for encouraging tourists. It is an area that needs more research, for there are few examples of this tourism focus for commemorative events in cities. Perhaps an exception (even the beginning of a trend) is how the 2012 centenary of the *Titanic* is being used to promote tourism. This case is considered in detail later in this chapter.

Contrary examples of failure

In contrast to examples of commemorative events which succeeded in attracting tourists, it is also valuable to consider failures. To conclude this section, we examine two cases where the organisers of commemorative events strategically set out to attract tourists, but failed to achieve the targets they had set. These case studies are instructive in revealing the problems of planning for one-off commemorative events and how the tourism expectations of events organisers may sometimes be over-inflated.

Expo Y 150

In 2009, Yokohama in Japan staged Expo Y 150. This was an international exhibition to commemorate the hundred-and-fiftieth anniversary of the port of Yokohama being opened to Western traders. In the seventeenth century, the Tokugawa Shogunate had adopted a policy of severely restricting international trade and contact. By the nineteenth century, the expanding Western powers were increasingly pressuring Japan to open itself to trade, which finally occurred at Yokohama in 1859. Once exposed to outside influence, Japan experienced a rapid period of modernisation and political and economic change. The five-month exhibition was budgeted with an attendance of 5 million visitors. Instead it received only 1.24 million. As recriminations started, the event organisers began legal action against three travel companies for failing to deliver contracted numbers of tourists (Takebe 2010). Part of the problem may have been that the event was staged too closely to the Shanghai World Expo.

The Millennium Dome

The Millennium Dome in London was built to commemorate the millennium (that is, start of the 2000s, a new thousand year period or millennium). A permanent exhibition centre, it commenced with a year-long international exhibition in 2000. Its business plan was based on 12 million visitors over the year, essentially just above its break-even point. However, that projection had been agreed upon before the organisers had decided on ticket prices, the contents of the exhibition, a marketing plan or transport logistics. The final numbers were only 4.5 million paying customers for 2000 (National Audit Office 2000). Compounding its problems was a disastrous opening night on New Year's Eve 1999. Four-thousand guests had been invited, but not provided with physical tickets, access to car parking or adequate transport alternatives. Most of them had to enter via the one working electronic security gate. Amongst the disgruntled VIP guests were newspaper editors, the head of the BBC and the major sponsors (Shone and Parry 2010).

Longer-term destination marketing

In addition to visitors to the specific commemorative event, the destination may use the anniversary as the trigger for generating publicity which will result in later flows of tourism. This is quite common with events in general. During the Olympics, for example, there will be sustained television marketing of the host city which is aimed at encouraging viewers to consider it for future travel (Frost and Laing 2011). The newsworthiness of commemorative events provides this opportunity for effective marketing. However, it is important to understand that commemorative events only provide a limited media window. It is an area that needs more research, but the media spotlight may only shine for a few days or a week around the key anniversary date. However, once that crucial date is past, it is quite likely that the media promotion will significantly fall and so may tourism. Furthermore, there may be a significant lag – perhaps 50 or 100 years – before that spotlight comes around again.

The following three examples illustrate how recent commemorative events have been used to anchor destination marketing campaigns:

1   India used the fiftieth and sixtieth anniversaries of Independence to launch international campaigns encouraging visitation. Similarly, the 2012 centenary of the establishment of New Delhi as the capital of India was also used as a tourism marketing campaign. Intriguingly, marketing for the latter was not tied to any actual events, but rather that this was simply a good time to visit.
2   In 2011, the two-hundredth anniversary of the (Re) discovery of Petra was the core of a tourism campaign for Jordan. The campaign was particularly noticeable in London, where attractive images of this iconic ancient city were plastered over hundreds of buses.
3   Also in 2011, the centenary of the Northern Territory in Australia was adapted to the marketing of this popular destination. The centenary's slogan of '100 years of the territory, over 50,000 years of stories', seemed dually applicable to the identity of local inhabitants and to the encouraging of tourism.

In all of these instances, the primary purpose of the marketing was not to attract visitors to the events staged for the commemoration. Rather, the aim was to use the anniversary to gain attention, to promote a message that something significant once occurred there which was now being commemorated and to implant the idea that it is worth a visit *in the future*. In these cases, it is important to understand that policy makers saw these anniversaries as so newsworthy and of sufficient international appeal to use them as the foundation for expensive marketing campaigns.

Tourism legacy of the commemorative event

The third way in which commemorative events stimulate tourism is through their legacy, particularly of built structures. This includes infrastructure, constructions for the event which become attractions in their own right (for example, the Eiffel Tower) or purpose-built interpretive centres (for example, the Titanic Visitor Centre in Belfast's newly branded Titanic Quarter). This legacy of commemorative events is discussed in greater detail in Chapter 10.

The 2012 centenary of the *Titanic*

The passenger liner *Titanic* sank on 15 April 1912, after hitting an iceberg in the North Atlantic Ocean. On her maiden voyage, she was at the time the ultimate in technology and luxury. Lacking adequate numbers of lifeboats, 1,514 of her passengers and crew died, with only 710 surviving. While not the greatest maritime disaster of modern times in terms of numbers, the sinking of the *Titanic* has an unsurpassed notoriety and worldwide recognition. As Mendelsohn argued:

> The inexhaustible interest suggests that the *Titanic*'s story taps a vein much deeper than the morbid fascination that has attached to other disasters. The explosion of the *Hindenberg*, for instance, and even the torpedoing, just three years after the *Titanic* sank, of the *Lusitania*, another great liner whose

passenger list boasted the rich and famous, were calamities that shocked the world but have failed to generate an obsessive preoccupation.

(2012: 2)

The interest in the disaster is generated by multiple interpretations and perspectives. In particular, there are six overlapping 'storylines' that contribute to public interest:

1   *Tragic romantic.* The tragedy is understood in terms of individual human stories – both real and fictional. The principle of 'women and children first' in the limited lifeboats opens up stories of separated lovers. There are also instances of individual heroism and sacrifice, as in the band which kept playing through the sinking in an attempt to maintain calm.
2   *Technical engineering.* The liner was an engineering marvel, pronounced as unsinkable. However, even its name suggests an unfolding Greek tragedy – its over-confident creators mirroring another Titan in Prometheus with their quest, and arguably hubris. A series of human errors contributes to the sinking, demonstrating that no matter how modern or advanced technology is, it can never be infallible. Fascination with the technical aspects was extended by the successful 1985 expedition reaching the wreck deep underwater, retrieving artefacts and filming the site.
3   *Personal and family connections.* Individuals related to those involved in the tragedy hold a special personal connection. Such relationships are a feature of many commemorative events, but are particularly prominent in the case of the *Titanic*.
4   *Dark.* Lennon and Foley (2000) position the *Titanic* as the beginning of the modern fascination with dark tourism. This, they argue, is partly due to the extensive media coverage over time and partly due to how the sinking illustrates our concerns with modern technology.
5   *Luxury and celebrity.* Much attention is given to the first-class passengers, particularly in fictionalised versions. Their privileged position both fascinates and repels. 'The *Titanic*'s story irresistibly reads as a parable about a gilded age', argues Mendelsohn, 'in which death was anything but democratic, as was made clear by a notorious statistic: of the men in first class … the percentage of survivors was roughly the same as that of children in third class' (2012: 5).
6   *Playful.* The *Titanic* is an internationally recognised popular culture icon, which may be used playfully in many contexts without dark overtones. Examples include commemorative events focussing on the fashions worn by the first-class passengers, it featuring in the *Dr Who Christmas Special* and its use as an inflatable children's slide at community events (see Figure 4.1).

These storylines both overlap and conflict. For example, a dark perspective adds depth to the romantic story, but is at odds with the playful approach. In 2012, the staging of a series of commemorative events for the centenary took place

Figure 4.1 Titanic inflatable slide at the Yakkerboo Festival in Pakenham, Australia. Photo by B. Harvey.

against this background of multiple stories. As a number of these events had aspirations of encouraging tourism, they provide a valuable case study of the paradoxical issues arising from combining tourism and commemoration. Though a wide range of events were staged to commemorate the *Titanic*, for simplicity our focus is on the main three, all of which purported to have tourism implications.

Even though the tragedy occurred in a remote part of the North Atlantic, it was possible to stage an event at the exact spot, 100 years on. Two tourism operators provided commercial products, with chartered cruise liners converging at the sinking location. These were the *Balmoral*, which had followed the *Titanic*'s route from Southampton and the *Azmera Journey*, which sailed out of New York. Both contained paying passengers. A number, who featured heavily in media reports, were descendants of those who sailed on the *Titanic* (Addley and McDonald 2012). A key part of the re-enactment was passengers and crew dressing up in early twentieth-century costumes and meals were replicas of those served on the original voyage. The anniversary was marked with a memorial service and the laying of wreaths.

Liverpool in England was where the *Titanic* was registered and the home for many of the crew. Its Merseyside Maritime Museum ran an exhibition – 'Titanic and Liverpool: the Untold Story' to coincide with the anniversary. Less conventionally, the city council staged the event 'Sea Odyssey: A Giant

Spectacular' from 20 to 22 April. This theatrical performance was loosely based on a true story involving a Liverpool girl's letter to her father on the *Titanic*. The 'actors' were giant puppets, which moved around the streets of the city accompanied by musicians and supporting performers. In some ways, it was a curious production to commemorate the tragedy, its impossibly colossal spectacle and technical audacity over-shadowing all else. Staged in the main parts of the city, it was watched by an estimated 600,000 people. Tellingly, Liverpool City Council pronounced it a great success, claiming that it generated a tourism impact of £32 million. Such a figure seems unlikely, as it equates in general terms to 160,000 visitor nights being generated by one three-day event. Again, it illustrates the pressure to over-estimate the tourism benefits to ward off any criticism.

The third event occurred at Belfast in Northern Ireland. This was where the *Titanic* was built. A 'Titanic Festival' included 'Titanic: The Musical', seven plays and a MTV concert. The highlight was the opening of Titanic Belfast, a purpose built museum costing £100 million. Situated on the site of the former shipyards where the *Titanic* was constructed, it marks the beginning of the redevelopment of this derelict area as a new Titanic Quarter. The new museum is planned as the flagship of the precinct, anchoring future housing and retail developments.

For Belfast, the *Titanic* centenary represented a once in a lifetime opportunity to reimagine its destination image. For decades the city has been associated with sectarian conflict. With the global focus on the *Titanic*, the city could use its connection to strategically rebuild a more positive and attractive image. This promise of economic renewal provided the impetus for investing in the Titanic Belfast museum. Tim Husbands, CEO of the museum, argued that it was 'a product that could transform the face of tourism in Northern Ireland' and would have an annual economic impact of £24 million (quoted in Addley and McDonald 2012). It was noticeable that this new beginning for Belfast was the 'hook' in media stories leading up to the centenary. The relevant UK newspaper headlines, for example, promised that it would 'relaunch' Belfast (Atkinson 2011) and 'do for the city what the Guggenheim did for Bilbao' (Addley and McDonald 2012).

Each of these events combined a different mix of *Titanic* storylines, appealing to various market segments. The commemorative cruises highlighted romance and personal connections, and most importantly it offered the chance to experience a simulation of the luxury. Liverpool's spectacular bravely mixed a human interest story with playfulness. *Titanic Belfast* focussed on the city's role in building what was then a technological marvel, rather than the sinking.

Of the three, Belfast's was the most expensive, hanging the reimagination of the city's image and the development of a whole new precinct on the promise of the publicity that the centenary would bring. Even before it opened, there were doubts about its viability. The Northern Ireland Audit Office had reservations that the new museum would attract the 290,000 paying visitors it needs each year to break even (Addley and McDonald 2012).

In the course of the centenary, Belfast struck one major obstacle. Up to April 2012, media publicity gave prominence to the Belfast development. However, during the actual week leading up to the anniversary date, there was a great increase in the number of news stories about the centenary, but Belfast was generally missing from these. Instead it was the cruises that dominated in the media. Furthermore, there were a wide range of film and television productions screened in that week, but these were mainly fictional stories or accounts of Bob Ballard's 1985 rediscovery. Table 4.2 lists the productions screened in Australia during this period.

For Belfast, the problem was that there was so much media attention given to the centenary of the *Titanic*. With such an extensive coverage, its connection and new tourism offering may have been blotted out. At this stage, it is too early to tell if this will be of long-term significance. It may take five to ten years before we can judge whether or not this commemorative event delivered the tourism benefits which were promised.

Table 4.2 Film and television productions for the centenary of the sinking of the *Titanic*, 2012

Date	Title	Details
5 April	*Titanic*	Cinema re-release in 3D of James Cameron's 1997 film starring Leonardo Di Caprio and Kate Winslet
6 April	*Titanic: The Mission*	Five-part reality television series, as engineers rebuild parts of the ship using methods from 1912
9 April	*Titanic 100: Final Word with James Cameron*	National Geographic television documentary, director James Cameron assembles a team of experts to investigate the mystery
11 April	*Titanic 100: Case Closed*	National Geographic television documentary examining theories of why the *Titanic* sank
14 April	*Bob Ballard: Titanic's Nuclear Secret*	National Geographic television documentary examining technology used by Ballard in his 1985 rediscovery of the *Titanic*
14 April	*Titanic*	1953 American feature film starring Barbara Stanwyck
14 April	*A Night to Remember*	1958 British feature film starring Kenneth More
15 April	*Titanic 100: Bob Ballard's Save the Titanic*	National Geographic television documentary examining how the wreck may be preserved
15 April	*Inside the Titanic*	BBC television documentary 'reconstructing' the sinking
15 April	*Lost Worlds: Unsinkable Titanic*	Canadian television documentary
18 April	*Titanic*	Four-part ITV television drama written by Julian Fellowes

5   It happened at the world's fair

Jules Verne dreamed of travelling around the world in eighty days. At the Esplanade and the Champs de Mars you can do it in six hours.
(Bulletin Officiel de l'Exposition Universelle de 1889,
quoted in Mathieu 1996: 59)

Major exhibitions and re-enactments are two varieties of events closely associated with commemorations. Re-enactments (explored in Chapters 6 and 7) seem an obvious medium for promoting the need to remember and reflect upon the past. In contrast, exhibitions are a curious choice, seemingly full of contradictions. These include:

1   In focussing a global spotlight on a host country and the historical incident being commemorated, there are objectives of improving international status and reinforcing identity. However, aspects of the exhibitions and commemoration may attract unfavourable comments as well.
2   The scale and expense of an international exhibition provides the opportunity for a major global impact, but also carries a high risk of financial failure.
3   While ostensibly aimed at the international community, the great majority of attendees will be local people.
4   Typically exhibitions look forward, rather than backwards to the past. Indeed, many are noted for their futuristic vision. Identity is imagined in terms of what societies will be in the future, rather than through the reflections on the past which are normally associated with commemorative events.
5   The relationship between the exhibition and the commemorative event may be quite tenuous. The commemorative event may provide little more than an excuse for a show. Or it may be that added advantage which just helps a city to win a bid for funding and endorsement.

Table 5.1 lists 28 major exhibitions which have utilised commemorative events as themes. Variously termed as expositions, expos, exhibitions or world's fairs, they were conceived as large scale, mass-market events. Completely portable, often gained through competitive bidding processes and targeting the global media, such international exhibitions qualify as mega-events. Even where they were repeated, such manifestations only occur at long intervals, as in the cases of the centenary and sesquicentenary expositions in Philadelphia or the Columbian exhibitions. Of the 28, 14 (50 per cent) were held in the USA and 8 (29 per cent) in Europe. In contrast, only one was in Asia, one in South America and none in Africa or the Middle East. Typically, the event commemorated was constructed as of national importance, such as foundation, discovery or independence. In a few cases the national significance seemed stretched, as in anniversaries of states or cities.

There is a clear *golden age* of commemorative exhibitions. Twenty-one of the 28 (75 per cent) were held between 1876 and 1940. In contrast, the next 70 years saw only a further seven (25 per cent), with only one staged in the last 20 years. This decline in incidence seems surprising, particularly given a perception that commemorative events in general are increasing (a phenomenon discussed further in Chapter 11). It suggests that commemorative exhibitions are historical artefacts, once highly popular, but now falling away in importance and relevance. This is certainly the case with the USA. As Gold and Gold comment, 'it is difficult nowadays to realise how much significance expositions once had in the USA' (2005: 83). Between 1876 and 1940, the USA hosted 13 commemorative exhibitions. Since World War Two, the USA has only staged one and the commemorative element was quite tenuous. Indeed, the American love affair with the world's fairs seems well and truly over. None has been staged since 1984. The bicentenary expo was cancelled and the US is no longer even a member of the international Bureau de Expositions (Frost and Laing 2011).

It is interesting to consider commemorative exhibitions that were announced, but then cancelled (Table 5.2). With some, the choice of historical event to be commemorated was quite intriguing. A world expo themed on the fiftieth anniversary of the Russian Revolution coinciding with the Cold War would have had some interesting implications, as would have the one in Rome planned to commemorate the twentieth anniversary of Fascism and Mussolini. The planned 1917 Japanese exhibition is a reminder that this rapidly industrialising country was an enthusiastic participant at all of the preceding US world's fairs (Rydell 1984). In considering the causes of cancellation, there is a sharp division. World War One doomed the two 1917 exhibitions. World War Two stopped the Italian one planned for 1942 and the two in the mid 1950s struggled to raise capital during post-war reconstruction. In contrast, the cancellations of the more recent three illustrate widespread unease about potential public debt and the declining passion for international exhibitions, particularly in the USA (Findling 1994).

National identity, international prestige

In linking these exhibitions to major national commemorations, the ambitions of organisers, sponsors, exhibitors and other stakeholders went well beyond those of normal large-scale trade and commercial events. As Hoffenberg explained, 'exhibitions were part of a self-conscious reworking of fluid national and imperial identities' (2001: xiv). These aspirations were well summed up by Wilbur Atwater

Table 5.1 Commemorative exhibitions

Year	City	Event	Commemorating
1876	Philadelphia	Centennial Exposition	Centenary of Declaration of Independence
1884–5	New Orleans	World's Industrial and Cotton Centennial Exposition	Centenary of first export shipment of cotton from American South
1888	Melbourne	Centennial International Exhibition	Centenary of European settlement
1889	Paris	Exposition Universelle	Centenary of French Revolution
1892	Madrid	Columbian Historical Exposition	400th Anniversary of Columbus's 'discovery' of the Americas
1893	Chicago	World's Columbian Exposition	400th Anniversary of Columbus's 'discovery' of the Americas
1897	Nashville	Tennessee Centennial Exhibition	Centenary of statehood
1904	St Louis	Louisiana Purchase Exposition	Centenary of US purchase of Louisiana from the French
1905	Portland	Lewis and Clark Centennial Exposition	Centenary of Lewis and Clark expedition
1907	Hampton Roads	Jamestown Tercentennial Exposition	300th Anniversary of European settlement
1911	Turin	Esposizione Internazionale dell'Industria e del Lavoro	50th Anniversary of the proclamation of the kingdom of Italy
1922	Rio de Janeiro	Exposção Internacional do Centenario	Centenary of Brazilian independence
1926	Philadelphia	Sesquicentennial Exposition	150th Anniversary of Declaration of Independence
1930	Antwerp	Exposition Internationale, Coloniale, Maritime et d'Art Flamand	Centenary of Belgium

1930	Liège	Exposition Internationale de la Grande Industrie, Science et Application d'Art de Wallon	Centenary of Belgium
1933–1934	Chicago	Centenary of Progress Exposition	Centenary of founding of Chicago
1936	Dallas	Texas Centennial Exposition	Centenary of Texas independence
1936	Fort Worth	Frontier Centennial Exposition	Centenary of Texas independence
1939	New York	World's Fair	150th Anniversary of inauguration of George Washington as first President of the USA
1939–40	Wellington	New Zealand Centennial Exhibition	Centenary of Treaty of Waitangi
1940	Chicago	Diamond Jubilee Exposition	75th Anniversary of the Emancipation Proclamation
1951	London	Festival of Britain	Centenary of the Great Exhibition (Crystal Palace)
1964–5	New York	World's Fair	300th Anniversary of British takeover (renaming New Amsterdam as New York)
1967	Montreal	Expo 67	Centenary of Canadian Federation
1988	Brisbane	Expo 88	Bicentenary of European settlement
1992	Seville	Expo 92	500th Anniversary of Columbus's 'discovery' of the Americas
1992	Genoa	Expo 92	500th Anniversary of Columbus's 'discovery' of the Americas
2009	Yokohama	ExpoY 150	150th Anniversary of the port of Yokohama being opened to the West

Sources: Allwood 1977; Rydell 1984; Rydell 1993

Table 5.2 Cancelled commemorative exhibitions

Date	City	Commemorating
1883	New York	Centenary of peace treaty ending War of Independence
1917	Tokyo	50th Anniversary of Meiji restoration
1917	Montreal	50th Anniversary of Canadian Federation
1942	Rome	20th Anniversary of Fascist rule
1954	St Louis	150th Anniversary of US Purchase of Louisiana from the French
1955	Paris	Centenary of first Paris Universelle Exposition
1967	Moscow	50th Anniversary of Russian Revolution
1976	Philadelphia	Bicentenary of Declaration of Independence
1992	Chicago	500th Anniversary of Columbus's 'discovery' of the Americas

Source: Allwood 1977; Gold and Gold 2005

from the Smithsonian Institution, who was involved in the planning of the 1893 Chicago World's Columbian Exposition. He argued that,

> the exposition should not be merely a show, a fair or a colossal shop, but also and pre-eminently an exposition of the principles which underlie our national and individual welfare ... the progress we have made, the plane on which we live and the ways in which we will rise higher.
>
> (quoted in Rydell 1984: 7)

There were two target markets involved. The main one was domestic. The great majority of the attendees were from the host country. The commemorative exhibition served to reinforce the view that they were part of a nation, that their nation was distinct and special, that it was the centre of a political or commercial empire and that it was making exceptional progress. As discussed in Chapter 2, this link between commemorative events and the imagining of the nation is very strong and these exhibitions were major examples of this connection.

The second market was international. It was important that these exhibitions attracted foreign exhibitors, media, dignitaries and visitors. They served to validate the rhetoric of national importance and progress. They showed the citizens of the host nation that their country truly was of international standing and worthy of respect within the global community. It scarcely mattered if such outsiders were proportionally quite small amongst the attendees, or whether or not their favourable commentary was sincere rather than just diplomatic. The contribution of international attendees was simply to reinforce the image of the nation that was being presented.

Revolutionary Victorian exhibitions

The centennial exposition at Philadelphia attracted 10 million patrons. Modelled on European exhibitions, it signalled a long and passionate interest in these types of events in the USA. This would become the template for how Americans approached commemorations for at least the next 70 years. It had further significance, in that previous commemorative events were usually held for just one day. The centennial of Independence could have simply focussed on 4 July. Instead, a new model was implemented with the exhibition starting in May and running through to November (McDonald and Méthot 2006).

Philadelphia also represented a major change in exhibition design. The Great Exhibition of 1851 had been contained within the Crystal Palace, a single, large and spectacular building. Philadelphia broke away from this model by having a showground containing multiple exhibition pavilions. Essentially, it was impractical and highly risky to build a single structure large enough to house all exhibits and patrons. The alternative was to have larger grounds with smaller buildings. This allowed the separation of exhibitors (particularly the different countries) and encouraged a greater range of fantasy architectural design. By covering a larger area with multiple pavilions, there was more for patrons to see and less crowding. From Philadelphia onwards, most exhibitions would follow this pattern (Gold and Gold 2005).

The Paris Exposition attracted 32 million attendees, roughly the then population of France. It was particularly noted for its design features, which later exhibitions would strive to duplicate or outdo.

The great success of the Paris exhibition was the 300-metres-tall Eiffel Tower, which was climbed by almost 2 million patrons (Mathieu 1996). Audacious in its design, the tallest building in the world, it served no other purpose than to be the iconic symbol of the exhibition. Taking their cue from this mega-structure, much of the rest of the exhibition was constructed of iron, promoting a message of French modernity and engineering excellence. As Paul Gauguin exclaimed, 'Iron, iron and more iron … the Exposition represents the triumph of iron' (quoted in Mathieu, 1996: 59). A further example of *Belle Epoque* gigantism was Eugene Mercier's monstrous barrel of champagne (see Figure 5.1). Two stories high, it held the equivalent of 200,000 bottles of this iconic French luxury product (Guy, 2007). A hundred years later it was restored for the two-hundredth anniversary of the French Revolution and placed on permanent display at its headquarters in Épernay (see Figure 5.2).

There was an intriguing contrast between the exhibitions in Philadelphia and Paris. Both commemorated revolutions. However, it seemed that France's exhibition was a bit too close to home for most of its neighbours. After all, the French had executed their king and the exhibition site of the Champs des Mars had been developed for revolutionary festivals. Accordingly, nearly all European monarchs declined to attend, the only exception being the King of the Belgians. Queen Victoria was not amused. Not only did she not go, but none of her family attended and the British Ambassador to France was specifically recalled, so that no official representative could be available. Furthermore, many aristocratic and moneyed French were alienated and organisers were initially worried that this might have a major effect on its viability (Greenhalgh 1988).

Figure 5.1 Interpretive panel at Eugene Mercier, showing the giant barrel en route to the 1889 Exhibition. Photo by W. Frost.

Figure 5.2 Interpretive panel at Eugene Mercier, showing restoration of the giant barrel for its centenary and the bicentenary of the French Revolution. Photo by W. Frost.

Once upon a time in the West

At Chicago (1893), St Louis (1904) and Portland (1905), the USA staged a trio of commemorative exhibitions that reinforced a mythology of frontier progress and Manifest Destiny. The term Manifest Destiny had been coined in the 1840s and referred to a widespread belief that it was clearly the USA's destiny to expand westwards across North America and further into the Pacific and South America (Laing and Frost 2012). This view was the justification for war with Mexico (1846–1848), which resulted in the gaining of Texas, California, Arizona and New Mexico; the rapid settlement of the West and the consequent displacement of Native Americans; the annexation of Alaska (1867) and Hawaii (1898) and war with Spain (1898), resulting in the acquisition of the Philippines and Puerto Rico.

These three commemorative exhibitions took an important role in propagating Manifest Destiny. Symbolically, they lionised a cavalcade of related historical incidents. Taken together, these key events were the foundations of American history, demonstrating the elements and logic of Manifest Destiny. Columbus, the great explorer, had crossed the Atlantic and discovered the Americas. The original colonies had declared their independence (already commemorated in 1876). In 1802, the fledgling government had the foresight to purchase the lands westwards from the French. What was contained within the territory acquired was unknown, so again a farsighted decision was made to send out an exploring expedition. Columbus, the Louisiana Purchase, Lewis and Clark – this was a very simple history lesson for Americans, justifying Manifest Destiny and their continued and inexorable expansion.

Chicago, with 27 million visitors and St Louis with 19 million attendees, were enormously successful events (Rydell 1984). The products and innovations on display and the very structure of the exhibition grounds reinforced this core idea that America's identity as an increasingly major international power was being celebrated. While these were international exhibitions, it was America that was on show to a predominantly American audience.

Ostensibly, exhibitions are about products and technology. However, at these three commemorative exhibitions the star attractions were people. Specifically, these were indigenous people swept up into the new American Empire. Chicago set the scene by borrowing the idea of ethnological villages from Paris, though really they were anthropological zoos where attendees could be titillated by fantasy voyeurism of primitive peoples and their customs. These were strategically well-paced along the narrow *Midway*. The official exhibition buildings at Chicago were spread across two public parks. Linking them required a pedestrian passage, which was dubbed the Midway Plaisance, or Midway for short. This was lined with various exhibits and sideshows, creating a popular precinct which bordered on the carnivalesque. So successful was this enforced design feature, that it was repeated at most later American exhibitions. At St Louis it was known as the Pike, at Portland the Trail and at the Jamestown Tercentenary, it was prosaically the Warpath (Rydell 1984).

Amongst the various exotic groups, the most popular by far were from the newly conquered Philippines. Government authorities were keen to convince the public of the righteousness of the war and demonstrate how the former Spanish colony would be an asset rather than a liability. For exhibition organisers, such an exhibit fitted exactly with the overall theme of continuing expansion. As the official exhibition guidebook at St Louis argued, 'the time is coming when the purchase and retention of the Philippine Islands will seem as wise to our descendants as does the Louisiana Purchase seem to us who live today' (quoted in Rydell 1984: 167).

At St Louis, the US government supported the 'Philippine Reservation', providing 1,200 Filipinos. Over half of these were members of the Philippine Scouts and Constabulary, paramilitary units demonstrating progress, assimilation and order. However, this was not what the public wanted. The sensation of the exhibition was a few hundred indigenous people, particularly, though not just, the Igorots. These Filipinos were presented as wild and savage tribes, wearing few clothes and performing ancient and mystical ceremonies. The success of this display at St Louis meant they became a staple for nearly all exhibitions up to World War One, though later versions were often organised by very dubious entrepreneurs (Rydell 1984).

While these three commemorative exhibitions looked forwards to further American expansion, they also looked backwards at the taming of the Western frontier and the disappearance of such a key element in the American national identity. In addition to the various displays of exotic tribes were exhibits of Native Americans. In 1876, the centennial exhibition had coincided with a major campaign against the Sioux, culminating in the wiping out of Custer's command. At Philadelphia, the *Atlantic Monthly* warned its readers, 'the red man, as he appears in effigy and photograph in this collection, is a hideous demon, whose malign traits can hardly inspire any emotion other than abhorrence' (quoted in Rydell 1984: 26). By the time of Chicago, resistance had been crushed and the survivors driven on to reservations. As the US government aggressively pursued a policy of forced assimilation, the displays at these exhibitions gave visitors a last chance to see what they imagined was a vanishing way of life.

At St Louis, juxtaposed to the Philippine Reservation was an adjacent display of local Native Americans, including the captive Geronimo (Goyaałé). This combination 'underlined continuities with America's past and with the national experience of subduing "savage" populations' (Rydell 1993: 20). Again the message was more than matter-of-fact history; the layout of the displays reinforced the view that it was America's Manifest Destiny to continue on this path of expansion and conquering indigenous peoples in the future.

The Apache leader Geronimo had surrendered in 1886 and was incarcerated at Fort Sill in Oklahoma Territory. From 1898, he was allowed leave to appear at local expositions and 4th-of-July parades. The Native American display he was a part of at St Louis had two aspects. Traditional handicrafts and skills were demonstrated, but more importantly in terms of US government policy, the Native Americans were shown attending a 'model school'. While the children learnt the 3Rs, the older ones were shown being trained in modern vocational skills (Debo 1976). In showcasing this policy of assimilation, the authorities demonstrated their benevolence and enlightenment. They also reinforced the message that the domestic frontier was truly settled and safe.

As one of the older members of his group, Geronimo was not forced to learn new skills. His putative role was displaying the ancient (and anachronistic) methods of making bows and arrows. His real role was being on show as the one and only Geronimo, a bona fide terrifying celebrity. His was an interactive exhibit and visitors could freely talk to him. He would sign an autograph for 25 cents and for between 50 cents and two dollars he would sell his photograph (Debo 1976; Rydell 1993).

St Louis delivered an elegiac vision of the West to its masses of visitors. They could experience the ageing Geronimo, but he was now stripped of his threat. Indeed, rather than a bloodthirsty savage, he was increasingly romantically viewed as an heroic resistance fighter. Visitors could view him with their own eyes and see him as human. Following on from St Louis, Theodore Roosevelt invited Geronimo to ride in his inauguration parade. The voluminous cheers of the crowd prompted one of the organisers to complain to the president, 'Why did you select Geronimo to march in your parade, Mr President? He is the greatest single-handed murderer in American history'. To which Roosevelt replied, 'I wanted to give the people a good show' (quoted in Debo 1976: 419).

The myth of the frontier was also foremost in two other events presented to coincide with the Chicago exhibition. These were not part of the official program – perhaps we would now call them part of the *fringe* – but they had a significant impact on how the West would be viewed in the future. These were presentations by historian Frederick Jackson Turner and frontiersman William 'Buffalo Bill' Cody. Writing to commemorate the centenary of these appearances, historian Richard White (1997) argues that while both told quite separate stories of the American experience they had similar conclusions about the significance of westwards expansion.

In central Chicago, the American Historical Association hosted the World Historical Congress. The timing and placement were deliberate to line up with the attraction of the Columbian Exposition. Other global organisations sought a similar alignment between their conferences and this exhibition, including the Congress of World's Religions and the World's Congress of Representative Women (Greenhalgh 1988). At the World Historical Congress, a young 31-year-old historian – Frederick Jackson Turner – presented a paper entitled 'The Significance of the Frontier in American History'. Starting with the startling revelation that the US Bureau of Census had decided that settlement had now reached such an extent that it could no longer draw a frontier line on the map, Turner argued that American national characteristics, including identity, practices, philosophy and institutions had evolved as adaptations to the continued movement westwards. The USA, he argued, was *exceptional*, distinct from all other nations, due to its frontier history. As he argued at Chicago, it was:

> To the frontier that American intellect owes its striking characteristics. That coarseness and strength combined with acuteness and inquisitiveness; that practical, inventive turn of mind, quick to find expedients; that masterful

grasp of material things, lacking in the artistic but powerful to effect great ends; that restless, nervous energy; that dominant individualism, working for good and for evil, and withal that buoyancy and exuberance which become of freedom – these are the traits of the frontier.

(Turner 1894: 39–40)

What became known as Turner's *frontier thesis* would be highly influential and contentious as historians debated the complexity of the American historical experience. A good example of the influence of the frontier thesis may be seen in a commemorative essay by pioneer environmental historian Roderick Nash. In 1970, he wrote an article to mark the upcoming centenary of the establishment of Yellowstone as the world's first national park. In this article he used Jackson's theory of American exceptionalism to argue that the concept of national parks was a distinct American invention arising from the USA's 'unique experience' with wilderness, the frontier and democracy (Nash 1970: 726). Whilst a popular view in the USA, such an application of the frontier thesis causes difficulties when we consider how quickly national parks spread to other countries. By the time of the Columbian Exposition, they were also established in Australia, New Zealand and Canada and under consideration in other countries. If the USA was uniquely shaped by its frontier, what was happening in other countries with frontiers? How did this gel with great enthusiasm for national parks in countries as diverse as Japan, Italy, South Africa and India? Though a theory of considerable merit, Turner's frontier thesis has tended to encourage a parochial view of American history, isolating it from trends and patterns in other countries.

Opposite the exhibition itself, 'Buffalo Bill' Cody leased a vacant block to present his 'Buffalo Bill's Wild West and Congress of Rough Riders of the World'. Cody had been touring his show since 1883. In 1889, he took it to Paris for the Universelle Exposition and had been primarily performing in Europe ever since. Chicago (and its crowds) offered an attractive homecoming opportunity. He had approached the exhibition organisers, but they did not have the space to accommodate him. The entrepreneurial Cody simply set up next door, grabbing a free ride on the exhibition's publicity (Carter 2000).

The flamboyant 'Buffalo Bill' had grown to be the embodiment of the tough and resourceful frontiersman. Revered as one of the remaining pioneers, he had outlived other legendary figures. Whereas his contemporaries Custer, Wild Bill Hickok and Sitting Bull had all died violently, Cody had survived (Laing and Frost 2012). His Wild West Show promoted a romanticised fantasy view of the frontier, with Cody first and foremost as the action hero. At Chicago, his show was watched by 25,000 people a day. Included in the program were displays of sharpshooting (featuring in particular Annie Oakley), horse riding, lassoing and bronco riding, frontier re-enactments (Indians attack a settler's cabin, a wagon train and the Deadwood stage) and a grand parade (Carter 2000). Before the advent of motion pictures, Cody delivered an unprecedented spectacle for increasingly urban American audiences.

Between the wars

After World War One, the fashion for commemorative exhibitions seemed over. A sesquicentennial exposition in Philadelphia in 1926 was a major commercial failure. Then, in the depths of the Great Depression, Chicago staged another commemorative exhibition. Partly, this was to mark the centenary of the city's founding and partly to mark 40 years since the Columbian Exposition. It was a huge success and spawned a new wave of exhibitions throughout the rest of the 1930s.

The success of commemorative exhibitions in the 1930s was linked to new approaches in their theming. In the late nineteenth and early twentieth century, most exhibitions proclaimed the march of empire. In the instability of the 1930s, this no longer seemed appropriate. The USA, in particular, had become more isolationist and its focus was on domestic problems. As the nation struggled to lift itself out of the Great Depression, commemorative exhibitions were enlisted in the fight. Their themes, displays and marketing, 'were designed to restore popular faith in the stability of the nation's economic and political system and, more specifically, in the ability of government, business, scientific, and intellectual leaders to lead the country out of the depression' (Rydell 1993: 9).

Chicago, in particular, highlighted a partnership between science, business and government. With the assistance of the Smithsonian Institute, the organisers constructed displays illustrating basic scientific theories. These included chemistry, biology, physics, electrical engineering and medicine. In their exhibits, private industry demonstrated the practical applications of this knowledge. While there was a significant focus on industrial applications, this was balanced by displays of model homes, complete with labour-saving devices. Whereas Chicago in 1893 had taken a 'department store' approach with shelves of products on display, Chicago in 1933 emphasised interactivity with demonstrations allowing patrons to try out new products. For example, through test drives and hard selling, General Motors sold 3,000 cars at the exhibition. The clear message was that the future would be brighter in employment and lifestyle (Findling 1994). The displays at this exhibition strongly emphasised a future fashioned by advances in technology and 'were exercises in cultural and ideological repair and renewal that simultaneously encouraged Americans to share in highly controlled fantasies about modernizing' (Rydell 1993: 10). Completing the partnership was government. Chicago was a showcase for Roosevelt's New Deal, which had just been launched (Rydell 1993). Federal agencies exhibiting included Agriculture, Commerce, the Census, the National Parks Service, Fisheries, the Panama Canal Administration and the National Advisory Committee for Aeronautics. As with business, their message was that co-operation and the wise use of technology would assist national social and economic recovery (Findling 1994).

The controlled messages at Chicago required a new approach in emphasising education. Attendees came for fun, but the intention was that they would also learn. Frank B. Jewett, an executive with the American Telephone and Telegraph Co. and President of the Science Advisory Committee for the Chicago Centenary of Progress Exposition, set out what should happen:

[Visitors will] pass through the fair and go out of it, largely without any consciousness of having been educated … [but they] go out educated to the idea that science is the root of most of the material things and many of the social things which make up modern life.

(quoted in Rydell 1993: 96)

The World's Fair at New York in 1939 highlighted concerns about the brightness of the near future. Whereas Chicago had proclaimed science as the antidote to the Great Depression, New York took place under the threat of expansionist totalitarian regimes in Europe and the Pacific. Ostensibly to commemorate the hundred-and-fiftieth anniversary of George Washington's inauguration as first President of the USA, its themes focussed on the desirability of democracy. It presented its collection of modernist buildings as a 'democracity', foreshadowing a future based on America's political paradigm. For some regimes this was intolerable. Nazi Germany refused to participate, though Fascist Italy and the USSR were enthusiastic participants. The British, keen to curry American support with war on the horizon, avoided their usual emphasis on their empire and provided a replica of Magna Carta as the centrepiece of their exhibit. The interpretation for this display emphasised that a history of democracy was part of a shared heritage between the USA and Britain (Greenhalgh 1988). This rewriting of history, according to Greenhalgh, seemed very dubious. However, it must be seen in a broader context of a wide range of cultural propaganda designed to gain the American public's support for Britain. For example, at the time of the New York World's Fair, Hollywood was churning out pro-British historical epics with British stars, such as *The Adventures of Robin Hood* (1939).

After World War Two

The war caused a long hiatus for international exhibitions. It was not until 1958 that Brussels hosted the first one since hostilities ceased. The Festival of Britain in 1951 stands out as an anomaly. A commemorative event to mark the centenary of the Great Exhibition, it was not really an exhibition itself. Rather, it was more an artistic and cultural festival. Accordingly, while noting its place amongst international exhibitions, we consider it in detail in Chapter 8 on cultural commemorative events.

In the USA, long the home of world fairs, exhibitions failed to recover their popularity. In the 1960s there was a brief flurry of interest, but none has been held since New Orleans in 1984. This decline in American interest in exhibitions was mainly due to the success of theme parks from the 1950s onwards. Chief of these was Disneyland, established in 1955. Heavily mediatised, it was both a tangible visitor attraction using characters and images from Disney's films and a television show. In form and structure, it used many of the features of the successful pre-war American exhibitions. Mixed in with rides and parades, there were displays paying homage to America's westwards expansion (Frontierland) and glimpses into the possible future (Tomorrowland).

The irony in the increasing competition from theme parks, was that these new developments were inspired by the successes of earlier exhibitions. Walt Disney was heavily influenced by his father having worked on the construction of the Chicago Columbian Exhibition. Many of the ideas about how theme parks were structured and laid out were copied from the successful American exhibitions (which in turn drew heavily on the 1889 Paris Exhibition). This may be seen, for example, in the way that the Disney Castle is the tall focal point of Disneyland, serving not only as an iconic marker, but providing directional clues to patrons. This is a similar role to that of the Eiffel Tower and many smaller towers in American exhibitions. In turn, Disney's success influenced later exhibitions. Disney himself was recruited to design and build displays at the 1963 New York World's Fair. These included 'It's a Small World' and 'The Hall of Presidents'.

The five cities hosting commemorative exhibitions since the late 1960s – Montreal, Brisbane, Seville, Genoa and Yokahama – have some striking similarities. None were capitals or the main cities of their countries. All could be categorised as second-tier cities. Accordingly, they all looked to exhibitions as a means of elevating their image and appeal to tourists and business. Perhaps more than with any of the earlier commemorative exhibitions, these were instances where the commemorative event was manipulated to stimulate public opinion and gain government support.

Montreal's staging of Expo 67 was due to 'frustrated international aspirations' (Gold and Gold 2005: 113). Though the largest city in Canada, it was not the capital. Economically, it was slowly declining relative to Toronto. Socially, it suffered from sectarian differences between French- and English-speaking groups. The success of Expo 67 was a great boost to civic confidence, encouraging it to bid for the 1976 Olympics.

Holding an international exhibition in Brisbane was a curious choice to commemorate the first European settlement in Sydney. This mirrored the similarly strange decision of Melbourne to host the commemoration in 1888. However, as noted in Chapter 2, Australia is a singular example of staging its national commemoration based on the arrival of European settlers rather than independence. The choice of Brisbane in 1988 was driven by the Queensland state government. Originally, the Australian Bicentennial Authority was not interested in an international exhibition. Essentially, Expo 88 was created and staged by state authorities and thrust upon an uninterested federal agency. While ostensibly a national event, its organisers were primarily interested in showcasing Brisbane and attracting tourism and economic development to Queensland (Bennett 1992; Craik 1992).

Tourist or local events?

Considering the recent international exhibitions in Brisbane and Yokahama once again raises questions of the tourism impact of commemorative events. As discussed in Chapter 4, there is a paradox in the expectations of events commemorating historical occurrences. Due to their local or national significance, organisers and stakeholders view them as worth staging. However, to gain appropriate public funding, there are often promises that they will generate tourism flows. After all, as the argument goes, if they are significant anniversaries, people will want to visit and take part in the experience. For many of the exhibitions in the nineteenth and early twentieth centuries, particularly in the USA, there were not high expectations of international tourism, given the limits and cost of ocean transport. These were primarily directed towards domestic markets. The Chicago Century of Progress Exposition, for example, received 23 million visits in 1933. Of these, 5 million were estimated as coming from local people (who made an average of ten visits each). The other 18 million (78 per cent) were counted as out-of-towners or tourists. However, these were nearly all from other parts of the USA (Findling 1994).

In modern times, the convenience and cheapness of jet air transport encouraged the belief that such exhibitions could attract high flows of tourists. Brisbane, in particular, had strong aspirations of encouraging international tourism. Traditionally, Queensland has a strong tourism economy based on its tropical coastline. The intention was that Expo 88 could reinforce this destination image to the southern states and the growing international market. This complemented the expectation that the 1988 Bicentenary of European Settlement would generally increase overseas tourism (Hutchinson 1992).

However, visitor data collected for Expo 88 told a different story. Of the 16.5 million visits to the exhibition, 65 per cent were local people from Brisbane and South-Eastern Queensland. Many of these had season passes. Early on, organisers had promoted season passes as a way to encourage local enthusiasm and generate cash flow. In this they had been successful, but there was a later problem in that repeat visits by patrons with season passes generated no marginal revenue. For Expo 88, those with season passes made an average of 12 visits each, higher than expected. In contrast, only 5 per cent of visits were by tourists from overseas. Furthermore, there were displacement effects. Nearby destinations and attractions reported falls in visitor numbers. After Expo 88, visitor arrivals to Australia decreased (Craik 1992).

Looking forward through remembering the past

Considering these cases of past successful commemorative exhibitions, there is a clear thread which joins them all together. While staged to remember a past event, the format of the international exhibition encouraged people to look towards the future. Whether this was through imperial or technological fantasies, these exhibitions were effective institutions for encouraging the imagining of both present and future national identities.

The great commemorative exhibitions are a curious episode in the way that societies stage events to remember and reflect upon the past. At times, particularly in the late nineteenth century and the 1930s, these were the main vehicle chosen by countries to mark their significant anniversaries. The USA warmly embraced them and seemingly every major exhibition had to have a commemorative theme. However, looking back from the early twenty-first century, they seem an anachronism, a curiosity from the past. We simply now do not use international exhibitions this way. World expos still flourish, though there has been a geographical shift, particularly towards Asia. This new wave of exhibitions does not seem to have the need for the commemorative element. That said, we need to be careful that we do not dismiss this phenomenon too quickly. It was thought to have disappeared in the 1920s, but came back. Perhaps its time will come again.

6   The re-enactors' world

It's not that we pretend that this is real, but it gives you an even greater respect for those men who really endured it. We can never reproduce what war was like, nor should we want to, but our endeavour is to never allow the sacrifices made by those who have gone before us to be forgotten.

(Chuck Hillsman, Civil War re-enactor, hundred-and-twenty-fifth anniversary of the Battle of Gettysburg, quoted in Linenthal 1991: 101)

If history is worth remembering, it is also worth re-enacting. There is a widespread fascination with attempts to remember and reflect upon past events through the donning of archaic costumes and acting in the roles of historic characters. And there is also scepticism and sometimes downright hostility about such practices.

Re-enactment events are a subset of the *living history* approach to cultural heritage. Living history is a broad term applied to efforts to interpret the past for a modern audience by simulating historical characters, situations and technology. This occurs in a range of contexts. In addition to re-enactments as part of commemorative events, it can be found at outdoor museums, historic buildings and sites, theme parks and at other events, such as re-created medieval fairs and exhibitions. While often seen as a recent phenomenon, early manifestations of the living history approach occurred in nineteenth-century Scandinavia and the 1920s development of Colonial Williamsburg in the USA (Timothy and Boyd 2004).

As has been suggested by a number of heritage researchers, our interest in the past is directly fuelled by our concerns with the intense pressures of modern society. To escape modernity, modern urban people are increasingly drawn towards an idealised past. Immersion in what is perceived as a simpler, better, *more authentic* past, is an effective and attractive antidote or escape from the alienation and marginalisation of modernity (Laing and Frost 2012; Lennon and Foley 2000; Lowenthal 1985). Re-enactment events allow *both* participants and audiences to suspend their disbelief, disengage from the problems of the present and enter a version of the past for a short period. That version of the past is, of course, a fantasy, but it is also a seductive fantasy.

Living history has become a staple of modern reality television. Its popularity suggests that it connects with a wide audience seeking this immersion in the past. These television re-enactments provide a template for event organisers and audiences as to how the past should be re-created and what is important in these reproductions. Examples of these television re-enactments include:

- Tony Robinson's *Worst Jobs in History*. His long-running *Time Team* often includes re-enactments of historical jobs and crafts, a practice known as *experiential archaeology*.
- *Rome Wasn't Built in a Day*, in which the English National Trust commissioned modern builders to construct a Roman villa using only Roman techniques and materials.
- *The Super Sizers Go* .... The hosts, restaurant critic Giles Coren and comedian Sue Perkins dress and eat in the style of a particular historic period for a week.
- The *Country House*, *Frontier House* and *Outback House*. In these, ordinary families live, dress and work in period houses. This cluster of shows, presented more seriously (or academically) than the others, has particularly attracted analysis by heritage researchers (for examples, see Elder 2009; Schwartz 2010).

The spectacle and colour of staged re-enactments events make them a great favourite of the mass media. While no longer a novelty, they still provide a striking contrast to other contemporary news stories. Packaged as educational and remembering important points in history, they also suggest linkages with reality television and epic feature films. In their performance structure, use of actors and reliance on convincingly realistic costumes, film and re-enactment events are very similar. This cross-over is well illustrated by the use of thousands of Civil War re-enactors as extras in the feature films *Gettysburg* (1993) and *Gods and Generals* (2003).

While historic re-enactments mimic cinema and television productions, there is an important division. At the heart of historic re-enactment events is the magic of live performance. There are no computer generated special effects. Accordingly, re-enactments surprisingly seem more realistic and authentic. For an audience watching a live performance of a trebuchet firing a flaming missile, or medieval knights on horseback jousting, or Pickett's Charge at Gettysburg; the experience is profoundly different from viewing a simulation on screen. In some instances, re-enactments are staged at the locations depicted, which may be constructed as sacred or hallowed ground. Even the earnest amateurism of many of the participants provides a distinctive and satisfying feel of reality to the performance.

Re-enactments for commemorative events also differ significantly from those staged as a living history tourism product. At most modern museums, heritage sites and themed attractions, living history re-enactments tend to focus on social history, particularly the re-creation of everyday lives and activities from the relevant historical period. Accordingly, actors or volunteers dress as ordinary people engaged in work and mundane household tasks. They might be demonstrating archaic crafts (blacksmiths, cloth-making), cooking or washing without modern appliances, children will be in old-fashioned classrooms and someone will be riding a horse. It is a non-specific re-enactment, not of an actual day or person's life, but of generally what life was like in that historic period. In contrast, re-enactments for commemorative events focus on narrative history. They attempt to tell a story of what actually happened on a particular day. That includes battles, explorations and revolutions. While many actors play ordinary nameless folk, others will star as real people, playing protagonists such as General Custer and Crazy Horse, and William of Normandy and King Harold. History provides a script that must be followed. The story may be open to some negotiation, but the basic narrative must be accurately told through the performance.

However, despite the magic, spectacle and special nature of historic re-enactments, they have tended to be ignored, downplayed and even ridiculed by cultural heritage researchers. Crang, for instance, noted that during his doctoral research into re-enactments, he 'encountered persistent skepticism from colleagues, at a most visceral level' (1996: 422).

This academic distaste for historic re-enactments is due to three inter-related factors. First, there is a simple snobbery. Re-enactments are like other popular visitor attractions and entertainments, such as zoos and theme parks. They are *popular culture*, an enjoyable experience for a broad range of social groups, full of spectacle and easy to digest, but supposedly lacking the higher purpose and intellectual rigour of museums (Frost 2011). Second, the enthusiasm of the participants seems overwhelming, even scary. This is *serious leisure* gone wild. The obsession with historical detail in costume, character and artefacts suggest a social world that most researchers do not wish to delve too far into. Even if they did, the resources required from those who have engaged in immersive or auto-ethnographic research of re-enactments (for example Belk and Costa 1998 and Crang 1996), seems prohibitive. Third, modern trends in historiography militate against taking re-enactments too seriously. The emphasis on social history in living history re-creations fits the pattern of the modern Western curriculum. A focus on dates and narrative history does not.

In this chapter, our aim is to explore the phenomenon of historic re-enactments as common elements in commemorative events. We particularly wish to further investigate some of the paradoxes and peculiarities which we have touched on in this introductory section. To extend this discussion, we will next consider a range of examples of different types of re-enactment. We then focus on a range of key issues which are raised by the interaction between commemorations and re-enactments. This analysis is taken further in Chapter 7 through a detailed auto-ethnographic examination of the annual re-enactment of the Battle of Hastings in England.

Examples of re-enactment events

The following are a series of examples, rather than an attempt at a comprehensive typology. As essentially any historical incident can be re-enacted, our aim here is to focus more on how and why these examples were staged the way they were.

A field of battle dreams

Battles are popular candidates for re-enactment. They combine colour and spectacle with popular appeals to patriotism and national identities. Many provide opportunities to remember and reflect upon tragedy, bravery and sacrifice. For the re-enactors they allow a chance to 'play at war', temporarily escape from modernity, or indulge in their passionate interests in historical detail. Whether intentionally or not, battle re-enactments have the potential to reopen old wounds and prolong conflict.

A number are staged annually, whereas others occur only on special anniversaries. Some well-known examples are:

- Battles of the American War of Independence (1776–83). For the bicentenary, starting in 1976 a number of battles were re-enacted.
- Battles of the American Civil War (1861–5). Re-enactments have been held for all major anniversaries, most notably the centenary and upcoming hundred-and-fiftieth anniversary. These are large-scale events in terms of the numbers participating as re-enactors, size of the audience and media coverage.
- The Battle of Little Bighorn, Montana, USA. Two groups hold separate re-enactments annually.
- Waterloo (1815). Napoleon's final defeat, this is held annually in Belgium.
- Isandlawana. The 1879 massacre of an invading British army is re-enacted from time to time in KwaZulu-Natal, South Africa.
- Battle of Hastings. Staged annually by English Heritage. The subject of Chapter 7.
- Battle of Britain. Re-enactments featuring restored aircraft were staged for the sixtieth and seventieth anniversaries.

A number of intriguing patterns emerge from this list of examples. There is a strong emphasis on the eighteenth and nineteenth century. These attract large-scale interest and this may be due to the appeal of antique firearms. Archaic weaponry is a major feature of all these re-enactments and even for the relatively recent Battle of Britain, the appeal is in rare, obsolete and iconic aircraft.

Research into commemorative battle re-enactments is geographically skewed. Nearly all academic studies are of American examples and as a result we know a great deal about commemorative re-enactments of the War of Independence, the Civil War and the Battle of Little Bighorn (Elliott 2007; Linenthal 1991; Stanton 1997). Outside the USA, analytical research is sparse. For example, while we know that medieval battle re-enactments (such as the Battle of Hastings) are popular; they are occasionally referred to in cultural heritage studies (for example Walsh 1992), but have not been researched in depth. An intriguing exception is a recent study of the re-enactment of the 1804 Battle of Castle Hill as part of a convict rebellion in Australia (Gapps 2010). This highlights the need for further research across a range of countries.

What is not re-enacted is just as important as what is. A dearth of examples from outside the Western world is clear. However, that raises questions of why. Is it simply cultural? Are these just Western obsessions? Furthermore, if battle re-enactments are stimulated by a desire to escape modernity, are they more likely to be staged in the future in countries undergoing rapid economic development, urbanisation and consequent reimagining of national identity? Re-enactments of recent wars are noticeably absent. There are, for example, no re-enactments of World War One battles. With the upcoming centenary of World War One, it will be intriguing to see if any are staged. In their work on dark tourism, Lennon and Foley (2000) have argued that conflicts from recent memory (approximately the last 100 years) have a special resonance. It may be that battles from the last 100 years are still too dark and embedded in personal memories to be commemorated in this form.

Foundation of the nation

These re-enactments are relatively rare, as constitutional changes often do not translate very well into engaging or spectacular events. While of symbolic importance, they are often celebrated with fireworks, parades and concerts to reinforce their impact on the nation, rather than re-enactments. During the American bicentenary, for example, the signing of the Declaration of Independence in Philadelphia was re-created, but was held indoors and could not be viewed by a large live audience. Similarly, for the bicentenary of the French Revolution in 1989, there was a re-enactment of the Declaration of the Rights of Man. However, its impact was muted by the actors being in modern dress (Crisp 1992).

The pageantry, scale and spectacle of parades are typically utilised to mark national foundation events. These contain elements of historic re-enactment, particularly costumed participants from the crucial time period. However, these also contain a great deal of invention, as they re-enact modern idealised notions of what it might have been like at the time. For example, when the Shah of Iran used 3,500 people to re-enact a historical pageant to commemorate the founding of the Persian Empire by Cyrus 2,500 years earlier; authenticity was not at all as important as the modern political statements being made (Lowenthal 1985).

Frontier days

In the USA, the period from around 1900 to 1940 saw much interest in living history and commemorative re-enactments. Foremost in this trend was the restoration of colonial Williamsburg, which commenced in the 1920s, though many towns, both large and small, staged historical pageants and re-enactments (Elliott 2007; Timothy and Boyd 2004). Fuelling this was a sense that the pioneers were ageing and their stories needed to be collected, remembered and honoured. Laura Ingalls Wilder, for example, was encouraged to write down her recollections of being a young girl on the frontier. The resulting *Little House on the Prairie* (1935) was an instant best-seller (Laing and Frost 2012).

Matching the tales of pioneering and homesteading were memories of outlaws. In the modern West these dominate commemorations of the frontier. The town of Tombstone in Arizona is noted for the 1881 Gunfight at the OK Corral. It stages an annual 'Helldorado Days Festival' on the anniversary. The appeal of the re-enactments rests on a combination of the archetypal Western action and the attention to detail in the arming and costuming of the actors playing the dandified gambler/sheriffs – the Earp Brothers. For the hundred-and-twenty-fifth anniversary in 2006, a special re-enactment was staged. In addition to the mandatory gunfight, there was an elaborate funeral procession for the killed outlaws, winding its way to the cemetery on Boot Hill.

In Australia, there is a similar nostalgic passion for dressing in old-time clothes and remembering bushrangers. Re-enactments featuring the infamous Ned Kelly have been staged in the towns of Glenrowan and Beechworth (Frost *et al*. 2008). The gold rushes are also a keen subject for re-enactment. In 2001, to commemorate the hundred-and-fiftieth anniversary of the discovery of gold, two towns re-enacted the first discovery. Both towns – Warrandyte and Clunes – argue that they were the place where gold was first discovered and the re-enactment was a means of reinforcing legitimacy for their competing claims. Chewton, another small gold town, annually re-enacts the Monster Meeting of 1851 (see Figure 6.1), when miners protested against unfair taxation. In 2010, we took part in this re-enactment, marching from the pub to the exact historical site, where re-created speeches were interspersed with modern interpretations of folk songs. Joining us was Tony Robinson, who filmed the re-enactment for his documentary series *Tony Robinson Discovers Australia*.

Figure 6.1 Re-enactors at the Monster Meeting, 2010. Photo by J. Laing.

In the footsteps of explorers

Re-enactment is a popular means of commemorating notable expeditions of explorers, both for adventure travellers testing themselves through duplicating arduous journeys and for communities whose identities are linked to these discoveries. The latter occurs in settler societies and often results in elaborate public events which conflate foundation with European discovery. Examples include:

- In South Africa, 1988 was the five-hundredth anniversary of the arrival of Portuguese navigator Bartolomeu Dias. A replica fifteenth-century caravel was constructed and sailed from Portugal and his beach landing in South Africa was re-enacted (Witz 2009).
- In Australia, the 1951 fiftieth anniversary of federation was celebrated with re-enactments of iconic explorers, including Cook (1770), Phillip (1788), the crossing of the Blue Mountains (1813) and Sturt (1830) (Gapps 2009). It is interesting that such re-enactments were not part of the 2001 centenary of federation.
- Between 2003 and 2006, 15 signature events were conducted across the USA for the two-hundredth anniversary of the Lewis and Clark expedition. These included re-enactments of their arrival at various places along the expedition's route (Ray *et al.* 2006).

Restaging sporting events

In 1977, the Melbourne Cricket Club staged the Centenary Test between Australia and England. This was to mark the first cricket *test match*, which had been played on the Melbourne Cricket Ground in 1877. That match is widely acknowledged as the world's first major international sporting contest, predating the Olympics and the Soccer World Cup. The initial idea was for a players' reunion, as had happened at the sixtieth anniversary in 1937, but as plans took shape the idea grew of a commemorative match. Earlier re-enactments of historic sporting matches had tended to follow a living history approach, with participants in historical costumes providing an *exhibition* match, often following archaic rules. However, the organisers of this match took a different approach. Rather than a re-enactment, they played a full-scale serious test match between the current teams of the two countries (Batchelder *et al.* 2002; Haigh and Frith 2007).

The resulting match illustrated the vagaries of such an approach. The Centenary Test was close and exciting, regarded as one of the best games ever. Its five days were watched by a crowd of approximately 250,000. The organisers could not have wished for a better example of what they were commemorating. In contrast, the test match staged to commemorate the 1980 centenary of tests in England was a dull draw and the gloss was taken off it by choosing to hold it at a different venue (Lord's) to the original (the Oval). Another special test to commemorate the bicentenary of European settlement in Australia in 1988 was also a tame draw. These two instances demonstrate the problem that restaged sporting events cannot be controlled to ensure they are memorable sporting contests.

Figure 6.2 Meeting the re-enactor playing Banjo Paterson at the Man from Snowy River Festival. Photo by W. Frost.

Literary re-enactments

Corryong, in rural Australia, stages an annual Man From Snowy River Bush Festival (see Figure 6.2). It was originally held in 1995 as a centenary commemoration of the 1895 publication of *The Man From Snowy River* by A. B. 'Banjo' Paterson. That commemorative event proved to be such a success that it was decided to hold it as an annual festival. The centrepiece of the event is a re-enactment viewed by approximately 5,000 people (the town's population is only 1,200). An actor dressed as Paterson talks about his life and legacy and recites some of his poetry. This is followed by a spectacular re-enactment by professional stuntmen of the horseback chase which is the central to the story of *The Man From Snowy River* (drawing heavily on the imagery from the well-known film version). For this small and remote country town, this event is its major festival of the year and the main opportunity to attract tourists and reinforce its pioneer identity (Laing and Frost 2012).

Literary re-enactments may also be participatory. Bloomsday is held annually on 16 June in Dublin. It commemorates the 1922 novel *Ulysses* by James Joyce. This is the story of one day in the life of Leopold Bloom, that being 16 June 1904. Participants, often in Edwardian costume, follow Bloom's path through the city, with appropriate stops for readings and much drinking beer in pubs. The event began with the fiftieth anniversary in 1954. Interestingly, this was the anniversary of the date of the fictional action in the book, not of its publication. In 2004 there was a major commemoration for the centenary, titled ReJoyce 2004 (Laing and Frost 2012; see also Chapter 8). Lostwithiel in Cornwall hosts an annual Charles Dickens Evening. This is held at Christmas time, focussing on his book *A Christmas Carol* (1843), in order to commemorate the links between the town and Dickens. For the festival, the townsfolk and visitors dress in early Victorian costume, some as characters from this and other works by Dickens. As with Bloomsday, the date commemorated is of the fictional action in the novel.

Key issues

Re-enactment events are more than simply dressing in costume and retelling a historical story. They also bring to life many key issues in society. These are events with strong meanings relating to society and identity and these meanings are often hotly contested between various stakeholder groups. In this second half of the chapter, we focus on some of these deeper issues, beginning with a discussion of ritual structure and then moving on to contestation and authenticity, before concluding with an examination of the serious leisure aspects of re-enacting.

Ritual structure

In his seminal work, Falassi (1987) argued that most events follow a *ritual structure*, which is a series of common rites or components. He argued that this structure was rarely deliberately planned by organisers, but rather grew organically or sub-consciously as a response to our basic human needs and beliefs. In essence, these are a series of underlying meanings, common to many commemorative events and often in evidence during re-enactments.

According to Falassi, the chief rites are:

1   *Valorisation.* Time and space are claimed for the event through an opening ceremony. These are now marked as different from normal time and space.
2   *Purification.* There are ceremonies to cleanse and safeguard the festival and its participants.
3   *Passage.* Rituals which mark transition from one stage of life to another, particularly for young people.
4   *Reversal.* Normal behaviours and roles are reversed. The illicit may be respect-able. A common form is the coronation of a 'fool' as the king of the festival.
5   *Conspicuous display.* The most valued objects are displayed, for example, religious relics are paraded.
6   *Conspicuous consumption.* Abundant, even wasteful, consumption, particularly of food and drink.
7   *Dramas.* Treasured stories are told through dramatic or musical performances.
8   *Exchange.* Symbolic exchanges of money, valuables or tokens. In Europe, the wealthy might distribute gifts and money to the poor.
9   *Competition.* Typically games and sporting contests, often between rival groups. Such games may be a substitute for armed conflict.
10 *Devalorisation.* A closing ceremony marks the return to normal time and space, perhaps with a promise of a future repeat of the festival.

A number of these rituals are particularly apparent and meaningful at commemorative re-enactments. Ritual 7 – dramatic performance – covers the whole theatricality of the re-enactment, though other ritual components are folded into that. Valorisation and devalorisation signify that the participants are symbolically going back in time. Equally importantly, these rituals demonstrate that the space for the commemoration is hallowed ground, in the cases of battlefield sites of great tragedy and sacrifice. At the re-enactment of the Battle of Hastings, for example, the event ends with the modern convention of a minute's silence, both honouring those who died and providing a means to return participants and audience from the medieval to the modern.

The ritual beginning and ending – valorisation and devalorisation – require the anachronistic use of an announcer. Equipped with a microphone and sometimes in modern dress, the announcer is a mediator who directly addresses the crowd and explains what they are about to see and experience. The announcer may also attempt an interpretation, even providing an *official* version of what it all meant. This creates an intriguing paradox, for real historic events are typically chaotic and confused. At its extreme, as we saw at Hastings in 2011, the announcer may explain that neither commander has a clear view of the battlefield nor a full understanding of the positions of all troops.

Conspicuous display is apparent in the level of detail and perceived authenticity of historic costumes, artefacts, weapons and other paraphernalia. This may be viewed as a form of competition between the participants. The historical narrative constrains what participants may do to demonstrate their attributes and egos. They cannot change history, by, for example, winning the day if they are on the losing side. However, they can outperform their fellow enthusiasts by the authenticity of their appearance.

Reversal may take the form of buffoonery and humour, even if this is inappropriate for the situation or character. The difficulty for many re-enactors is that humour allows them to get a desired reaction from the audience. This seemingly validates their performance, laughs and smiles showing that they are being enjoyed and appreciated. Accordingly, the temptation is to either drop out of character to make a humorous aside, swap banter with the announcer, or play up the comic aspects of the historic person.

Contestation

As discussed in Chapter 2, commemorative events relating to national identity are often highly contested, as different groups champion their views as to what is important within national memory.

When national commemorative events include re-enactments, this dissonance is magnified. Battles, in particular, are by their very nature contested. Even centuries later, they may highlight unresolved tensions and conflicts. In re-enacting battles, organisers encounter the difficulties of how they will represent and interpret the battle and the different positions of the opposing sides. Even whether or not it is appropriate to re-enact a battle becomes a point of contention. In this section, we consider a series of examples of re-enactments provoking contestation. These range from events reinforcing official nationalism interpretations, through to those where marginalised groups have sought to reclaim re-enactments and their narratives and on to situations when the factual veracity of what is being re-enacted is questioned.

Reinforcing the hegemony of official nationalism

Official nationalism occurs where governments and ruling elites present a hegemonic view of the nation's history. Such an interpretation is forcefully, even coercively presented as the *true* version which all citizens must enthusiastically embrace. As discussed in Chapter 2, commemorative events are critical to this process of imagining of a national memory. In organising these events, re-enactment may be pivotal to dramatically portraying this official interpretation. The choice of what to re-enact privileges particular historical incidents and characters as vital to the nation's history. As absolute reconstructions, these re-enactments not only present one view of history as correct, but implicitly negate all other possible versions.

A striking example of this hegemonic usage of re-enactments occurred in 1988. The White minority government in South Africa keenly supported the five-hundredth anniversary of the arrival of Portuguese navigator Bartolomeu Dias. A fifteenth-century caravel was constructed and sailed from Portugal. It arrived off the coast on the anniversary date of 3 February and re-enactors representing Dias rowed ashore, 'discovering' South Africa. For the apartheid regime, under international pressure for change, this was an opportunity to gain positive international media coverage. They used this re-enactment to present an image that since South Africa was multicultural and was slowly moving towards reform, there was no justification for external intervention (Witz 2009).

However, while a unified message was intended as the outcome of the re-enactment, marginalised groups strove to present an alternative interpretation. That the beach that Dias had landed on (and which had to be used for an authentic re-enactment) was a Whites-only beach, became the focal point for dissent. Though organisers attempted to have token Black involvement, the re-enactment was eventually boycotted. This resulted in the absurdist scenario, that the re-enactor playing Dias was greeted by White re-enactors playing Blacks. As Witz summarised the encounter, 'in a most astonishing reversal "whites" had to masquerade as "blacks" in order to perform apartheid's last festival' (2009: 151).

In settler societies, this is a common problem with re-enactments. How are the vanquished indigenous people encouraged to play their part in telling stories of 'discovery' or conquest? In early twentieth-century USA, Native Americans were often involved, either through economic incentives or through the persuasive powers of government agencies. Accordingly, at the fiftieth anniversary of the Battle of Little Bighorn in 1926, a reported 10,000 Native Americans were present. After a re-enactment of the battle, the cavalry re-enactors and the Native American participants rode in from opposite directions, shook hands and observed a minute's silence. They then rode off in pairs, symbolising the modern policy of friendship and assimilation (Linenthal 1991). As discussed below, such an official statement would break down by the time of the centenary.

In Australia, re-enactments of various explorers were staged for the fiftieth anniversary of Federation in 1951. As the re-enactors reached towns on their route, they encountered parties of Aborigines, who would ceremonially challenge or threaten the intruders before giving way and allowing entry. However, as with the Dias anniversary, these re-enactors were White, 'blacked-up' to play the role of the indigenous peoples. Such displays were organised by local communities rather than the central coordinators. The enthusiastic participants were often children, representing either local schools or scout groups. Actual indigenous people, at this stage still not counted as citizens, were excluded from these events (Gapps 2010).

Changing interpretations

An excellent example of the contests implicit in battle re-enactments is the efforts to stage the Battle of Little Bighorn in Montana, USA. It is valuable to look at this in detail, drawing on the excellent study of the cultural heritage of Little Bighorn by Elliott (2007) and of American battle commemorations by Linenthal (1991).

After the battle in 1876, commemorative events were staged in most years. Major re-enactments were staged in 1909 and for the fiftieth anniversary in 1926. As the site was under the control of the War Department, they were happy to allow such activities. However, in 1940 the battlefield was transferred to the National Parks Service, who had a policy of not allowing re-enactments (Linenthal 1991). In 1964, the nearby town of Hardin decided to stage a major re-enactment of the battle as part of the commemorations of the centenary of the founding of the Territory of Montana. The script was written by Joseph Medicine Crow, a local Crow Indian, who had worked on the script of the 1941 Errol Flynn movie *They Died With Their Boots On*. However, Medicine Crow was sacked from that film after voicing his opinion that Custer was headstrong and foolish. Accordingly, he was keen to develop a more accurate and even-handed version of the story than Hollywood had tended to follow. Elliott (2007) argues that Medicine Crow's production was in the style of historical pageants popular in small-town America in the first half of the twentieth century. Rather than an attempt at an accurate reproduction, it was a series of historical vignettes and stories, culminating in the battle. One major difference was that whereas Hollywood films and most local pageants present the action from the White Man's point of view, the Indian perspective was foremost in this re-enactment. 'What made the Custer re-enactment special' according to *Newsweek* 'was that the Battle of Little Bighorn unfolded entirely from the Indian's point of view' (quoted in Elliott 2007: 233).

The 1964 re-creation was a great success, involving co-operation between local White businessmen and Indian groups. It had been particularly successful in drawing tourists to this remote and economically depressed part of Montana. Not surprisingly, Hardin decided to stage a re-enactment each year on the anniversary of the battle. During the 1960s, it typically attracted good crowds. However, in the early 1970s, interest in Custer and the re-enactment seemed increasingly out of tune with the *zeitgeist*. Increased activism for Indian rights marginalised the production. In 1972, part of the venue was vandalised by opponents. After 1973, with the centenary looming in three years time, it was decided not to hold any more re-enactments.

Then in 1990, the re-enactment was revived, once again following Medicine Crow's script. Partly this was due to economic problems encouraging the local government to explore tourism opportunities. Controversy over the decision by the National Parks Service to change the name of the National Monument from the Custer Battlefield to the Battle of Little Bighorn stimulated major national media coverage. A third factor was the success of Kevin Costner's *Dances With Wolves* (1990), generating broad interest in Lakota culture and history. Later decisions to allow monuments honouring Indian deaths at Little Bighorn also seemed to have defused tensions (see Chapter 11 for a further discussion of changing attitudes).

The successful revival of the Hardin re-enactment and increased public interest led to a Crow family – the Real Birds – developing their own re-enactment event. Though smaller, they had the advantage of being able to stage their event on their land adjacent to the National Parks Service National Monument. As a result, there are now two rival re-enactments, both held on the same weekend to commemorate the battle. Such rivalry comes with claims and counter-claims of ownership and who best stages an authentic re-enactment.

Contestation at Little Bighorn reflects the ever-changing meanings that groups in society attach to historical events. The initial re-enactment was an attempt to claim heritage back from Hollywood, to show an Indian point of view. In the 1970s it foundered as out of step with community values. Its revival in the 1990s again resulted from changing perspectives and the appearance of a rival demonstrated that other stakeholder groups laid claim to the same heritage. Post 9/11, interpretations have changed again, both Indians and cavalry being seen as doing their duty and part of a strong US military tradition. This view is best summed up by Ernie LaPointe, a Vietnam veteran and great-grandson of Sitting Bull. In 2006, LaPointe visited Steve Alexander, who regularly plays Custer at the Hardin re-enactment. Alexander (who is discussed in greater detail later in this chapter) owns Custer's house in Monroe, Michigan and wore a replica Custer uniform for their symbolic meeting. Asked how Sitting Bull would have felt, LaPointe replied 'Sitting Bull didn't dislike Custer, he realized he was a military guy following orders' (quoted in Philbrick 2010: 305). While such an interpretation is now widely popular, it remains paradoxical. Custer was in command with quite broad orders and *he alone* made the fatal decision to divide his command and attack (Philbrick 2010).

Contested facts and gatekeepers

While there is much disagreement about the Battle of Little Bighorn, the essential facts are beyond dispute. What about a re-enactment where some stakeholders argue that a crucial part of a historical incident never actually took place? In restaging the Battle of Hastings, English Heritage is careful regarding the idea that the battle was lost when Harold was mortally wounded by an arrow in the eye. While this is a long-held and popular view of what happened, there actually is hardly any evidence that he was killed this way (Howarth 1977). The conundrum is whether or not to re-create the legend that most of the audience are familiar with. Or is it better to try to educate them with a historically more accurate interpretation? At Hastings, English Heritage has taken the latter approach.

At the most extreme are debates over whether a historical event even occurred at all. From 1957 to 1964 the US National Parks Service staged a re-enactment of how the idea of national parks was invented. This was based on a report of a campfire discussion by an exploring party in Yellowstone in 1870. During this, Cornelius Hedges proposed that the area should be protected as a national park rather than be open to private development. However, as the centenary of this incident approached, some National Parks Service staff became increasingly worried that it had never happened and was simply a later invention. If the story was false, they were then perpetuating a myth through their popular re-enactment. Accordingly, a decision was made to cease staging the event. Interestingly, the modern consensus is that the discussion and decision to push for protection probably did take place around that campfire, and that Hedges did convince his fellow explorers of the need for official protection, though the term national park itself was not coined until later (Frost and Hall 2009; Schullery and Whittlesey 2003). This instance provides an instructive example of *gatekeeping* at a re-enactment event. Through making a decision on what was historically accurate or not, the National Parks Service set themselves up as arbiters of what was appropriate and correct for re-enactment. As a government agency they were decreeing an official version of history and effectively excluding other interpretations.

Reconciliation

Reconciliation is an important element in many commemorations (see Chapters 3 and 11). Some re-enactments, particularly of battles, stress reconciliation, either through ceremonies and rituals or through interpretation. To illustrate this, we consider the example of the Battle of Gettysburg, drawing on the work of Linenthal (1991). The crucial battle of the American Civil War, it was fought from 1 July to 3 July in 1863 and through those dates has a close temporal and symbolic alignment with Independence Day on 4 July. It is also linked with Abraham Lincoln's Gettysburg Address, delivered at the commemorative dedication of the National Cemetery for soldiers killed in the battle.

Soon after the end of the war, various regiments began to stage annual reunions at the battlefield. These initially commemorated martial fraternity rather than national identity. However, under the presidency of Rutherford B. Hayes, there were concerted efforts to restore the South and rituals of reconciliation became popular. At the 1887 commemoration, 300 Confederate veterans walked en masse across the battlefield, retracing the steps of Pickett's Charge, a desperate and disastrous attempt on the last day of the battle to smash through the main Union lines. In turn, 1,000 Union veterans waited at the stone wall that had been their defensive stronghold. As the two groups met, they shook hands across the wall.

This re-enactment of Pickett's Charge followed by a ceremonial handshake became the staple of all commemorative events at Gettysburg. At the fiftieth anniversary in 1913, 55,000 veterans attended, camping out on the battlefield despite an average age of 72 years. At the time it was thought that this would be the last reunion, but the event persisted. Finally, in 1938, it was decided that the seventy-fifth anniversary would be the last, billed as 'The Last Reunion of the Blue and the Gray'. Some 1,900 veterans attended, with an average age of 94. Once again symbolising reconciliation, a single veteran from each side was selected to approach the wall, reach over it and shake hands.

At the centenary in 1963, there were no longer any veterans. Instead there were costumed re-enactors, a pastime that had grown rapidly in the 1950s. Despite opposition from the National Parks Service and the federal Civil War Centennial Commission, a re-enactment was held on the battlefield before 40,000 spectators. The Confederate re-enactors followed the path of Pickett's Charge up to where Union re-enactors stood at the wall. Both groups joined to salute a monument and sing the national anthem. For the hundred and twenty-fifth anniversary in 1988, the National Parks Service had banned re-enactments and instead staged a commemorative ceremony. In what we now would call a *flash mob*, approximately 1,000 re-enactors materialised from nearby private land and began staging their re-enactment. In doing this they drew off 3,000 of the crowd at the official ceremony. As had first been staged 101 years previously, the costumed re-enactors concluded their guerrilla performance with the ceremonial handshake across the wall.

Authenticity

Re-enactments are dominated by the quest for authenticity, though Crang powerfully argues that this is a 'quixotic quest' (1996: 416). Arguably, authenticity is an impossible dream. We can never re-create the past, only a facsimile of it (Lowenthal 1985). Furthermore, gaps in our historical knowledge have to be filled by best guesses and the limitations of event logistics often force the compression of time, narrative and incidents (Crang 1996). Authenticity at cultural heritage visitor attractions, particularly those involving living history, is an ongoing and strongly contested academic debate. Research into historical re-enactments provides a valuable insight into how people perceive authenticity.

For living history re-enactments, particularly of battles, authenticity is mainly focussed on costumes and equipment. This draws criticism that this is really antiquarianism rather than history, that detail and minutiae are privileged over providing interpretation (Crang 1996; Lowenthal 1985). This problem is magnified in three ways. The first is that many people are not comfortable with a normative approach to interpreting history and feel it should be centred on facts, that there is a positivist one version of history and any variance from this is a subversive *rewriting of history*. Second, re-enactment event organisers will always face a difficult balancing act between education and entertainment. Third, many historical re-enactments attract participants who are primarily interested in clothing, weapons and other artefacts. Accordingly, their displays and performances will reflect their interest and they will see the re-enactment's authenticity as primarily dependent upon the quality of these historical trappings.

This focus on the perceived authenticity of costumes and artefacts is central to the re-enactors' ethos and is a constant in research studies. Researcher Cathy Stanton was 'struck by the way re-enactors privileged sensory data – sound, taste, smell, sight – in the creation of their encampments' (1997: 40). She found that she gained acceptance for her ethnographical research through her musical ability, which allowed her to play the part of a young boy in a Civil War fife and drum band. Stephen Gapps, also taking an auto-ethnographic approach, noted that being a re-enactor meant he was 'looking for evidence of not just what happened, but also how it *looked*' (2010: 58). Carnegie and McCabe utilised a web-based survey to question a wide range of re-enactors. They found that 're-enactors invested a huge amount of time, research, money and skills and enjoyment in developing a collection of material objects associated with authenticating the detail of their chosen period' (2008: 358).

The quest for authenticity is waylaid with compromises. Battle re-enactors may be obsessed with the authenticity of their uniforms and weapons, but discipline is another matter. Stanton (1997) notes, for example, that real Civil War soldiers would be ordered to undertake guard duty at nights, yet no re-enactor is interested in taking their experience to that level. In 2010, when we participated in the re-enactment of the 1851 Monster Meeting, we were not required to dress the part of gold miners. Some did, but for most of us our costume was simply bush hats. However, what was not negotiable was the use of flags and banners. In particular, no one was allowed to fly the iconic Southern Cross flag, for this was not created until the later Eureka Rebellion in 1854.

Another factor which adds to the authenticity of re-enactments is the immersion of the actors in their roles. Rather than simply explain how people acted in the past, they demonstrate this by in-character performances. Performers at re-enactments of Hastings or Waterloo, for instances, are not just dressed as soldiers, they are wholeheartedly taking on the persona of characters from this time period. This not only means dressing the right way, but behaving and talking as people did in these times. At many battle re-enactments this extends to living, eating and carousing in tented encampments, not only during the course of the public event, but after hours, perhaps for a number of days.

Some re-enactors go to extraordinary lengths to immerse themselves in their character. Steve Alexander annually plays Custer at both re-enactments of the Battle of Little Bighorn. He also played the role in the 2005 US Presidential Inauguration Parade. When playing Custer, Alexander is always careful to stay completely in character. A serious enthusiast, Alexander started giving talks about Custer while dressed as his hero. His uncle found the performance disjointed and advised he shift to presenting in the first person, as:

You are up there in front of us, you've got the regalia on and you are saying 'Custer did this, and Custer did that'. You need to say *I* did this and *I* did that.

(quoted in Elliott 2007: 94)

A similar approach is taken by Michael Beattie who plays the Australian bushranger Ned Kelly in an annual commemorative event in the country town of Beechworth. Part of the events is a re-enactment of the captured Kelly being brought into town and tried in the still existing courthouse. Normally a local tour guide, Beattie parallels Alexander in building upon a physical resemblance, engaging in detailed research to ensure his grooming and clothes match and always remaining in character (Frost and Laing 2011).

Dropping in and out of character may be confusing and dissatisfying for some audience members. At the 2010 re-enactment of the Man From Snowy River, a performer played the role of author 'Banjo' Paterson. With an impressive costume and demeanour, he recited some of Paterson's poetry. However, in parts of the performance he drew parallels between soldiers in World War One (during which Paterson was a war correspondent) and the Iraq War. He also sang a song in praise of bushranger Ned Kelly, presenting a view which the real Paterson would absolutely not have held. Such inconsistency raises questions of how to balance impersonation and contemporary performance.

In some instances, the exactness of reproduction is not important. In 1936 Jean Cocteau re-enacted the circumnavigation of the globe described in the novel *Around the World in Eighty Days*. Cocteau could have worn period costume appropriate to the 1872 setting of the story, but chose not to. While he followed the rough itinerary of the fictional Phileas Fogg, he did not duplicate his movements and adventures en route. Rather he used the re-enactment to experience and write about the places visited as they were now in 1936.

Serious leisure

The concept of *serious leisure* was developed by Stebbins to describe the growing phenomena of people in 'systematic pursuit of an amateur, hobbyist, or volunteer activity that is sufficiently substantial and interesting for the participant to find a career there in the acquisition and expression of its special skills and knowledge' (1992: 3). While those involved in serious leisure develop their interest in the same way as one would develop a career, the rewards are not in money, but in personal fulfilment and status through achieving excellence in a field which fascinates them. Developing that expertise may take years of painstaking study and practice and that commitment is important to the ensuing satisfaction. Empirical research by Hunt (2004) into re-enactors in the UK concluded that their primary motivations could best be understood in terms of serious leisure.

Belk and Costa (1998) examined historical re-enactment as the pursuit of serious leisure in their study of US Mountain Men events. These focus on re-creating the lifestyles of Mountain Men – trappers travelling well beyond the frontier in the period 1825 to 1840. At certain times of the year, Mountain Men would come together to trade at events known as Rendezvous and it is these meetings that are re-enacted. Strictly speaking these are not commemorative events, for while they are focussed on remembering and honouring the Mountain Men, they are not linked to any specific talismanic dates. Nonetheless, Belk and Costa's detailed study provides great insight into the world of serious re-enactors.

Belk and Costa participated in 13 Rendezvous events, all held around the Rocky Mountains. These lasted an average of three days, were held in forested public land and involved the establishment of short-term camping communities dressed in period costume and engaging in traditional activities. As Belk and Costa analysed these:

> Rendezvous participants socially construct and jointly fabricate a consumption enclave, where a fantasy time and place are created and experienced ... The modern mountain man rendezvous as a fantastic consumption enclave is found to involve several key elements: participants' use of objects and actions to generate feelings of community involving a semimythical past, a concern for "authenticity" in recreating the past, and construction of a liminoid time and place in which carnivalesque adult play and rites of intensification and transformation can freely take place.
>
> (1998: 219)

This transformation takes serious time and effort. Newcomers, known as *pilgrims* are expected to participate in quite a number of events before being fully accepted into this fantasy social world. Developing Mountain Men costumes and accoutrements is a slow and cumulative process. While gear can be purchased, part of the fantasy is engaging in ceremonial bartering as the Mountain Men did nearly 200 years ago. Great respect and status is gained by those who are adept at making their own authentically-styled costumes. Others are valued for expertise in archaic crafts such as flint-making, tanning hides, horsemanship and bead-work. A third vehicle for excellence is in exercising appropriate braggadocio during the carnivalesque evenings, outshining others in prodigious displays of swearing, vernacular language, tale-telling and drinking (Belk and Costa 1998).

New worlds from the old

What do these attempts to re-create the past tell us about how re-enactors view the past? Do they tell us something about how they see the modern world? As discussed in Chapter 1, commemorative events allow people to both remember the past and reflect on what that means now. Dressing in costume, playing a historical character and demonstrating expertise in old skills are fun and part of the fun is taking them seriously and excelling at this. However, should we go deeper? Is there something about re-enacting that profoundly affects its participants, shaping their place in the modern world?

In her study of American Civil War re-enactors, Cathy Stanton argues that there are deeper psychological benefits beyond communitas and simple blowing off steam. To conclude this chapter, it is valuable to examine her findings.

Studying Civil War re-enactors in the mid-1990s, Stanton found that at least half were male, White, middle class, conservative and military veterans (1997: 67). Many were confused and bitter with changes in society. Vietnam loomed large in these discussions, a military failure which they saw as indicating a lack of political leadership. As one informant told Stanton, 'The white male Anglo-Saxon of today really doesn't know what he's supposed to be'. He felt that many were drawn to re-enacting 'as just looking for a simpler day, where they can go out and not feel guilty' (1997: 83).

Stanton viewed this attitude as common to most of the re-enactors she studied. She argued, 'these reenactors live in age when "immutable" truths are being challenged, and they use re-enactment – either as a means of defence, escapism, or gradual accommodation – as a way of responding to those challenges' (Stanton 1997: 77). In the conclusion of her study, she reflected:

> It is fascinating to speculate on the choice of the Civil War itself as a means of expressing a view of a more unified and stable social world ... Are reenactors, themselves children of a generation who experienced first-hand the exhilaration of a sense of national cohesion , perhaps striving to capture that sense through the simulation of war?
>
> (Stanton 1997: 84–5)

Such an argument raises further questions. If Civil War re-enacting is a response to the problems of modernity in the mid-1990s, how do we explain its popularity at other times? Most specifically, we are fast approaching the hundred-and-fiftieth anniversary of Gettysburg. All indications are that this will be the largest re-enactment yet, including a new generation of participants who are not from Stanton's earlier research cohort. It seems reasonable that many of these will share similar demographic characteristics to Stanton's group, and that they may be using re-enactment as a means of dealing with contemporary issues. The difference will be that in a post 9/11 USA, they will have their own worries about the future and their role in the world.

7   A day at Battle

Reporter: King William, congratulations on a wonderful victory.
William: Thank you, David.
Reporter: You must be very pleased with the boys.
William: I certainly am, David; they did a wonderful job.
Reporter: Did you expect to win?
William: Well, I never had any doubts, David. The boys have been fighting very well on the continent, but this was the big one they were all looking forward to.
Reporter: Were there any anxious moments?
William: Well, right at the start, David. Our lads weren't used to the sloping ground …
Reporter: Well now, what about that 'incident'?
William: Oh, you mean when Harold was knocked down. (He goes all serious). Well, that was a very nasty business, David, and we're sorry about it. But I think it was fair.

(The Complete and Utter History of Britain,
broadcast 1969, quoted in Wilmut, 1980: 190)

There is a rich history of comedians sending up re-enactors and commemorative events involving battles. The premise of the British television show *The Complete and Utter History of Britain* was to humorously represent various incidents from British history using modern media formats (much like the modern *Horrible Histories*). For the Battle of Hastings, it utilised the structure of a post match interview with a sporting star, with the earnest Terry Jones interviewing an upbeat Michael Palin as Duke William. The sketch concluded with a new take on the arrow in the eye, the moment in the battle that the writers could be confident that most of their audience knew about, especially since this was only a few years after the nine-hundredth anniversary of the Battle of Hastings. Indeed, the idea for the series came from a sketch by Palin and Jones in the 1967 series *Twice a Fortnight* (Wilmut 1980). In that, they re-enacted the battle on the pebble beach at Hastings. *Dr Who* also drew on this topicality, being involved in the battle in the episode 'The Time Meddler' (1965).

As members of *Monty Python*, Palin and Jones were involved in a sketch where the Batley Townswomen's Guild re-enact the Battle of Pearl Harbour. *Monty Python* took this fascination in re-enactment to the extreme in the film *Monty Python and the Holy Grail*. It culminates in an epic battle between King Arthur and the French for the ultimate possession of the grail. However, just as the two armies clash, the police arrive to arrest the re-enactors. This lampooning continues in modern comedy. David Walliams and Matt Lucas of *Little Britain* fame have recently made a spoof on airline reality shows, called *Come Fly with Me*. One episode features two men, Colin and Gavin, who are heading to the re-enactment of the Battle of Agincourt. They are barred from taking their swords on board their flight and are incensed at what they regard as heavy-handed bureaucracy by the French check-in staff ('We beat you at Agincourt!'). The staff try to smooth things over and suggest that they give the swords to their wives or girlfriends to take home. The response is instantaneous – 'We're re-enactors – do you think we have wives or girlfriends?!'

In 2011, we attended the re-enactment of the Battle of Hastings. This is staged annually at a village called Battle, located in Sussex, south-eastern England. The battlefield site is managed by the UK government agency English Heritage, who stage this commemorative event. The battle was fought on 15 October 1066. It was between the Saxons, led by King Harold, and the invading Normans, under Duke William. After a day long battle, King Harold was killed, according to legend when an arrow struck him in the eye. After that, Saxon resistance crumbled and the victorious William was crowned as the new king. These events are widely known as the Norman Conquest.

In this chapter, our aim is to extend our discussion of re-enactment events in Chapter 6 by utilising the Battle of Hastings as a detailed case study. We chose to examine this re-enactment in depth as it was a long-established, successful, annual event. However, we were also aware that despite this, it had not been the subject of academic study. It was occasionally mentioned in the events and heritage literatures, but always only briefly.

Furthermore, we are using an autoethnographic approach. We are conscious that autoethnography is a novel, even controversial methodology. It is used occasionally in events studies, particularly for re-enactments, though the term itself is rarely used (examples include Belk and Costa 1998; Gapps 2010; Kozinets 2001; Stanton 1997). We find it a valuable method for understanding complex phenomena, providing a rich and highly personal perspective, and we have been increasingly using autoethnography in our research. To us, it is a logical progression from the descriptive ethnographic research carried out by Turner and van Gennep, excerpts of which Falassi (1987) includes in his anthology of essays on the festival. In the case of this book, we are experimenting in using it as the basis of one chapter. It is, we stress, an experiment. Hopefully, it will encourage others to explore this and other pathways.

This chapter details our impressions, observations and reflections of the event. We have recorded these separately, rather than try and force a synthesis, as we see that there is value in contrasting the differences in our experiences. Accordingly, each comment is attributed to either of us through the use of our initials.

We prepared for battle on 15 October with the view that we would use this methodology. What was unexpected was that we experienced two commemorative events ...

***

WF I had a few strong memories of the nine-hundredth anniversary, which was commemorated in 1966 when I was seven years old. My parents bought us a weekly illustrated English magazine called *Look and Learn*. Aimed at children and educational in its objectives, it was very English in its content. For the anniversary it featured a number of stories, including a series over a few weeks which reproduced and explained the Bayeux Tapestry. That Norman depiction of the battle also featured in an attractive series of commemorative stamps put out by the UK post office. Finally, we lived on the outskirts of Melbourne. Not too far away is a town called Hastings. In 1966, they held their re-enactment. We did not go, but it must have been in the news. Every now and again my father would recall how it had got out of hand and there had been punch ups.

JL I have been fascinated with medieval history pretty much all of my life, mainly as a result of reading Arthurian tales as a child and later watching movies such as *Excalibur*, *Braveheart* and Kenneth Branagh's *Henry V* and the recent television series *Merlin*. We studied the medieval period in my second year of high school, and all the students seemed similarly entranced. I'm not sure what it is that held us all in thrall and still attracts me today. Perhaps I just like a good sword fight! It's also the romance of the codes of chivalry, knights on horseback, castles with fairytale turrets and fair ladies who swoon over their lovers. The weapons of choice – the sword and the long-bow – are beautifully made and elegantly designed. The battles I have read about are won through hard slog, discipline and courage, not the latest technology (although the soldiers at Agincourt might disagree!). Even the names of the leaders are spine-tingling – the Black Prince, Richard the Lionheart, El Cid. These battles are fought in places whose names live on down the centuries, such as Crécy, Stirling Bridge and Bosworth Field. And then there is the Battle of Hastings, which everyone associates with the fight for the English crown. All these ingredients seemingly make it the perfect re-enactment.

WF We arrived in Hastings and it was Hastings Week. However, while this festival was centred around the date of the battle, the celebrations in Hastings seemed unconnected. This seemed to be because the battle and the re-enactment were at Battle, a different place. As a visitor, I sort of thought of the battle as being at Hastings, but the locals had a different view. Indeed, unless you knew the event was on, you could walk around Hastings and see no suggestion of its existence. The Hastings Visitor Information Centre was promoting Hastings Week, though its focus was on what was happening in the town, not way off in Battle. When we told the manager at our hotel where we were going, she seemed quite surprised. I got the feeling she thought it was quite naff. Instead she emphasised that there would be a bonfire and fireworks that night down at the beach. There was quite a strong tradition of bonfires along this coast she explained, laughing that 'we seem to be a Pagan lot around here'.

JL Hastings is a familiar sight from interminable viewings of *Foyle's War*, with its small cottages complete with chimney pots arrayed on the chalky hills overlooking the sea, winding streets and the presence (and screech) of seagulls. It does not have an impressive stronghold like Dover or Rochester. Only the small ruins of Hastings castle suggest its royal connections and allude to the fact that one of the most decisive battles in English history was fought just up the road at Battle. I'm also struck at how blasé people seem to be about the re-enactment. It seems that this event is seen as a local rather than a regional affair, with the encounter between King Harold and Duke William justly claimed by the town of Battle, rather than Hastings. I felt this was an opportunity missed, given that Hastings has aspirations to position itself as a trendy weekend seaside getaway close to London, rather like Brighton has done. It has some things in its favour, including some excellent fish restaurants, boutique accommodation and the attractive heritage seascape. Yet the connection to the famous battle is so strong in most people's minds and central to the destination image that it seems an obvious one to make in order to boost tourist numbers. Are they influenced by the spoofs and Pythonish jokes, and see the re-enactors as 'geeks' or eccentrics; not quite the type of sophisticated tourist they want to appeal to?

WF Arriving by train at Battle, we just followed the crowd out of the small rural station. Young children in medieval outfits were a sure sign we were going in the right direction. The re-enactment was to be held at Battle Abbey. This was established by King William as a thanksgiving for victory. Operated by English Heritage, the battle site is in its grounds. Normally, visitors experience it by following a trail of interpretive signs. However, on the weekend closest to the battle's date, English Heritage stage two re-enactments, one on the Saturday and one on the Sunday.

WF We arrive at the battlefield, literally a grassy field. The 'arena' is marked out by a simple wire fence. There are no stands or seats. It's just find a place on the grass. We take our cue from the crowd. Find a good vantage point. Next to the fence allows us an uninterrupted view. Later in the day the crowd will be six or seven deep. Relying on my meagre knowledge of military history, I tactically survey the ground. Surely, Harold will occupy the high ground forcing the Normans to come up the hill. Accordingly, I suggest we sit at the top of the hill to have a good view of the Saxon defence. I, of course, am wrong. Whatever history says, in this battle the armies will clash *across* the hill, leaving the crowd and food vendors to camp on the high ground. With my orientation skills completely wrong, we eventually realise that we will sit opposite the Norman lines.

JL Before the proceedings begin, we talk to a man and his young son, sitting nearby. The man mentions that his son is a medieval devotee ('he loves everything about it!'). I ask whether his son watches *Merlin*. Of course, the answer is affirmative. No doubt many of the children here, dressed in mock chain mail, leggings, and armour and wielding small swords, knives and axes, are fans of the show. A number engage in mock fights with each other, echoing what we will shortly see in the re-enactment. All seem enthusiastic – none seems to have been press-ganged here by their parents – and a carnival-like atmosphere is building, as people unpack their picnics and stake their spots.

WF The announcer from English Heritage paces up and down with a hand held mike. While there are lots of re-enactors around in armour and other medieval clothing, his costume is a tweed suit. Whether or not he is one, he's taking the role of the history professor, explaining what is happening, its meaning and implications. Watching the announcer at work, I remember the Battle of Hastings comedy sketch I had seen long ago (and which is quoted at the beginning of this chapter). He's a modern character, out of place in costume and manner. Clearly he's meant to be an interpretive mediator, providing some sort of linkage between the crowd and re-enactors.

JL The day is bathed in brilliant sunshine – the sort of golden autumnal day that one reads about in books. I forget to bring a hat, and spend the day with a programme up against my forehead, in an attempt to cut down the glare. I am even concerned that I might get sunburnt, which is not something I tend to associate with England in October, nor with a battle. I expected glowering skies and rain, which would add to the hardship and challenge of the event, both for the crowd and those people taking part. Instead, we are buying ice-creams with a wedge of flake chocolate in them and wearing sunglasses. Yet as it gets closer to the time when the first action begins, there is a definite sense of build-up and even an air of tension. We are all waiting for the clash of swords and the first glimpse of the opposing armies. The foot soldiers and their leaders emerge from the trees at the bottom of the hill and march onto the battlefield. It is an eerie and emotional sight, and I am immediately caught up in it all.

WF The announcer provides a back story for the upcoming action. For both the Saxons and the Normans he goes right back to the Romans. I find him a bit long-winded. He certainly speaks too long for the children surrounding us. I also find that some of the historical interpretation jars with my pre-existing knowledge. My understanding of the battle comes from the classic work *1066: The Year of the Conquest* by David Howarth (1977). I'd brought my copy on the trip, reading about half on the flight over. I understand how easy it is to get into the mind-set that there is only one right version of history and expect all visitor interpretation to conform to it. Without consciously thinking it through, I want him to tell me my version of the conflict.

JL As I know less detail about the historical event than Warwick, I enjoy hearing some context. The children are amazingly well-behaved throughout all this and I am struck by the lack of litter, which continues for the rest of the day. To me, this illustrates the respect that is given to the site, which is perhaps akin to a pilgrimage for some of the people present. I hear British accents most of the day and no French tourists appear to have made the journey across the Channel, even

Figure 7.1 Mock battles at the re-enactment of the Battle of Hastings, 2011. Photo by W. Frost.

though some signage is bilingual (French and English), the result of obtaining EU funding. How comfortable would they feel here today? I think they would fit right in – there is no rancour in the crowd and no jingoistic French-bashing. The passage of time has smoothed any conflict and the event is essentially a performance that we are watching, a drama that stirs the blood but not the passions.

WF The morning's entertainment is a form of tournament, a series of mock battles (Figure 7.1). These are contested by the re-enactors. Later today, they will need to follow the script. Here they are not constrained. It is a chance to demonstrate their own individual prowess and preparation. There is no distinction between Norman and Saxon. They are individuals. Each fight utilises a single type of weapon – sword, spear, battleaxe. Scores of re-enactors peel off in pairs, seemingly randomly and set to trying to best each other. Some strut and prance, shouting out insults and boasts, playing to the crowd. Victory comes from touching your opponent on an unprotected part of their body (counting coup). Once it commences, I realise how similar it is to the tournament *mêlée* described in Sir Walter Scott's *Ivanhoe*, which the eponymous hero demonstrates his worth by winning.

WF Very quickly most of the combatants are dead. If you can't win, there is an opportunity to die with great drama. The groaning and overacting bring nervous laughs from the crowd. This is interactive theatre. They know we are watching and they play to us. We have a new commentator now. He's dressed in medieval costume, but not armour. His persona is of the weapon master. He's old, the fighters are young. As he explains the technical details, he jokes with the crowd. An event marshal joins in. They are two greybeards overseeing the young men training. There are women out there too, though this is not over-emphasised.

JL The fighting is quite visceral and physical, and the men look genuinely exhausted as they retreat from hand-to-hand combat. We are sitting close enough to see the sweat on their brow and their grimaces. It's a reminder that people are involved in battles, rather than anonymous armies. It also shows how seriously these re-enactors take what they are doing. There is a sense of pride and swagger about some of the men as they leave the field, or walk through the crowd. It's not over the top, but more suggestive of their commitment and identification with their characters and the story in which they are taking part.

WF The warriors use blunt weapons. Against shields, their blows are hard. The death strokes, aimed at unprotected areas, are light. Right in front of us, two knights clash. At the first blow of a battleaxe, a shield is completely shattered. They both stop and look in amazement. The greybeard marshals rush up. For the next hour or so, there is a steady stream of medievalists coming over to look and laugh at the shield with a big hole in it. There's an edge to the laughter. Sure, the shield was not up to it, but it could have gone horribly wrong.

WF As the duelling combatants thin out, the commentator becomes more personal. He provides the names of individuals who are still fighting. Sometimes there are affectionate jokes. One knight fights with a sword and a dagger. The commentator is scornful of the second blade – it is nothing but a butter knife. It's effective though and the banter continues as the knight works his way up to the last few contestants. As each round progresses, one warrior stands out. This is Torstin, a German re-enactor. Seemingly no one can defeat him. He wins the first three tournaments. Some of us cheer, some boo. Again I am reminded of *Ivanhoe*. We are unsure whether we want him to win everything or not. Suddenly, there's a shout. Torstin is down and out. Nonetheless, he is the champion of the tournament, demonstrating his expertise in medieval combat to his peers in the re-enacting fraternity.

JL The name Torstin sounds authentically Saxon, so no wonder he's a crowd favourite. After the knights leave the field, we get to witness the men on horseback. They charge across the field, making a wonderful photo opportunity, as the commentator explains battle tactics and the importance of horses in these encounters. Having these small vignettes of battle re-enacted before the main event seems to serve two purposes. First and foremost, it provides a spectacle for the crowd while they are waiting for the main event. Just staging the battle on its own would only last for a few hours. This way, the event is spread over a full day. It also heightens the enjoyment of the battle re-enactment, helping to explain the panoply of weaponry, battle strategies and types of combat that would have been typical in William and Harold's day. By the time the battle is scheduled, the crowd is pumped and ready to see some action.

WF The lunch break. The audience are invited to visit the medieval encampments. We choose the Normans simply because they are closer. The re-enactors are enjoying themselves displaying their costumes, weapons and other paraphernalia. Earlier today at the English Heritage tent, children were allowed to look at weapons. However, they couldn't touch them due to occupational health and safety

Figure 7.2 Meeting the re-enactors at the medieval encampment, 2011. Photo by J. Laing.

regulations. In the Norman camp, it is 1066 and there are no such regulations. We watch as kids are encouraged to put on helmets and pick up swords and battleaxes (see Figure 7.2). Here, the spirit of Merlin is strong. Are young recruits being charmed? Certainly, most of the re-enactors are young. In their twenties, perhaps early thirties. Few look older.

JL We stroll around the camp and see people making handicrafts and preparing food, cooking in pots around a fire or seated inside tents. There are more bearded men here than a *Lord of the Rings* movie, and an air of quiet intensity. Women are ever-present here, whereas the battlefield is a domain for men, with women relegated to the role of water carriers.

WF After lunch, the real battle re-enactment commences. The commentator in the tweed suit returns. Now it's history by the script. No rugged re-enactor individualism allowed now. Torstin and others must play their assigned parts. Now is the time for epic spectacle. The two armies pour on to the field and are aligned in battle formation. There are approximately 400 re-enactors. That's far less than the actual battle, but it makes an impressive sight.

WF William, Duke of Normandy, and half a dozen of his minions ride up and down his battle line. These are the only re-enactors on horseback. The narrator/professor explains that these are the elite of the re-enactors. Horses trained for medieval work are expensive, English Heritage can only afford a few and it's a great privilege to take these roles. To give the crowd photo opportunities, the duke and his henchmen ride along the fence, waving their swords. It's also the opportunity for crowd participation. Egged on by the announcer, we either cheer or boo the invader. Most of us boo. I boo. Raised on a diet of Errol Flynn and Robin Hood, I must support the Saxons. That's part of it, but another key part is that we've slipped neatly into Falassi's rites of reversal (see Chapter 6). This is our opportunity as twenty-first-century people to shout and boo at authority figures. It's good humoured fun, no repercussions and we get to blow off steam. It's what our peasant ancestors have been doing at festivals for centuries.

JL I feel more allegiance towards William, perhaps because Harold's claim to the crown was slightly dubious, but also due to a sense that his victory paved the way for an economic, social and cultural flourishing and helped to make the England we see today. Given the crown is now descended from William, isn't he really just the forebear of the British establishment? Surprisingly, however, I can't remember what chant we gave in his support – probably just 'Guillaume', the French version of William. The battle-cry for Harold's army is more poignant ('Ut, ut' or 'out, out' in modern parlance), and I suspect more memorable as a consequence.

WF The re-enactor playing William does not respond to our taunts. A good touch. He's physically and majestically above us peasants. However, one of his toadies takes the bait. He rides forward and yells that we can expect higher taxes as reward for our disrespect. For a moment I fear he's going to channel Alan Rickman and cancel Christmas. Also, to convey a fearsome medieval knight, his voice should thunder like Michael Caine or Windsor Davies. This chap hasn't got it. His voice is thin and strained. He's more like Edmund Blackadder.

WF The battle commences. Various groups march back and forth, waving flags. One lone Norman knight charges forward. The flower of continental chivalry, he challenges Harold to single combat. The Saxons know nothing of such etiquette. He's hacked down. We cheer. A Norman bishop appears (of Bayeux?). He blesses the soldiers. He then draws his sword and charges into the affray. We boo.

JL Even as I am lost in what I am seeing, I am marvelling at the discipline of the participants and how much work has gone into staging this. Everyone is arrayed appropriately, and appears drilled to within an inch of their lives. Yet the potential for the unexpected is obvious, based on what we have seen in the morning's displays, and there is an edge to watching this – one slip, even with a blunt sword, and someone could be hurt. On this huge field, there are charges and set pieces involving huge numbers of men, but also the intimacy of individual combat, as the battle lines break up.

WF The isolated historical vignettes now blend into a general free for all. Charge after charge is made by the Normans, crashing into the Saxon defensive line, known as a shield wall. The Saxon defence holds, repelling each charge. The announcer becomes more frantic, trying to convey that William's opportunity is slipping. A rumour, he shouts, runs through the Normans that William has been killed and they begin to waver. The duke removes his helmet and gallops around the field, rallying his men.

JL I become so engrossed in what is happening on the field, that I almost start to forget that the outcome is predetermined and William will be victor. The men are throwing themselves into it and I wonder whether some of them might feel tempted to change history, rather than stick to the script. I am also wondering how they will handle the famous 'arrow through the eye' incident, given it is not certain whether this actually happened or just became one of the web of stories that are woven around a historically significant event like the Battle of Hastings. It's certainly one of the more dramatic ways to die on a battlefield, and gives Harold the cloak of a martyr who lost on account of a mere fluke or stroke of bad luck, rather than through lack of prowess or leadership. I'm struck at how difficult it must have been to have fought a battle without modern aids of communication. Arresting a wild rumour such as William's death or the infamous arrow incident would not have been easy and might easily sway the outcome of a battle.

WF The battle enters its final phase. The re-enactors have been in mock battle for nearly an hour. The individual choreography is rough and ready. If one is killed, he just gets up and keeps going. But now some start to lie motionless, signifying the heavy losses and the shortening of the Saxon shield wall. Quite suddenly it collapses. Harold has been killed. The announcer takes pains to explain that the arrow in the eye is a later invention – we simply don't know what actually happened. Resistance crumbles, William is now King of England.

WF The battle is over, what do we do? There is a final ceremony, consistent with Falassi's model, to close proceedings and allow us to return from the eleventh to the twenty-first century. The announcer thanks us, but then calls for a minute's silence. This is, after all, a site of a real battle, where thousands died for their cause. The re-enactor armies and the crowd bow their heads and there is complete silence. Then there is applause. The re-enactors march off to their camps for mead and ale. They will do it all again at a repeat re-enactment the next day. We troop to the railway station.

JL The minute's silence we have witnessed is an interesting link to a tradition started after the Great War, yet doesn't seem jarring in this setting nor affect the authenticity of the day in my eyes. It helps to bring us back to the modern day from the liminal realm of the event, and it is difficult to imagine how else they might have concluded the proceedings. A speech would have been phony, and just to leave us to drift away from the field would have been an anti-climax after all we had seen and heard. It also reflects the sentiment of the day, where there was often a good-natured round of applause for various exploits, whether Norman or Saxon. In the end, it was all part of a common history, rather than 'them' and 'us'.

WF Back in Hastings, we amble down to the beach. We've heard about a bonfire procession, but few details. My expectation is of a small group in medieval dress with torches, consistent with the battle. To our surprise, the beach contains a massive pyramid of wood, perhaps 20 metres high. Only now does it dawn upon me that this is a Guy Fawkes bonfire.

JL There are names of people written on some of the pieces of wood. We find out later that they are the names of members of the local bonfire society who have died over the past year. This makes the bonfire a kind of funeral pyre, rather than just a bit of fun, and very personal to the locals.

WF On the beach we fall into conversation with a couple in their fifties. Average suburbanites, except they are dressed all in black and carry backpacks with anarchist symbols. A costume perhaps? Borrowed from their children's wardrobe? They are members of one of the bonfire societies. It is only months later in reading Sharpe (2005) that I gain any understanding of these community institutions. Even then, I struggle as there's no Australian equivalent I'm aware of. They enthusiastically explain the iconography of the bonfire. Banks, politicians and hoodies are going to be symbolically burnt. I think back to the Guy Fawkes nights of my childhood, organised by the local scout group. Who did the local scoutmaster want to burn? In the present, I ponder why anarchists are against hoodies. Well, looting designer shops is hardly revolutionary, perhaps they've given anarchy a bad name.

JL I have a different take on the use of the hoodies as a symbol of evil, based on my time spent in London during the riots. I think they struck at the heart of people, even as far away from the capital as Hastings. They symbolised a society out of control, with law and order able to crumble so easily, and a section of the populace that felt let down and dispossessed and wanted to hit back and 'get even'. The social contract was broken. Scenes of looters, setting fire to buildings and attacking police formed an indelible memory. I think this use of the bonfire was a way for local residents, or at least a section of it, to regain control over their community. Part of me understands this, but another part feels a bit uncomfortable at the Marie Antoinette allusion conjured up by the sign at the top of the scaffold – 'Off with their hoods'. Did the organisers really want these people hanged, even symbolically? Yet the evening ends in fireworks, with oohs and ahs, and people huddled together. Perhaps this is cathartic, allowing the riots to be put behind and bringing people together. The streets are thronging with a steadily surging crowd, who seem ready to continue their night out. The hoodies, if present, are clearly keeping a low profile.

WF During the course of the evening, we see hundreds of people in fancy dress. They're in pubs, wandering the streets, queuing for fish and chips. Smugglers seem to be the most popular, afterwards I learn that this is the staple of the south-east coast Guy Fawkes Nights (Sharpe 2005). Next in popularity comes pirates. They're both male and female, young couples and families with children. As a researcher, I've examined how tourists are fascinated by outlaws, undertaking case studies in the American West and Australia (Frost 2006; Wheeler *et al.* 2011). I'm intrigued at the paradox between this love of law-breakers and our desire for a peaceful and ordered society. I had thought of it as only a feature of the frontier, a reimagining of a mythical Wild West. What I see at Hastings opens my eyes to wider possibilities. At the very least, it is a perfect example of Falassi's rite of inversion. This commemorative event provides a licence to adults to be children, to play at being naughty and dangerous. It's the biggest night of the year and it's easy to see why.

8   Cultural commemorations

Anniversaries are big business in the cultural world and have long been convenient events for promoting agendas.

(Browne 2008: 324)

A phenomenon as widely dispersed as the Darwin commemorations is bound to have had many causes, serving many purposes.

(Shapin 2010)

Cultural commemorative events reinforce cultural identities and heritage. They can focus on creative works – including books, works of art, music and other forms of performance – or their creators. Commemorations of such creativity may be strongly linked to national identities, though in many cases they may be so widely appreciated that their connections are universal. The link to national identities often makes such commemorative events popular with governments and the broad appeal raises hopes of encouraging tourism. Conversely, some cultural commemorations may be quite subversive and others of limited appeal outside a particular community.

It is important to understand that cultural commemorations have the potential for dissonance. Controversies may arise from differences about the meanings of the event itself as well as the person or thing that is the subject of the commemoration. Conflict may result from a perception that governments or organisers are trying to manipulate or rewrite history, utilising it for propaganda. There might be issues of gatekeeping and ownership, as in disputes between governments and the family of the deceased whose anniversary is being celebrated.

In this chapter, we explore three key themes with respect to cultural commemorations. The first is their potential for shaping identity, a sense of place and national pride. These are considered using case studies of anniversaries of Shakespeare and the Festival of Britain, which was held to mark the centenary of the Great Exhibition. The second theme is how these events shape, even dramatically alter, our views and understanding of their subjects. Here we consider three two-hundredth birthdays – Charles Dickens, Charles Darwin and Richard Wagner. The third section explores the link with nostalgia and attempts to reclaim the past, utilising Bloomsday as a case study.

Identity, image and nation building

Cultural commemorations regularly involve issues of personal or national identities. This might stem from a strong connection of the person or cultural phenomenon being celebrated with the destination staging the commemoration. It might also be linked to the potentially high regard and esteem with which they are held, although even a poor reputation might have implications for identity-formation and could even be changed through the aegis of a commemoration. These events may also contribute to a destination's image, by entwining the commemorative event with a particular place. Governments may therefore stage cultural commemorations for social rather than economic purposes, with the aim of fostering community bonding, and building social capital and a sense of nationhood by evoking pride in past achievements. These themes can be traced through the following two case studies.

The Shakespeare anniversaries

Shakespeare's funeral in 1616 was a quiet affair, as befits a man who was regarded as 'just another writer of popular entertainment' (Deelman 1964: 5). So how did the Shakespeare 'cult' begin, leading to his present status as the greatest dramatist and poet of his time, if not *all* time (Lynch 2007)? Shakespeare tourism or the *Shakespeare trade* dates back to the eighteenth century (Hogdon 1998; Hubbard and Lilley 2000). This coincides with the date of the first Shakespeare anniversary celebrations, which marks the start of the iconisation of Shakespeare, influencing how the English understand his works, and, in turn, themselves (Deelman 1964; Lynch 2007). Shakespeare is an instructive case study of the evolution of 'cultural renown' (Taylor 1989) through commemorative events, which shaped this process and underpinned his growing dominance as a national icon.

Apart from the constant performance of his plays, often updated to suit contemporary audiences, there are biopics such as *Shakespeare in Love* (1998), with Joseph Fiennes as the impecunious bard, in love with the winsome Viola and writing what will later emerge as *Romeo and Juliet*. There are modern twists on the plays, exemplified by *Ten Things I Hate About You* (1999), a teenage rendering of *The Taming of the Shrew* starring Heath Ledger and *The Tempest* played out in outer space in the sci-fi classic *Forbidden Planet* (1956). The Cole Porter hit musical *Kiss Me Kate* (1948), another spoof on *The Taming of the Shrew*, featured the song 'Brush up your Shakespeare' with its advice for men wanting to chat up a woman ('Just declaim a few lines from 'Othella'. And they'll think you're a helluva fella'). The creation of the new Globe Theatre beside the Thames attracts crowds for performances of the Bard's plays, alongside works by his contemporaries such as Marlowe. All of these maintain Shakespeare's familiarity across the generations, as do his ubiquity as required reading in the classroom. Like many of our peers, we studied plays such as *Macbeth* and *Julius Caesar* in high school. Hundreds of familiar words and phrases originated with Shakespeare (Macrone 1993). Shakespeare's quintessential role within English popular culture, as well as the shaping of English cultural identity, has led to the inclusion of *pop-up* Shakespeare on the London Tube in the 2012 Cultural Olympiad, part of the London Olympic Games.

The focal point for Shakespeare is the small town of Stratford-upon-Avon in Warwickshire, where visitors can see Shakespeare's birthplace, along with Anne Hathaway's Cottage (Watson 2006). The decision to hold celebrations to mark the bicentenary of the birth of Shakespeare in 1769 in Stratford was a bold one, given the dramatist was strongly identified with London, his place of residence and the locale of many of his successes (Lynch 2007; Stern, 2004). The two-hundredth anniversary jubilee marked the beginning of the identification of Stratford-upon-Avon as the place to celebrate and honour Shakespeare (Deelman 1964; Hubbard and Lilley 2000). The town still has an annual birthday celebration for Shakespeare in April and is largely dependent on Shakespeare tourism for its economic survival (Deelman 1964).

It was a difficult and crowded two-day stage coach ride from London at the time, which did not deter committed Shakespeare devotees, including James Boswell, author of *Life of Samuel Johnson* (1791). The actor David Garrick was the high-profile organiser of the festivities, which are often referred to as 'Garrick's Jubilee', thanks to his efforts to promote both Shakespeare and his own celebrity (Lynch 2007). Garrick was courted by the town council, who hoped to use the jubilee to raise funds to restore the Stratford town hall. He presented the town with a statue of Shakespeare and his efforts at creating the first Shakespeare-linked commemorative event led to Garrick being buried at Shakespeare's feet in Westminster Abbey. He was also a shrewd entrepreneur, and his musical commemorative tribute to the event which made his name, called simply *The Jubilee*, was performed 152 times at Drury Lane 'making it more popular, in the period as a whole, than all but three of Shakespeare's own plays' (Taylor 1989: 119).

The three-day jubilee celebrations of 1769 were marred in part by bad weather; the disinclination of the town council to bankroll proceedings; skyrocketing prices charged to visitors by local profiteers, including daily rates for rooms equivalent to a week's wages for a tradesman; and a heckler – the actor Thomas King (Deelman 1964; Foulkes 2002; Lynch 2007). The rain led to the cancellation of the street pageant, which would have allowed the whole town to participate in the event. Luckily the weather improved by the third day, allowing the Jubilee Cup and the fireworks to go ahead. Activities in the newly-built pavilion were limited to those who could afford to pay. Garrick took centre-stage in a production entitled 'An ode upon dedicating a building, and erecting a statue, to Shakespeare, at Stratford upon Avon' (Foulkes 2002). The heckler's interruption was supposed to be an ironic commentary on Voltaire's criticism of the poet, but his humour was not appreciated, with Boswell describing it as something which 'had better been omitted at this noble festival: it detracted from it's (sic) dignity; nor was there any occasion for it. We were all enthusiastic admirers of Shakespeare' (quoted in Lynch 2007: 254). The town struggled to cope with the numbers of visitors. While there was public criticism of the jubilee in its day, nevertheless it is viewed from the benefit of hindsight as a triumph, which confirmed Shakespeare's 'cultural pre-eminence' (Foulkes 2002: 1) from that day forward.

The next great Shakespeare anniversary was the 1864 tercentenary of his birth. Unlike the Garrick jubilee, with its pageants and fireworks, this was to have a practical and serious purpose, as befits a Victorian mindset. Unfortunately, the planned royal patronage of Prince Albert was prevented by his untimely death and his eldest son, the Prince of Wales, was approached but declined the role (Foulkes 2002). The future Edward VII, unlike his parents Victoria and Albert, was not a great fan of Shakespeare. Transport to Stratford, however, was no longer a problem, with the advent of the railways, which augured well for attendance. The organisation of events took place on two fronts in England – London and Stratford – as it was felt that a 'double celebration' was appropriate, given the interest in Shakespeare (Foulkes 2002). There were also events held in the United States, including Boston. Committees were formed, and swiftly had to deal with conflict over leadership and the legacy of the anniversary. The Stratford committee wanted to endow university scholarships for students from Shakespeare's former childhood school. They got a statue from the town council instead, much to the chagrin of those who sought an educational outcome of the celebrations. There were disputes over the choice of performers, with the engagement of Stella Colas and Charles Fechter, both French actors, seen as an insult to their English equivalents. In the event, only Colas appeared on stage during the tercentenary, with several English actors withdrawing in protest at the perceived Gallic raid on the turf of their national hero (Foulkes 2002).

Despite this ill-feeling, the show went on, over a period of two weeks rather than the mere three day extravaganza of the jubilee. Stratford was fortunate to experience better weather than it did in 1769 and excursion trains were provided from surrounding areas, allowing copious numbers of visitors to flock to the town. A pavilion was built for up to 5,000 people to enjoy a programme ranging from dinners and a ball, to concerts and theatrical productions (Foulkes 2002). There was even a performance of Handel's *Messiah*, a metaphor for the sacralisation of Shakespeare. Speakers from Germany emphasised the greatness of Shakespeare and his link with 'great nations' (Foulkes 2002). While they sought to claim a common literary heritage, based on Saxon blood, the boost to English national pride was not lost on those present. Despite the rhetoric, once again, the exclusivity of the pavilion resulted in the townspeople missing out on most of the festivities other than a street pageant, leading to local angst at being shunted sideways. The pageant was organised and funded by the local people, rather than via the committee, and demonstrated community feeling about Shakespeare and his connection with their local identity (Foulkes 2002).

London's events were less successful than their Stratford equivalents. A planting of a sapling given by Queen Victoria (she was absent, still in mourning for the death of Prince Albert) was overshadowed by protesters over the treatment of Garibaldi. Performances of Shakespeare which were intended to have a long run were forced to close early, due to lack of patronage and the selection of lesser-known Shakespeare plays over audience favourites (Foulkes 2002). The committee lacked a leader in the mould of Garrick, and the ease of visits to Stratford lured those who saw the town as the rightful home of the tercentenary and Shakespeare celebrations.

Later commemorations built on the strength of their predecessors. The three-hundredth anniversary of Shakespeare's death was celebrated in 1916 but World War One affected the celebrations (Hoenselaars and Calvo 2007). The four-hundredth anniversary of his birth in 1964 was however an extravaganza. More American destinations came on board, with New York celebrating Shakespeare's anniversary year with a number of productions (Danziger 1964). The centrepiece however of the celebrations was Stratford (Deelman 1964). It remains the place most associated with Shakespeare, and Shakespeare continues to be one of the most beloved and admired playwrights and poets; the direct result of the commemorative anniversaries of the eighteenth and nineteenth centuries, particularly Garrick's jubilee.

The Festival of Britain

In 1951, the UK staged the Festival of Britain. Its official purpose was to 'show our faith in Britain's future and commemorate her achievements in the past', through a celebration of the centenary of the Great Exhibition of 1851. In reality, the commemoration of the Great Exhibition was little more than a pretext for the festival (Hillier 1976: 12). Planning was already far advanced when it was realised that the Great Exhibition did not play a part in the festival, and a model of the Crystal Palace was hastily constructed (Hillier 1976; Strong 1976). The Festival Director, Gerald Barry was 'determined that the Festival would not become a mindless exercise in nostalgia' (Festival of Britain 2011: 11). The Festival of Britain can therefore be compared to the Philadelphia Exposition of 1876, which was also ostensibly a commemorative event – officially celebrating the centenary of the signing of the Declaration of American Independence, but effectively staged to raise public morale after war and foster hope in the future (Hillier 1976).

The festival clearly contributed to a political agenda. While there were calls to postpone it when South Korea was invaded in 1950, the decision was made to go ahead, as it was argued by Gerald Barry to be a 'moral and spiritual weapon' against anti-democratic forces. The festival emblem showed Britannia above a four-pointed compass, in the patriotic colours of red, white and blue. As Strong (1976: 6) notes, this festival was part of a long line of 'secular state festivals in which government set out to present to the masses the ideals and goals of a new society, framed within a view of history recast in the terms of romantic nationalism'. While glorifying Britain, the festival's iconography was also insular and failed to embrace Europe and the Commonwealth. Nor did it recognise the political changes occurring in the post-war world (Strong 1976).

The staging of the 1951 Festival of Britain at a time when the country was still in the midst of rationing after World War Two was designed to be a 'tonic to the nation' (in Barry's words) and give a boost to public morale. Britain was in the grip of post-war blues and was given official sanction to shake them off and celebrate. The official leaflet noted: 'The visitor will see a Britain full of hope and brightness'. Some criticised this sanguine, even saccharine view of the festival, arguing that it came at a time when Britain's economy was going backwards and in a time of crisis (Forty 1976). Others argued that the festival encouraged people to think that happiness could be satisfied by material wants and a coat of fresh paint (Forty 1976). The 'enforced jollity' stuck in some people's throats (Lucie-Smith 1976: 189). The timing of the festival could be seen as macabre, at a time when men were still fighting in Korea and it was felt by some that public money could be used for better things (Egan 1976). An alternative view is that the festival had a far deeper emotional significance for the British than perhaps some appreciated at the time or in retrospect. It could be understood as a tribute to the fallen – to the sacrifices Britain had made in the war (Festival of Britain 2011). This is borne out in the support it received from visitors and the fond memories that surround it, which lasted well beyond the initial euphoria of the festival period (Banham 1976). Casson (1976: 81) also argues that it had a 'spiritual' dimension, coming on the heels of a hard-won victory: 'It was noticeably unboastful and nobody was taught to hate anyone'.

The festival was intended to attract tourists back to Britain, particularly from Europe and the United States, by showing a Britain that was 'open for business' and recovered from wartime. As Barry, in a BBC recording in 1950, observed: 'We mean to look our best next summer'. Buses were sent to Europe to publicise the festival (Banham 1976), complete with exhibition space and information in different languages. The festival provided the opportunity to regenerate the South Bank, which was a slum area in 1951, and marked the rebirth of the arts. Strong (1976: 6) refers to the festival and the coronation 'as culminations of a great reawakening ... after years of privation ... The Festival of Britain is the single gigantic event which crystallizes the whole era'. Others see the Festival of Britain in less deferential terms. Plouviez (1976: 166) observes that whereas the Great Exhibition showcased Britain's might as an 'industrial power', the festival marked a time when Britain 'started being the world's entertainers, coaxing tourists to laugh at our eccentricities, marvel at our traditions and wallow in our nostalgia'.

The South Bank Exhibition was the centrepiece of the festival and attracted nearly 9 million visitors. It was likened to a 'small city', with 14 pavilions focused on different themes. These included the Lion and the Unicorn pavilion, which explored British values and the national character, and the Homes and Gardens pavilion, which provided up-to-the-minute examples of rooms decorated in bright colours by fashionable designers such as Terence Conran. Two pavilions were dedicated to film and television, with the television pavilion showing visitors the new medium, which most found a novelty. Only the Royal Festival Hall was designed to be permanent. The Dome of Discovery, which was the largest aluminium structure in the world at the time, was dismantled after the festival concluded (Feaver 1976). Ray Davies of the Kinks remembers being taken to the site with his father. When he asked what it was all about, his father replied: 'It's the future' (Festival of Britain 2011: 15). Davies directed the Meltdown festival as part of the 2011 sixtieth anniversary celebrations, which celebrated music since the 1950s.

The South Bank area featured gardens festooned with fountains, flags, balloons, public art, lighting, and 13 restaurants and cafés. This was a revelation after the war. People danced outside at night in their overcoats to the strains of an orchestra (Forty 1976). To crowds used to blackouts and air-raids, the experience of eating outside and the amount of lights used was thrilling, even decadent. Even fresh paint was a novelty (Forty 1976). The 90-metre high Skylon structure, lit up at night, became the symbol of the exhibition, which Feaver (1976) compares to the Trylon at the 1939 New York World Fair. It was supposed to be purposeless, yet its presence on the South Bank was seen as a symbol of the policies and activities of the outgoing Labour government, resulting in the incoming Conservative government demolishing it (Festival of Britain 2011).

From an early stage of planning, it was envisaged that the festival would involve the whole country, not just London (Banham, 1976; Hillier, 1976). The South Bank Exhibition therefore formed part of what the organisers called a *constellation of events*. These additional nine events were:

1   the Festival Pleasure Gardens at Battersea, including a funfair, treewalk, firework displays, a children's zoo, street performers and shows;
2   the Living Architecture exhibition in East London, which focused on the rebuilding of Britain after the war and was used to kick-start the East End after the heavy bombing it sustained;
3   the exhibition of books at the Victoria and Albert (V & A) Museum in South Kensington;
4   the Science exhibition at the Science Museum in South Kensington;
5   the Exhibition of Farm and Factory in Belfast;
6   the Exhibition of Crafts and Living Traditions in Edinburgh;
7   the Exhibition of Industrial Power in Glasgow, which harked back to the Great Exhibition, in that it focused on Britain's prowess in heavy engineering and new technology of the future, including atomic research;
8   the Festival ship *Campania*, which sailed to ten cities, carrying versions of the South Bank Exhibition;
9   the Land Travelling Exhibition, a show about the British people and the things they make and use, which travelled to Birmingham, Leeds, Nottingham and Manchester.

The festival concluded its four-month run on 30 September 1951. More than one in three Britons attended. Russell (1976: 167) refers to the organisers' assertion that the festival was an "autobiography of the British people ... written by ourselves' ... and 'reflected what we were like at that particular time'. As with many commemorative exhibitions (see Chapter 5), the promotion of national identity was a key objective.

The sixtieth anniversary of the Festival of Britain was celebrated in 2011. Artistic Director Jude Kelly observed in the official program: 'We aren't holding a new Festival of Britain – we're celebrating the original'. Festivities included a museum of 1951 at the festival centre, with a free exhibition on the first Festival of Britain. The Festival emphasised inclusivity: 'This site was never about the few – it was built for the many. It set a glorious and permanent marker down about the use of public space for the imagination to flourish and for creativity to be celebrated' (Festival of Britain 2011: 1). The official guide posed the question: 'As we begin the next 60 years as a festival site, we are asking the questions, what do we believe in today and what kind of future do we want?'

Dissonant heroes – Dickens, Darwin and Wagner

Issues of identity entwined with commemorative events also bring to the fore allied concepts of pride and shame. Not all cultural greats are admired, and we may wish to forget some, while remembering others. Sometimes this is the result of learning more about the famous person after their death, with the spate of biographies that accompany an anniversary giving us a more rounded picture in some instances. Other reputations are resurrected as the result of an anniversary, or the celebrations are used to acknowledge the change in attitude towards a famous person. As we explore in this section, anniversaries connected with Charles Dickens, Charles Darwin and Richard Wagner have been used in this way to reflect changing and contested understandings of their achievements and characters.

Charles Dickens: icon or imposter?

The two-hundredth anniversary of the birth of Charles Dickens on 7 February 2012, attracted widespread media interest and exposure, but also saw a re-evaluation of his image based on a number of new biographies that were released to mark the occasion. In his day, he was a popular figure, whose literary fame was augmented by regular speaking tours, notably his visits to America, and acting roles on stage. He was a flamboyant showman, a larger than life figure, who worked hard at his own celebrity (John 2010a). His fame is in no danger of waning. Indeed, Dickens is as widely known and loved today as he was to Victorian audiences. The term *Dickensian* is often applied when referring to the Victorian era, with the 'Dickensian childhood' broadly understood as meaning one which is bleak, loveless and poverty-stricken (John 2010a). His characters such as Scrooge, Fagin, Mr Micawber and Miss Havisham are familiar to a wide audience through regular dramatisation of his works in television series, musicals and films, and he appears in his own right as a character in a 2005 episode of *Doctor Who*. He has even spawned a theme park – Dickens World in Chatham, Kent (John 2010a; Laing and Frost 2011).

The two-hundredth anniversary celebrations were multifarious and took place in a number of different places associated with Dickens or his books. Events in London included a ceremony to lay a wreath at his tomb in Westminster Abbey, with readings by people such as actor Ralph Fiennes and a member of the Dickens family, a visit by Prince Charles to the Dickens museum, and a day of events in Southwark Cathedral, near the debtors' prison where Dickens' father was incarcerated, which included an exhibition of artefacts, a choral evensong with readings, a guided walk, the pealing of bells and a talk by his biographer, Claire Tomalin. The town of Portsmouth celebrated its famous son by commissioning a project (the Dickens Community Archive project) to connect local community groups with the town's archives and records. Six of the groups were then chosen to contribute to a Dickens 200 exhibition at the city museum. They also held a church service at the cathedral, involving readings by Simon Callow and Sheila Hancock, and unveiled a new statue to Dickens. A 24-hour global read-a-thon saw Dickens' books read publicly in places as diverse (and surprising) as Kazakhstan, Korea and Syria. Exhibitions to mark the occasion were held at institutions such as the Morgan Library and Museum in New York, the Museum Strauhof in Zurich and the Centre Culturel de l'Entente Cordiale in Condette, France. And Penguin Books ran a competition to find Dickens' most beloved character. The result was unsurprising – Ebeneezer Scrooge from *A Christmas Carol*.

Not all events were confined to Dickens' birthday. Many extended festivities across the year, hoping to gain more mileage out of the occasion. Portsmouth staged a *Great Expectations* festival, which took place between 22 June and 1 July 2012, while the Museum of Childhood held a conference on 'Dickens and childhood', which was apt given the number of famous Dickens' characters who are children (i.e. David Copperfield, Little Nell) and the way he depicts the severities and deprivation of many a Victorian childhood. The Dickens Museum in London (see Figure 8.1) took a more innovative step. They closed their doors between April and December 2012, to allow a £3.1 million restoration project to go ahead. The works have been funded by the National Heritage Lottery fund, and involve structural works as well as upgrades to the display and interpretation of the collection, to allow a more satisfying visitor experience. The anniversary was also the impetus for creating an online and publicly accessible archive of Dickens' magazine and newspaper journalism, (*Dickens Journals Online* – www. buckingham.ac.uk/djo).

Until recently, Dickens was chiefly characterised as a paternalistic social progressive (John 2010b), who campaigned for better working and living conditions for the poor and a reformed legal system. He exposed the pointless bureaucracy, unfeeling and brutal administration, greed, and tragic outcomes of Victorian institutions such as the workhouse, the debtors' prison, the law court and children's homes, through his novels such as *Oliver Twist* (1838), *Nicholas Nickleby* (1839), *Bleak House* (1853) and *Little Dorrit* (1857). His best loved novel, *A Christmas Carol* (1843), contributes to the mythology of Christmas (John 2010a). Indeed, it helped to popularise many holiday rituals through its depiction of the Cratchit family celebrations, with culinary treats ('There never was such a goose … Oh, a wonderful pudding!') and festive cheer around the hearth.

The anniversary led to Dickens being viewed as a more complex character than had previously been the case. Many of the events focused on the social issues of his day and thus the role that Dickens played in exposing them to the world. This followed the traditional line of Dickens as a social reformer. An example is the Museum of

Figure 8.1 Charles Dickens Museum, London. Photo by J. Laing.

London's exhibition 'Dickens and London', which 'promises a "haunting journey" using sound and projections to explore wealth, poverty, prostitution, childhood mortality and philanthropy in Victorian times' (Maddox, 2012: 3). However, other events utilised readings, particularly from Claire Tomalin's new biography, *Charles Dickens: A Life* (2011), which show Dickens in a different light. While he did care passionately about social justice, and his works arguably stand the test of time, Dickens' private life brings forth questions over his own moral character. He exposed his wife to humiliation through airing her shortcomings and his misery in the newspapers, while conducting an affair, with the young actress Ellen Ternan (Tomalin 2011). Douglas-Fairhurst's biography is equally candid about Dickens' 'occasional eruptions of racism and sexism' (2011: 243) and poses the question of whether Dickens married 'the wrong sister' and details the writer's relentless, almost obsessive drive, shameless self-promotion and fear of failure. The changing perceptions of Dickens can be summed up in an article in *The Economist* in 2011, which reviewed the two new biographies of Dickens under the headline 'Beloved bully'. His birthday celebrations have given us licence to continue to revere the novelist, yet comprehend that the man had flaws.

Charles Darwin

The Darwin anniversary in 2009 was a double celebration, marking 200 years since the birth of Charles Darwin and 150 years since the publication of his work

The Origin of Species. Concerns were raised in some quarters at the potential political and religious agendas that were being pushed through the auspices of the commemoration. Perhaps this was naive, given Browne's (2008: 324) contention that 'scientific anniversaries … provide an opportunity to push an agenda, and even adapt the past, so telling us what we like best to hear'. The most obvious example was the use of the Darwin anniversaries to counter arguments against his evolutionary theories.

Darwin's work on natural selection posited the idea that variations in a population result in some genetic traits becoming more common, where they assist the individual to survive and thus reproduce. His comment in the penultimate chapter of *The Origin of Species* – 'The belief that species were immutable productions was almost unavoidable as long as the history of the world was thought to be of short duration' directly contested the view that the world had been created fully formed as described in the Bible (*creationism*) and sparked controversy that has been raging ever since. High-profile atheists such as Richard Dawkins have used Darwin's work to support their contention that there is no God: 'Darwinian evolution, specifically natural selection … shatters the illusion of design within the domain of biology' (Dawkins 2006: 118). The Darwin commemorations in 2009 became, in particular, a platform to rail against the creationist worldview, with the National Secular Society contending: 'Darwin's 200th birthday has become a rallying point for scientists opposing creationism' (Shapin 2010). Dawkins was especially prominent in many commemorative documentaries and panel discussions connected with the anniversaries, and held Darwin up as a fellow poster-boy for atheism. This glosses over Darwin's agonies over his growing loss of faith, a source of grief to his beloved wife Emma, and his belief, as he articulated in his 1887 autobiography: 'The mystery of all things is insoluble by us; and I for one must be content to remain an Agnostic' (quoted in Healey 2001). With multiple interpretations, the anniversaries had become 'a struggle among scientists for Darwin's soul' (Shapin 2010).

Another example of dissonance with respect to the 2009 Darwin anniversaries related to the ownership of the theory of natural selection itself. Alfred Russel Wallace independently came up with the same theory as Darwin, and sent the latter an abstract detailing his findings, which Darwin labelled 'a striking coincidence' (Healey 2001: 240). Darwin arranged for some of his unpublished writings to be published alongside Wallace's essay, to make it clear that 'Charles had reached his conclusions earlier and independently' (Healey 2001: 241), and was motivated to get his tome, *On the Origin of Species*, out in print as soon as possible. While some would argue that Wallace was hard done by, a new book by Stott (2012) – *Darwin's Ghosts: In Search of the First Evolutionists* – posits that both scientists arguably leveraged off the work of others, including Aristotle, Leonardo da Vinci and even Darwin's own grandfather Erasmus, who have gradually expanded the boundaries of knowledge in this area. Stott's point is that no scientist works in a vacuum, and the work of predecessors is necessarily part of the solution to many scientific conundrums. While others such as Shapin (2010) call Wallace 'undercelebrated', he acknowledges that Darwin went further in 'mapping out the grand literary and political strategy to make natural selection stick in the culture'. Nevertheless, the anniversary celebrations were remarkably silent on the earlier works, which led some to question the bias towards Darwin. Beccaloni and Smith, in a letter to *Nature* magazine in 2008, argue that the hundred-and-fiftieth anniversary of the *discovery* of natural selection should have been celebrated to a greater degree, acknowledging Wallace's role and achievements, as well as Darwin's.

Darwin was also recast as a 'green hero' (Shapin 2010), in another revision of history to suit modern sensibilities. This is based on his lyrical prose with reference to nature in *The Origin of Species*, most famously illustrated by his depiction of 'an entangled bank, clothed with many plants of many kinds, with birds singing on the bushes, with various insects flitting about, and with worms crawling through the damp earth'. His wonder at this complexity and the laws which make this possible has been translated into ecological zeal. Commemorative documentaries extol his work in awakening environmental concerns and label him 'the father of ecology' (Shapin 2010). It ignores Darwin's passion for shooting birds, although it must also be said that he paradoxically abhorred cruelty to animals and took enormous pleasure from his gardens (Healey 2001). It is a stretch however to equate this to a green crusade. His own wife was more revolutionary in this regard, waging a public campaign about issues such as the brutality of steel animal traps, often in Darwin's name (Healey 2001).

The anniversaries were used as a vehicle for destinations wanting to leverage off their connection with Darwin for different purposes. Cambridge, where Darwin studied as an undergraduate, was keen to emphasise its academic bona fides. It held a Darwin festival in 2009, with speakers such as David Attenborough and Richard Dawkins. Through this type of event, it hoped to portray itself as 'providing intellectual support for evolutionary thinking' (Williams 2008: R182) and a seat of august learning, instrumental in shaping the mind of the young Darwin. Shrewsbury, the birthplace of Darwin, was looking to boost tourism through the Darwin connection. It has staged events on Darwin's birthday for some years, and created a memorial garden in 2009, which was supposed to evoke his 'entangled bank' (Williams 2008).

Lest it be mistakenly believed that this dissonance and multiplicity of meanings is purely a modern phenomenon, it should be pointed out that the 2009 celebrations had a clear precedent in the 1959 centenary. As Kolchinsky (2010) notes: 'Each Darwin anniversary has initiated a reappraisal of evolutionary thought and a revaluation of the significance of his works to world outlook and world culture, reflecting not only the level of evolutionary knowledge, but also the socio-political and ideological environment in various countries'. In 2009, celebrations included high-profile exhibitions at institutions such as the Natural History Museum in London, and the Australian National Maritime Museum; a competition to commission a commemorative ceiling in the British Museum in what is now called the Darwin Room; a scheme to send 12 artists to the Galapagos Islands to highlight environmental degradation; and a re-enactment of the voyage of HMS *Beagle*, where Darwin collected much of the data that he would later analyse and dissect through the pages of *On the Origin of Species*. The 1959 anniversary was similarly marked by a swathe of events. Smocovitis (1999) referred to plans for a re-enactment of Darwin's voyage on the *Beagle*, and an establishment of a memorial park in the Galapagos Islands, which were mirrored by the 2009 initiatives. There were also parallels with respect to religious controversy, with Sir Julian Huxley's 1959 Convocation Address in Rockefeller Chapel used as a 'secular sermon' to pronounce that 'Evolutionary man can no longer take refuge from his loneliness in the arms of a divinized father-figure whom he has himself created' (Smocovitis 1999: 303), much to the consternation of many people present. The University of Chicago hosted the Darwin Centennial Celebration, and used it to highlight its intellectual gravitas, and 'share some of the glory associated with Darwin' (Smocovitis 1999: 322), much as Cambridge University did in 1909 and again in 2009. The three anniversaries collectively helped to 'reassert the primacy of natural selection against other evolutionary rivals' (Browne 2008: 324). Interestingly, the scientist R. A. Fisher, also renowned in research into natural selection and in Cambridge on the occasion of the 1959 centenary, had this to say about Darwin anniversaries: 'A centenary celebration is an occasion for retrospect, yet, I submit ... that the purpose of retrospect is to prepare ourselves for the future, by avoiding the unnecessary repetition of the errors of the past' (Edwards 2011: 428). The historical pretext for the commemoration is thus almost irrelevant, in the fight to win the scientific and cultural war.

Richard Wagner

The fiftieth anniversary of the death of composer Richard Wagner was used in the early Nazi years to push the agenda of the Third Reich. Wagner's anti-Semitic views were well known, as was Hitler's devotion to Wagner as the voice of a pure Aryan Germany. The nexus between the Nazis and Wagner 'is felt to be so firm and so self-evident that it is sufficient reason alone to maintain a ban on Wagner as one form of commemorating the Holocaust' (Vaget 2001: 662). After World War Two, Wagner was shunned for his racial beliefs. Most famously, the Israeli Philharmonic Orchestra boycotted Wagner's music, and the centenary of Wagner's death in 1983 was low-key. In recent years, attempts have been made to embrace the music rather than the man, with the Israel Chamber Orchestra now willing to play his compositions, and Jewish conductors such as Daniel Barenboim campaigning to lift the boycott (Vaget 2001). The debate revolves around whether his work should be tainted by his political and racial beliefs, or left to stand alone 'neither predetermined nor bound by its creator' (McClatchie 2008: 190). The reassessment of Wagner is not based on excusing his prejudices, but rather on disassociating them from his body of work.

The 2013 anniversary, marking 200 years since his birth, continues this trend of celebrating the extraordinary achievements of the composer of great works such as the mighty *Ring* cycle. It goes further, preferring to ignore or sweep under the carpet his unpalatable racism in favour of emphasising his role as an 'ardent democrat' and his 'uncompromising striving for artistic self-realisation' (Presse

News Leipzig 2012). Leipzig, his birthplace, plans events such as the opening of the new Richard Wagner Museum, complete with a permanent exhibition called 'The Young Richard Wagner – 1813 to 1834' and a Wagner festival, and is using the slogan 'Richard – Leipzig born and bred' to emphasise his ties to the city. Perhaps the shift away from Bayreuth for this commemoration is aiding the resurrection of Wagner, with the focus now on his music rather than his moral character. This represents the antithesis of the Dickens anniversary, which contrastingly recaptured the man and put him centre stage. The German National Tourist Board is assisting Leipzig with its promotion of the bicentennial, along with Tourismus and Marketing GmbH in Bayreuth (www.leipzig.de). Further evidence of Wagner's rehabilitation is the Wagner200 initiative, which aims to produce *The Flying Dutchman* for children aged between 6 and 14 years, using young artists. There seems to be no suggestion that the use of Wagner in this context might be inappropriate, although it is telling that the selection of an opera steered clear of German Rhine legends, choosing instead a libretto associated with the mythology of another country – the Netherlands.

Reclaiming the past: nostalgia and Bloomsday

Commemorations may also be exercises in looking back and celebrating a past that never was. They may contribute to identity building, shaping our view of ourselves, even if based on a rose-coloured view of history. This last case study is an exercise in nostalgia. Bloomsday commemorates the day immortalised in James Joyce's *Ulysses* – 16 June 1904. The date was chosen by Joyce for a sentimental reason – it was the day he first met and kissed Nora Barnacle, the woman who was to become his wife. *Ulysses*, as its title implies, uses Homer's *Odyssey* as a central motif, with the sojourns of Leopold Bloom through Dublin akin to the meanderings of the Greek hero Odysseus. The book is drenched in vignettes of Dublin – 'the sights, smells, sounds and music of a city' (Kaplan 2004). It is carefully crafted but often obscured by the dense and wildly unstructured prose, which makes it one of the most enigmatic and frustrating of texts in the modern oeuvre:

> He approached Larry O'Rourke's. From the cellar grating floated up the flabby gush of porter. Through the open doorway the bar squirted out whiffs of ginger, teadust, biscuitmush. Good house however: just the end of the city traffic. For instance McAuley's down there: n.g. as position. Of course if they ran a tramline along the North Circular from the cattle market to the quays value would go up like a shot.

James Joyce and his literary oeuvre are so inextricably linked to Ireland and its capital Dublin in particular, that one can be forgiven for forgetting that Joyce left Ireland in 1904 in disgust (Spangler 2002). His arguably most famous work, *Ulysses* (1922), was started in Trieste (Italy), when Joyce was a teacher of English at the Berlitz School of Languages (Morris 1992; Spangler 2002), and he remained a cynical and often scathing observer of Irish politics, religion and conservative culture from afar, only returning to Ireland on brief interludes. The central character in *Ulysses* is a Hungarian Jew, and it has been argued that Joyce meant the novel to shine a spotlight on racial tension and anti-Semitism in Ireland (Magalaner 1953). Joyce was largely ignored by his Irish compatriots. While Joyce's works were banned in many countries, due to their sexual content, no one bothered in Ireland, due to the belief that there was not enough interest in his books and thus no potential danger to public morality. Contemporary views about Joyce are mixed. In some conservative quarters, he is still seen as subversive and anti-Church and state (Spangler 2002). To others, he has been reclaimed as one of Ireland's favoured sons, along with his fellow one-time pariah, Oscar Wilde, 'to make Ireland and its culture more saleable to the outside world' (O'Connor 1998: 245).

The first Bloomsday was celebrated in Dublin in 1954, commemorating 50 years after the action portrayed in the book. Spangler (2002: 123) describes the decision to stage the event as something which 'must have appeared a radical and subversive act to conservative, Catholic and nationalist Irish'. It was a small affair, organised by two local enthusiasts – John Ryan, an editor of the periodical *Envoy*, and Brian O'Nolan, a writer. They were joined by four friends, who retraced the journey taken by Bloom and the artist Stephen Dedalus in *Ulysses*. Their intentions to completely re-enact the novel were well-intentioned but unrealised. They only made it as far as Davy Byrne's pub, which occurs about half-way through the book, and 'spent the afternoon at the bar' (Spangler 2002: 122). It took a while to grow as an event, with numbers remaining small throughout the 1960s and 1970s, involving participants who were mostly academics (Spangler 2002). This might be due to the perception at that time, as articulated by J. B. Priestley (1960: 340) that 'nobody thinks of [Joyce] as an Irish novelist'.

Bloomsday started to take off after the celebrations for the centenary of Joyce's birth in 1982, when Ireland was repositioning itself within Europe as a modern and forward-looking country – the 'celtic tiger', experiencing an economic boom and cultural revitalisation (Spangler 2002). The centenary celebrations provided a platform for a series of high-profile events, such as a 30-hour reading of the novel on Irish radio, a ceremony to unveil a bust of Joyce in Dublin and street theatre, involving performers recreating scenes from the book in Edwardian dress. The announcement of a new James Joyce Cultural Centre completed the festivities and marked the return of Joyce to national favour (Spangler 2002). There are now gold plaques across the city in the locations Joyce wrote about; a permanent change to the urban landscape which cements Joyce's place in the city's cultural narrative and the hearts of many Dubliners.

Bloomsday these days is celebrated right across the globe (Kaplan 2004) and is big business for Ireland, with the Irish Tourist Board making much of the celebration and the links of Joyce with Dublin to attract international visitors. Souvenirs such as Joyce T-shirts and coffee mugs are readily available in the shops (O'Connor 1998; Spangler 2002). Around 10,000 people take part in the event each year and Beja (1985) refers to the 'religious aura' that pervades

Dublin on this date. In 2004, the centenary of the fictional date immortalised in *Ulysses*, the President of the Republic of Ireland, Mary McAleese, toured the James Joyce Cultural Centre. Her visit evinces the political dimension of the day and provides the imprimatur of the state to proceedings (Sauter 2009). It has been argued, however, that this success and support comes at a cost. The marketing of the Bloomsday celebrations to tourists is based on stereotypes of the Irish as unsophisticated, romantic dreamers who love music, singing, dancing, drinking and a life of leisure – an image reinforced by John Ford's *Quiet Man* (1952). The Irish pubs of Bloomsday advertising are welcoming to strangers, and hark back to idyllic rural notions of the *craic*. This runs counter to the pubs depicted in Joyce's fiction, which are places contributing to moral decline and xenophobia (Spangler 2002). This *regressive nostalgia*, where the events of the past are bathed in a rosy glow and there is a yearning for a past that never was (Spangler 2002), also ignores the reality of pubs in contemporary Dublin, many of which cater for an 'urban, professional clientele' (Spangler 2002: 127). Furthermore, there have been disputes about ownership. James Joyce's grandson Stephen failed to attend the centenary of Bloomsday in 2004, as a result of his dispute with the Irish government. He threatened to sue them for copyright infringement if they went ahead with plans to conduct public readings of *Ulysses*, and was angered by their amendment of copyright laws to allow an original copy of the manuscript to be placed on display in the National Library in Dublin (Sauter 2009).

Bloomsday is in some senses still true to its roots as a largely grassroots initiative. Many of the street performances and guided walks are led by amateurs and private citizens, rather than organised centrally, and events do not attract an entrance charge (Sauter 2009). Typical activities include guided walks, street performances and readings, often by individuals dressed in Edwardian costume. Spangler (2002) describes the intimacy of the various events, and high levels of interaction between the audience and participants, an interplay described by Sauter (2009: 474) as 'theatrical playing', which contributes to a sense of authenticity and connection to others. The deliberate avoidance of issues such as political and religious conflict during these events might be viewed as an example of *active nostalgia*, a manifestation of a desire for a better future – an Ireland that is 'more peaceful, more inclusive than it is today' (Spangler 2002: 133). This kind of nostalgia may act to bind people together, and becomes part of a collective identity. As Spangler (2002: 135) notes: 'The value of Bloomsday ... is that it functions as a cultural performance that negotiates community through enactment'. Like many cultural commemorations, it has a social purpose; helping its participants discover who they really are.

9 Commercial commemorations

All brands have a history. Some brands have a heritage. And a few have made their heritage a valuable corporate asset.

(Urde *et al.* 2007: 9)

The marketing and events literatures are surprisingly silent on commemorations that have a commercial purpose, despite their pervasiveness and global reach. Perhaps the lack of troubling questions or dissonance relating to commercial products has made these commemorative events less interesting in the eyes of researchers. There is similarly a paucity of business-events research that considers promotional events and product launches, let alone the product commemoration. We argue that the latter's distinctive qualities as a form of commemorative event and their special position within a corporate public relations campaign make them worthy of further investigation.

Product commemorations differ from other forms of commemorative events in three main respects:

1   Sider and Smith (1997) refer to commemorations as 'attempts at closure'. Commercial commemorations, in contrast, are aimed at highlighting the longevity and iconic nature of products and emphasise their continuation into the future. They keep memories, as well as the products, alive.
2   Product commemorations are largely, if not exclusively driven by economic objectives such as sales growth or enhancing brand awareness or brand loyalty. The company or organisation is planning the anniversary and associated events to improve their financial bottom line. The interest from a research perspective however is the way in which these commemorative events have an effect on the market from a social or cultural standpoint. Why are people still interested in this product, what role does the anniversary play in this process and what are the impacts of these commemorative events on participants and the broader market?
3   Product commemorations are largely uncontroversial and do not attract dissonance or conflict, as is often the case with other commemorative events. The products selected for commemoration are normally beloved and popular,

which is the very reason they have lasted so long and are thus in a position to be commemorated at all. They might have attracted debate or notoriety when they first came on the market, such as the Barbie doll or the Beatles' *Sergeant Pepper's Lonely Hearts Club Band*, but quickly become accepted and ubiquitous, achieving global reach and maintaining that position over time. In some cases they are *heritage brands*, 'with a positioning and a value proposition based on [their] heritage' (Urde *et al.* 2007: 5). This narrative often lends itself to a commemoration, to emphasise the brand's longevity and history.

In this chapter, we explore these differences, and how businesses are using product commemorations as a way of gaining a marketing edge in a crowded marketplace. We also examine the reasons why they generate demand from a customer perspective. Different types of products may elicit different responses from the public and we advance three different concepts to explain the social and cultural effects of celebrating their anniversaries.

First, these commemorations are often linked to nostalgia for the past, particularly for things connected with our childhood, such as toys. Second, media products such as records or films, like toys, may enter popular culture and attract a devoted fan base, who use these anniversaries as a way to validate their obsessions and the social worlds or sub-cultures within which they reside. Third, in the case of luxury products, commemorations are a form of myth-making and contribute to the prestige and value of the brand in the eye of the consumer. Accordingly, this chapter is divided into three parts, examining these factors in detail and providing case studies of commercial commemorative events.

Toy stories

The nostalgia associated with toys is well-recognised (Orpana 2010; Peers 2004). They are an important part of our childhood, and particularly in the case of long-established brands, 'bind consumers to their pasts and to the communities that shared those brands' (Brown *et al.*2003: 20). These old brands are comforting: 'a safe haven in an unsafe world' (Brown *et al.* 2003: 20), and represent 'anchors of meaning' (Holt 2004: 1) that contribute to constructing self-identity. Some of the iconic toy brands still in existence include Lego, Meccano, Hornby, Tonka, and Mattel's Barbie doll.

Interest in toys is not limited to children. Many adults collect toys from their childhood, finding discarded treasures in junk shops, collector fairs or online, through sites such as eBay (Orpana 2010). Collectors' clubs and societies for toys abound and attract devoted members who eagerly seek out both originals and replicas of vintage toys (Peers 2004). Television shows such as *James May's Toy Stories* (2009) and episodes of programmes aimed at collectors such as *Antiques Roadshow* in the United Kingdom and *The Collectors* in Australia also cater to toy enthusiasts and the general public's nostalgia.

Anniversaries of the original launch of toys are an opportunity for tapping into this wistfulness for our youth and the 'personal and cultural associations' we make with these products (Brown *et al.* 2003: 20). Commemorative events of toys are both a response to their enduring popularity and a device to keep this alive, in a modern world of brand homogeneity and brand-saturated markets. In the following section, we look at two well-known toy brands – Lego and Barbie – and how each has generated a dedicated set of fans, communities of collectors, and a cross-generational appeal. Both were born in the post-war baby boom and are still hugely popular today. However, there are key differences in how the opportunities arising from their anniversaries were capitalised upon.

Lego: Danish ingenuity

Lego is in one sense the most straightforward concept possible – a basic studded plastic brick that can be used to build anything from the *Harry Potter* Hogwarts castle, to a Ferris wheel or pirate galleon. Its simplicity is the source of its genius, as its scope is only limited by the imagination of the user. The product is also consistent – the bricks have not altered their design since 1958, allowing children to use Lego pieces owned by their parents and combine it with modern pieces. The Lego ethos is to produce a toy that children will want to come back to and continuing playing with, long after its purchase (Delingpole 2009). It has been described as having 'revolutionized childhood itself' (Cendrowicz 2008). The Danish Lego company was founded in 1932 and the name itself takes its inspiration from the Danish words 'leg godt' or 'play well' (Cendrowicz 2008). The bricks were first sold in 1949, but the patent for this unique concept was not filed until 1958. Anniversary celebrations of Lego are thus linked to the latter date.

Lego fans can also visit Legoland theme parks, in Billund Denmark, Carlsbad, USA and Windsor, UK. Rides are themed around Lego product ranges such as Vikings and pirates (Bakir and Baxter 2011; Johns and Gyimóthy 2003). There are Lego versions of iconic landscapes and buildings from around the world and places where visitors can simply play with the bricks (Johns and Gyimóthy 2003). These themes parks are aimed at families and some liken the visit to a form of pilgrimage: 'Adults felt it was their duty to take their children there and some also relived memories of their childhood. This nostalgia was especially noticeable in older people' (Johns and Gyimóthy 2003: 12). Visitors also come to a large extent to experience Lego 'in different ways – the events and the park is an extension of play and entertainment that children already have at home' (Bakir and Baxter 2011: 415). In addition, travelling exhibitions such as 'The Art of the Brick' by artist Nathan Sawaya are popular, and highlight the flexibility of the product, and there are numerous conventions held around the world, such as the BrickFair Lego Fan Festival, BrickCon, and BrickWorld in the United States and Brickvention in Australia.

In 2008, the company celebrated the fiftieth anniversary of Lego. Over 400 billion bricks have been produced during that period (Cendrowicz 2008; Wienberg 2008) and seven new boxes of Lego are sold every second (Delingpole 2009). The Lego company is the world's fifth largest toy company on the basis of global sales (Cendrowicz 2008) and was voted the world's most respected and trusted company in 2009 by the Reputation Institute in New York (Wienberg 2008). Despite this public good will, Lego endured some difficult years financially, and was nearly forced into bankruptcy in 2004 (Robertson and Hjuler 2009). Its decline was the result of diversifying into areas that were unprofitable, including its theme parks and a line of craft sets (*Clikits*) promoted to girls. The company managed to turn its fortunes around, by taking a 'broad view of innovation', rather than seeing it only in terms of product development (Robertson and Hjuler 2009). Products that were not core to the business were divested, including the theme parks, which are now majority owned by the UK-based Merlin Entertainments. The anniversary celebrations also helped focus attention back on the core product, which has been rejuvenated through tie-ins and licensing deals with popular movie franchises, including *Star Wars*, *Harry Potter*, and *Pirates of the Caribbean*. Many of these figures have become collectors' items (Delingpole 2009).

The anniversary was marked mainly by product line innovation, rather than a series of events, which perhaps reflects the company's desire to stick to what it does best based on its bad experiences with over-diversification (Delingpole 2009). The Town Plan set dating from 1959 was reintroduced as an 'anniversary version', and was marketed as being in '1950s retro style' (Wienberg 2008), in a clear appeal to baby boom nostalgia. The search engine Google celebrated the occasion by using depictions of the brick to spell out its name (Wienberg 2008). This is a common gambit by Google, which often incorporates anniversaries into the style of its name on its website. Its founders are admirers of the toy, observing that playing with Lego in their youth helped them to learn to think creatively (Delingpole 2009).

Other high-profile fans of Lego include footballer David Beckham and singer Britney Spears, who have mentioned playing with Lego with their children through social media such as Twitter and Facebook. The fact that Lego did not capitalise on its celebrity connections during its anniversary suggests that it is primarily concerned with its dedicated and family-oriented fan base, which has remained loyal to the company over many years. The case of Barbie however is quite different, and celebrity links are applauded and encouraged, as evidenced during her fiftieth birthday celebrations.

Barbie: beautiful doll or bimbo?

The Barbie doll, launched in 1959, became a global phenomenon, which continues unabated today. She was not the first fashion doll (Peers 2004), and even had a design similar to the German doll Bild Lilli, based on a comic strip in the *Bild Zeitung* newspaper. Her fame, however, soon outstripped her predecessors. The creator of Barbie, Ruth Handler, saw Bild Lilli on a trip to Europe, and decided to create an American version named after her daughter Barbara, with a boyfriend, Ken, named after Handler's son (Peers 2004). Barbie was billed on her box as a 'teen age fashion model' (Pearson and Mullins 1999) and came complete with a soignée wardrobe of clothes that were reminiscent of those made by designers such as Dior and Chanel. Each outfit came with miniature accessories, including hats, gloves and jewellery, and was designated its own name, which evoked a glamorous and well-travelled lifestyle, such as *Roman Holiday Separates*, *Gay Parisienne* and *Evening Splendour* (Peers 2004). The quality and finish were extraordinary. Despite the couture clothing, Barbie wore a ponytail hairstyle, like many young girls in the late 1950s, sported casual outfits reminiscent of a college student, including cheerleader and graduation ensembles, and had a wholesome image, which appealed to parents (Pearson and Mullins 1999; Peers 2004; Varaste 2001). She was embraced by little girls the world over, but also spawned a dedicated adult collector market and has a large gay following (Peers 2004; Rogers 1999; Toffoletti 2007).

No other doll, nor arguably toy, has had the impact that Barbie has had, nor maintained its popularity over such a long time period. According to Rogers (1999), 99 per cent of girls aged between 3–10 years in the United States own at least one Barbie doll and the average is eight dolls per girl. Annual sales worldwide are about $1.5 billion (Dittmar and Halliwell 2006). These days, the standard Barbie doll is less couture and more a jeans and T-shirt girl (or dressed to kill in cheap disco frills and fripperies). Fantasy lines appeal to very young children, such as Barbie as a mermaid or wing-clad fairy (Peers 2004), often tied in with animated movies like *Fairytopia* and the *Princess Barbie* series. Collectors are still catered for with limited editions and special lines, aimed at a more cashed-up and discerning audience. Replicas of famous women in Barbie-form have been popular, such as Grace Kelly, Audrey Hepburn and Cher. Versions of Prince William and his wife Catherine have been created in their wedding garb to celebrate their first wedding anniversary.

Barbie is a fashion doll, rather than a representation of a baby or child, and as such, has been accused of sexualising childhood, fetishising the female form and encouraging girls to be obsessed about their weight and self-concept (Dittmar and Halliwell 2006; Toffoletti 2007). Her notoriety is puzzling given that 'it is the "baby doll" as infant who is anomalous over the total oeuvre of European dolls' (Peers 2004: 3). Barbie however is the feminist's *bête-noire*. If she were life-sized, she would topple over, as her vital statistics are notoriously unrealistic (BBC News 2009; Dittmar and Halliwell 2006), with abnormally sized breasts, a wasp waist, and long legs that are way out of proportion with her upper body. She stands permanently on tip-toes, so she can wear vertiginous stiletto heels (Hall 2004). Barbie evokes a series of conflicting meanings, ranging from a symbol of domesticity and materialistic 'shop-a-holic' to a powerful and independent career woman (Pearson and Mullins 1999; Peers 2004; Toffoletti 2007). The working woman image is interesting, in that Barbie was envisaged to have an occupation (albeit a stereotypically feminine one such as a nurse, ballerina, air hostess or model) 'at a time when few American women were employed outside the home' (Pearson and Mullins 1999: 256). The name Barbie however is now used as a pejorative label to denote an air-headed woman, usually fair-haired and buxom. Songs like Aqua's *Barbie Girl* (1997) send up this image, with lyrics such as 'I'm a blond bimbo girl, in the fantasy world, Dress me up, make it tight, I'm your dolly'. Some women have even endured plastic surgery to make themselves look like Barbie (Rogers 1999; Toffoletti 2007). Depending on your viewpoint, this can either be understood as an example of feminine anxiety over ideals of beauty or alternatively empowerment and self-determination (Toffoletti 2007).

Commemorative events have always been interlinked with the Barbie phenomenon. The fortieth anniversary in 1999 was marked by two exhibitions of designer-clad Barbies in department stores in Paris (Peers 2004). This is 'a marketing strategy that Mattel has perfected, namely, creating high-profile events that earn the company and its most famous product endless news media publicity' (Rogers 1999: 98). It has been labelled as Mattel's 'icon-constructing business' (Rogers 1999: 99).

In 2009, Mattel celebrated the fiftieth anniversary of the Barbie doll with the re-release of the original 1959 doll, in her black-and-white striped swimsuit, as well as iconic dolls from the years in between, such as the 1967 Twist n' Turn Barbie, the 1971 Malibu Barbie and the 1977 Superstar Barbie. The wording on the box says that this doll is 'recreated in loving detail. If you missed your chance before, or no longer have your beloved Barbie®, now is your chance to reconnect with a long-lost friend!' While selling products was important, special events were the lynchpin of the commemorative PR strategy.

There was a runway show in New York, part of Fashion Week, featuring 50 American designers, who created lines in tribute to Barbie. A corporate party was held in Malibu, California, in a life-sized Barbie house, emblazoned with the neon words 'Welcome to my dream house' and featuring pop art, such as a portrait of Barbie by Andy Warhol. This was not aimed at the masses but at the celebrity fan, although the publicity generated may have contributed to and reinforced brand loyalty (Murray 2005). Guests, such as the reality actress Lauren Conrad, author of *L.A. Candy*, and *Project Runway* host and model Heidi Klum entered on a pink carpet and viewed a wardrobe of 50 high heels and floral arrangements in the shape of bags and shoes. The party's theme matched LA's Tinseltown image. A Mattel representative noted that it was important that despite the recession, 'we recognize this monumental, epic moment for the Barbie brand' (Dubin 2009).

The party evoked memories of Barbie, but not the elegant clotheshorse of 1959. The emphasis on hot pink (often called 'Barbie pink', after the colour of the boxes) and link to a Californian celebrity lifestyle is a more recent trend for Barbie, and its use for the anniversary celebrations represents the reshaping of memory over time. As Gillis (1994: 3) notes: 'we are constantly revising our memories to suit our current identities'. It can also be argued that we view our memories through a haze, particularly those relating to childhood. The Barbie commemoration is no exception. Nora (1996: 3) observes that memory is 'a phenomenon of emotion and magic', which the Barbie anniversary celebrations drew upon and mythologised.

Ketchum PR, the company who organised the runway show and party, noted that sales of Barbie increased by 18 per cent and that 67 per cent of people surveyed knew that it was Barbie's birthday (www.megandunlevyeventplanning. wordpress.com/barbie-anniversary). Brand awareness was thus an important strategic outcome of these mediatised events (Murray 2005). Another was brand maintenance, which aims to 'remind consumers of what it was they found attractive about the brand identity to begin with' (Levine 2004: 103). The enduring appeal of the Barbie doll over 50 years was evidence of her credibility as an icon (Holt 2004) and heightened the desirability of owning one of the dolls. This builds brand loyalty and a devoted consumer base.

Commemorative events relating to the Barbie anniversary were not confined to North America. This acknowledges Barbie's global brand status (Rogers 1999). For example, Federation Square in Melbourne hosted an exhibition of 300 dolls, called *Forever Barbie*, which they billed as 'the largest collection of Barbie Dolls ever assembled in our hemisphere' and 'the world's inaugural comprehensive Barbie retrospective'. Tourism Victoria marketed it as one of Melbourne's 'kookiest exhibitions' (a deliberate use of 1950s vernacular) and a celebration of 'pop culture'. In Germany, the anniversary dominated the news media during the Nuremburg Toy Fair, with Chancellor Angela Merkel presented with her own customised Barbie, an example of Barbie's paradoxical embrace of female empowerment, despite being a much maligned icon of femininity.

A Barbie concept store covering six floors was opened with great fanfare in Shanghai, with spas and cafés. However, it closed in March 2011, reputedly due to problems with brand recognition, despite the link to the anniversary, and the sexiness of the product, which did not appeal to Chinese tastes (Bloomberg News 2011). This suggests that commemorative anniversaries are not a panacea for all products and that regional factors need to be taken into account; even with a product that enjoys global dominance.

Media products: films and music

Anniversaries connected with the media, including films, books and CDs, need a committed and participatory fan base to pull them off (Shefrin 2004). They also work their magic through media convergence, where there is a plethora of platforms that raise and maintain brand awareness, and may incorporate spin-off products such as toys, clothing and collectables (Månsson 2011; Murray 2005). The Internet, particularly social media, is a significant element in this mediatisation process, with fan discussion groups and blogs sharing information about re-releases and tie-ins and 'exhibiting a sense of ownership' over a brand or franchise (Shefrin 2004: 261). This paves the way towards an anniversary edition.

As Murray (2005: 417) notes: 'The optimum commercial goal is for a content package to achieve "classic" status, positioning it for anniversary re-release and repeat consumption long after the initial costs of its production have been amortized'. This leads to high profits and creates its own momentum, positioning the product nicely for the next anniversary celebrations. Collins *et al.* (2002: 347) argue that the re-release (usually based on the 'hook' of an anniversary) requires one of three basic prerequisites:

1   The product must 'ride on the crest of a fashion wave from a bygone era'. The Beatles' *Sergeant Pepper's* album fits into this category, as an example of 1960s psychedelia.

2   It has a position of dominance 'in a genre that is currently in vogue'. *Star Wars* for example is a premier example of the sci-fi genre.
3   It has cross-generational appeal. *The Wizard of Oz* is an example of a film that the whole family can enjoy.

These re-released products should not be seen merely as trivial or fun-filled forms of leisure. Their importance lies in the way they provide meaning in our lives and link people together. Kozinets (2001: 85) observes that 'entertainment products are key conceptual spaces that consumers in contemporary society use to construct their identities and their sense of what matters in life'. Watching a television programme like *Star Trek* may become akin to a spiritual or sacred experience for devotees. Fans may form a sub-culture, and share a common identity through their love of a particular product or brand, as well as a sense of being different from others (Kozinets 2001). These fans are actively engaged over a long period of time with 'a particular narrative universe' (Shefrin 2004: 273). Films such as *Lord of the Rings* or *Star Wars* invest their fans 'with feelings of legacy and inheritance' (Shefrin 2004: 268) and have spawned commercial tours to filming locations (Roesch 2009). These fans feel a responsibility to safeguard the film from being tarnished by association with inappropriate merchandise or events, and may lobby the directors or companies if they are concerned with the commercial or creative direction being taken. And this popular image of the obsessive nerd and their fandom has become a well-known archetype, as in the television series *The Big Bang Theory*.

We examine two iconic re-releases of products to celebrate milestone anniversaries – a pop album, and a cult film – and the role that fandom plays in these commemorations.

Fortieth anniversary of Sergeant Pepper's Lonely Hearts Club Band

There are a handful of albums that blew a generation's mind and changed the course of rock or pop history. People remember where they were when they first heard them, and listen to them over and over again. Their appeal spans the generations. Examples include the Who's *Tommy* (1969), Led Zeppelin's fourth album, usually referred to as *Led Zeppelin IV* (1971), Pink Floyd's *Dark Side of the Moon* (1973), Michael Jackson's *Thriller* (1982) and U2's *The Joshua Tree* (1987). Then there is *Sergeant Pepper's Lonely Hearts Club Band* (1967) by the Beatles. It was voted number one of the 500 greatest albums of all time by *Rolling Stone* magazine ('an unsurpassed adventure in concept, sound, songwriting, cover art and studio technology') – the iconic album from arguably the most famous pop group ever.

The Beatles' innovation and creativity revolutionalised rock and roll, and influenced culture at its broadest (Kohl 1996), including everything from fashion and cinema to religious trends. Over less than a decade, they changed from the four loveable 'mop-tops' singing 'She loves you' to the avant-garde experimentalists at the heart of the drug-addled 'swinging 60s', who sat at the feet of the Maharishi Mahesh Yogi and tripped out on acid. Riley (1987: 258) calls them 'a pivotal part of rock's story ... with an endless stream of original material [that] challenged what anyone imagined pop could become'.

Sergeant Pepper's Lonely Hearts Club Band took six months to record, instead of the normal three weeks for pop albums (Clydesdale 2006). It was the first example of 'the concept album as we know it' (Riley 1987: 267), with its conceit of a 'vaudevillian music-hall group' (Kohl 1996: 85), where 'a splendid time is guaranteed for all' and songs that flowed into and complemented each other. It was also the start of the 'studio years' for the Beatles, as they had now stopped touring, frustrated with the screaming fans and endless travel (Julien 2008). This allowed them to pour all their creative energies into their albums. The range of musical styles showcased in *Sergeant Pepper's Lonely Hearts Club Band* is eclectic and astonishing (Kohl 1996). The album met with immediate critical and popular acclaim and was played around the clock on radio stations (Kohl 1996). The cover was also one of the most memorable in history, with its cardboard-cut-out collage of famous people, including Marilyn Monroe, Bob Dylan and Oscar Wilde, accompanying memorabilia and lyrics printed for the first time on the back (Inglis 2001; Norman 2008). Interpreting the meaning of the individuals represented on the cover (as well as identifying some of the more obscure examples) became a national pastime (Inglis 2001). Unsurprisingly, *Sergeant Pepper's Lonely Hearts Club Band* won a Grammy award in 1967 for the best album cover and was rated by the BBC in 1999 as one of the top 20 British masterpieces of art and design of the twentieth century (Inglis 2001).

It was inevitable then that important anniversaries of the album's release would not go past unnoticed. The fortieth anniversary occurred in 2007 and was marked by a commemorative album recorded by current-day pop stars, such as Bryan Adams and Oasis, who sang new versions of the Beatles' *Sergeant Pepper* hits. These recording sessions were also played on BBC radio, in a two-part special, the first of which went to air on the anniversary of the original album's release. The artists were interviewed about the commemorative album and their views on the 1967 masterpiece. Interviews were conducted with people connected to the original album, such as the classmate of John Lennon's son Julian who allegedly inspired the song *Lucy in the Sky with Diamonds*, one of the myths behind the album to be explored (BBC News 2007). A fan on the Beatles Unlimited website (www.beatles-unlimited.com) wrote about the anniversary in terms of the way it affected their identity:

> Not only are we celebrating a musical legacy, marked with various anniversaries and milestones, but we are celebrating something which has very much become a part of us. It has become part of our personal fabric. It is as if it has, in a small part, defined who we are.

Daniels (2006: 28) argues that pop music of the 1960s is a 'principal medium of memory for the period'. Commemorating the release of the Sergeant Pepper album helps to keep that memory alive, and brings us back to the Summer of Love, when all things seemed possible. Memory and identity are intertwined concepts, in that 'the core meaning of any individual or group identity, namely, a sense of sameness over time and space, is sustained by remembering; and what is remembered is defined by the assumed identity' (Gillis 1994: 3). Thus, the memories evoked by the Sergeant Pepper anniversary and its associated commemorative events also help to shape and sustain the self-identity of the fans, in a symbiotic process that enriches their lives.

Twenty-fifth anniversary re-release of Star Wars

The re-release of *Star Wars* was good news for Lucasfilm in the wake of disappointing sales of licensed products linked to *The Phantom Menace*, the first of the *Star Wars* prequels. While a commercial success, the film was savaged by many fans (Brown *et al.* 2003; Shefrin 2004), with the annoying new character Jar Jar Binks coming in for particular criticism. The point was made 'that even a media brand with an impeccable track record at retail can falter badly if audiences deem the film anchor inadequate' (Murray 2005: 430). This was not the case with the original *Star Wars*, which was acclaimed by critics and fans alike. Tiffin (1999: 67) observes that the original trilogy 'has become an integral part of our modern popular culture, a myth in its own right'. The appeal of their re-release is trans-generational – with adults enjoying 'a nostalgia trip' and 'trickling sheepishly back to fill the theatres all over again' (Tiffin 1999: 67).

Following on from the successful re-release of *Star Wars* for the twenty-fifth anniversary, the thirtieth anniversary was marked by events such as *Star Wars* Celebration IV at the Los Angeles Convention Center. It featured stands and exhibits related to the *Star Wars* franchise, an autograph hall, an art show and talks by actors such as Carrie Fisher (Princess Leia). There was also a European version, staged in London, with machines from the film on display, and one in Tokyo, Japan. A convention were subsequently held in 2010 in Los Angeles to celebrate the thirtieth anniversary of *The Empire Strikes Back*, with the highlights including an interview of director George Lucas by Jon Stewart and an appearance by actor Mark Hamill (Luke Skywalker).

These commemorative events were very much for the fans and open to anyone to attend who could afford the entry fee. Unlike luxury product commemorations, discussed in the next section, these events were not pitched at an exclusive and rarefied crowd. This would have upset and alienated their fan base. Lucasfilm were clearly aware of their market and aimed to please. This was particularly important given the uneasy relationship between the company and fans over decisions such as re-mastering the original films to include new scenes and tidy up 'glitches', the disappointment with the new trilogy, especially *The Phantom Menace* and concerns that fans were not being consulted and listened to (Shefrin 2004).

Luxury products

These products are the deluxe and aspirational end of the spectrum, and have an emotional and charismatic appeal based on authenticity, excellence and a quality of *magic* (Dion and Arnould 2011). Examples include motor cars, expensive watches, and champagne. Their use or display denotes status (Han *et al.* 2010), although not all luxury products are beyond the reach of the mass market. Many couture houses, for example, gain significant revenue from mass market sales of their branded perfumes. Similarly champagne, although expensive in comparison with other alcoholic beverages and enjoying a hedonic and prestige image, is widely regarded as the drink of choice for all at special celebrations (Guy 2007). It is the brand heritage and aura of luxury which gives the product aspirational value (Dion and Arnould 2011; Urde *et al.* 2007).

Certain brands are evocative of extravagance and the best that money can buy – Ferrari, Mercedes, Rolls-Royce and Porsche (cars), Moët et Chandon and Krug (champagne), Rolex and Tag Heuer (watches). They also call to mind certain qualities, linked with a desirable and rose-tinted past. According to Brown *et al.* (2003: 20), these 'classic brands not only embody the moral values of craftsmanship and lasting value but also hark back to a time when the world seemed safer, more comprehensible, and much less commercial'. The irony is that their promotion via commemorative events is a commercial decision designed to promote the prestige of the product, amplify its desirability and thus boost sales. Many luxury brands can be conceptualised as 'heritage brands', in that they have (1) a track record of excellence and delivering on their values and promises; (2) longevity, (3) core values underpinning their strategies and performance, (4) symbols that express the brand's heritage, like a logo, motto or mascot and (5) an identity bound up in their history (Urde *et al.* 2007).

We turn to two examples of luxury brands that have celebrated important anniversaries – the E-type Jaguar and Perrier-Jouët champagne – and consider the types of commemorative events that are associated with this class of product and why they form an important element in perpetuating and strengthening the brand.

The E-Type Jag: 50 years of the British racing great

The Jaguar E-type, colloquially known as the 'E-type Jag', celebrated its fiftieth anniversary in 2011 (see Figure 9.1)with a series of high-profile and photogenic events, as befits the car that has been consistently labelled the most beautiful ever designed by Enzo Ferrari and 'the most famous automotive sex symbol' (Walsh 2011: 5). Its genius of design and ability to capture the spirit of its times led the Metropolitan Museum of Art in New York to buy one for display in its permanent collection in 1996. They marked the occasion with an exhibition on the design and engineering feats behind the car (Walsh 2011).

Originally SS Cars, the name of the company was changed to Jaguar in 1945 to avoid any connotations of links to the Nazis. The E-type was launched in 1961. It was a sensation, not just because of its sleek and almost feminine curves, but also its astounding performance, coupled with a price of just £2,160, which equates to about £38,000 in 2011 (Williams 2011). This is a surprising strategy for a prestige car brand, where the high price is normally more important in establishing status than engineering (Haig, 2004). The price of the E-type Jaguar at its launch was

Figure 9.1 Promotional poster in London for the fiftieth anniversary of the E-type Jag. Photo by J. Laing.

almost half the price of the Aston DB4 and a third of the cost of a Ferrari 250 GT (Walsh 2011). It was also available without waiting, straight off the showroom, until demand began to outstrip supply (Classic & Sports Car 2011).

Clamour for the car meant that Jaguar refused to lend it for use in films. They turned down the request by the producers of *The Saint* for Roger Moore as Simon Templar to drive the E-type coupé. There are also rumours that they turned down a similar request from the producers of the *James Bond* films, paving the way for the Aston Martin to become linked with the Bond legend. It did not stop the juggernaut however. Managing director of Jaguar, Mike O'Driscoll, calls the E-type 'Jaguar's most enduring and iconic symbol … one of the most exciting cars ever created' (Williams 2011). Production stopped in 1974, but the legend continues. While other cars celebrated fiftieth anniversaries in 2011, including the Mini Cooper, it was the E-type anniversary that took centre stage.

The car took on cult status from an early stage, fostered by the interest in and publicity generated by celebrity owners such as actors Tony Curtis, Steve McQueen, Brigitte Bardot and Sid James, footballer George Best and pop stars, including Beatles guitarist George Harrison, Rob Orbison, and Dave Clark from the *Dave Clark Five*. The latter used the car in their film *Catch Us if You Can* (1965) and on the cover of their album of the same name. Clark reminisced that 'Once I had an E-type, I knew I'd made it … It was a wonderful car for pulling birds' (Walsh 2011: 5). British racing driver legend Sir Jackie Stewart attributes the successful courtship of his wife to the many trips they took in his E-type Jaguar (Walsh 2011). It became 'as synonymous with the Swinging Sixties as the Beatles and the mini skirt' (Williams 2011). The Italian comic character Diabolik always drove a black 1961 E-type Jaguar, befitting his anti-hero status and the black edge to the stories.

Commemoration of the E-type Jag emphasised its history, which reflects Jaguar's status as a heritage brand (Urde *et al.* 2007). Events chosen to celebrate the fiftieth anniversary of this classic car were highly visible, and not just to enthusiasts. There were the predictable displays at car events such as the Nürburgring Old Timer Grand Prix (Germany) and the Pebble Beach Concours d'Elegance (USA). At Goodwood's Revival and Festival of Speed (UK), a sculpture was created; the only one they have ever displayed of a single car, to mark its anniversary. As the artist, Gerry Judah, observed: 'Together with the Concorde, it's one of the most beautiful machines in Britain's design history' (Walsh 2011: 11). A convoy of 50 E-types drove out of the Coventry Transport Museum in February (Coventry is the birthplace of Jaguar) and proceeded to the Geneva Motor Show in Switzerland (where it was launched in 1961). Classic Rendezvous and Supercar Day, the automotive festival held by Lord Pembroke at his Wilton estate (UK), featured an E-type coupé attached to a vintage silver Airstream caravan, in a salute to the 1960s. The Silverstone Classic (UK) in July featured E-type challenge races, as well as displays. The parade of 767 E-type cars around the circuit, led by the 90-year-old ex-Jaguar chief development test engineer Norman Dewis, set a Guinness World Record. Cars were shipped in from around the world by fans who wanted to be present at this historic occasion and attendance at the annual event swelled to more than 80,000, its largest crowd to date (Classic & Sports Car 2011).

Londoners going about their business on 6 June were greeted by a parade of 50 E-type Jaguars, which started at Forbes House, headquarters of the Society of Motor Manufacturers and Traders, and ended up at the 2011 Motorexpo in Canary Wharf, London. According to James Elliott, the Group Editor of *Classic & Sports Car* magazine:

> If the E-type's 50th has done anything, it has raised the profile of classic cars in general to new heights of public awareness ... There were hundreds of passers-by – kids, tourists, you name it – standing in the rain, clicking away merrily with their cameras.
>
> (Classic & Sports Car 2011: 160)

The convoy had its own police escort and travelled past some of London's more iconic tourist attractions, such as Buckingham Palace, Trafalgar Square, Admiralty Arch and Tower Hill, which made a spectacular background for newspaper photographs and television news footage. Professional cyclists preceded the parade, which was led by racing driver Nigel Mansell, a former Formula 1 world champion. While the event was successful in terms of a tribute to the sports car and emphasised the cachet of the Jaguar brand, it also raised money for UK Youth.

These types of events are centred on the spectacle of convoys or processions. This creates a carnivalesque atmosphere but also helps to build *communitas* amongst those enthusiasts who take part. They have a collective stake in the success of the commemorative event, in contrast to the Perrier-Jouët example discussed below, which is limited to the privileged inner sanctum of invited guests. Involvement in a high-profile event like a car show, attracting extensive media coverage, may give these individuals a sense of pride in showing the world that they are 'Jaguar drivers' and contributes to their personal as well as group identity (Holt 2004).

Developing commemorative events associated with a car also acknowledges the powerful place of the car within our culture. Pickett (1998) refers to the fetishistic attraction of automobiles, the sexual quality that underpins the comments by E-type Jaguar owners of its 'pulling power'. The design features of the car are also likened to a female, which contributes to 'narratives of desire' (Stephen 1998) and the fantasy of racing cars.

In addition to the car events and rallies, Bonhams conducted auctions of two E-types at Goodwood, both of which were raced competitively. A series of commemorative merchandise was produced by Jaguar, a form of commemorative legacy, such as cuff-links and luggage. Fibreglass models of the E-type coupé were produced by Spirito Design, in consultation with Jaguar's design team and with the imprimatur of the factory, with just 50 produced for collectors. The model was unveiled at the 2011 Silverstone Classic. Books were also favoured as a souvenir. The second edition of Porter's book *Jaguar E-type: The Definitive History* (2011) was produced by Haynes, while Jaguar produced a collectors' coffee-table book for the fiftieth anniversary – *E-Type: 50 Years of a Design* – which came in two versions – a premium one retailing at £49 and a limited-edition VIP version for £299, bound in a reproduction of the E-type's original upholstery (http://www. jaguar.com).

These events put the car – and its maker – in the spotlight, but were not undignified or over the top, as befits an anniversary held in the wake of the global financial crisis. There is often a fine line in terms of taste in promoting high-end and high involvement products such as luxury cars, or as discussed below, French champagne. Manufacturers tend to err on the side of caution, and may often link the anniversary to good causes or charities, or a link with artistry or good design, which perhaps makes the luxury more palatable and the celebrations potentially less shallow.

Two-hundredth anniversary of Perrier-Jouët champagne

The French champagne house Perrier-Jouët was founded in 1811 (see Figure 9.2). Its neighbours along the famous Avenue de Champagne in Épernay include Moët et Chandon, Pol Roger and Mercier. Perrier-Jouët is a brand with a distinctive art nouveau design created by Emile Gallé in 1902. Wine consumption has been argued to be an aesthetic experience, which 'could be uplifting or profound in its impact' (Charters and Pettigrew 2005: 128). Champagne in particular has an

Figure 9.2 Perrier-Jouët headquarters in Épernay, France. Photo by J. Laing.

association with pleasure and a reputation as the drink of choice for celebrations. Expectations were thus heightened for the events held in London and Paris for the two-hundredth anniversary of Perrier-Jouët in 2011. Like Jaguar, the brand has a high heritage quotient (Urde *et al.* 2007), and leveraged off this in its anniversary celebrations.

Both cities hosted a lavish party, with the theme of 'living legacy'. The London version took place in Il Bottaccio, a townhouse in London's Hyde Park Corner. One hundred invited guests, drawn from various creative endeavours, including artists, milliners, fashion designers, actors and ballet dancers, were invited to bring along their 'mentor, muse or protégée' and enjoyed a reception serving flutes of Perrier-Jouët's Belle Epoque 2004, and a dinner orchestrated by chef Albert Roux. The tribute to creativity was a perfect fit for the champagne house, according to its global sales director, with its 'rich legacy of craftsmanship, artistry and inspiration'. It also acknowledges the viewpoint that 'a good wine is like a good work of art' (Charters and Pettigrew 2005: 132). At dinner, guests were treated to an array of Perrier-Jouët cuvées, with the highlight being the Belle Époque 1998 jeroboam, with which toasts were made to the future. The world's first 'legacy champagne' was on display; a limited edition case created and signed by the artist Daniel Arsham housing two magnums of Belle Époque 1998 vintage, which is designed to be stored in a private Perrier-Jouët cellar for up to 100 years. It is thus a treat for future champagne drinkers to enjoy. Only 100 of these bi-centenaire packs have been created for the two-hundredth anniversary celebrations, and the majority are available from the Épernay boutique (by appointment only) or through the Pernod Ricard network. Following dinner, an exhibition of portraits of the guests by Lorenzo Agius was displayed, with a written dedication by each guest to their source of inspiration. These were later converted into a commemorative book, copies of which were presented to all the guests.

In Paris, the party was held at the École des Beaux Arts, which again was a link to the qualities of artisanship and craftsmanship associated with the brand. The focus was on family legacy and photographs were taken of guests by Studio Harcourt, and exhibited during the evening. Guests included glamorous mother and daughter models Jerry Hall and Georgia May Jagger, designer and restaurateur Sir Terence Conran and his daughter Sophie, and actress Catherine Deneuve and her son Christian Vadim. They represented the rich and famous, but had a certain style or élan. These were not chav reality stars or B-grade celebrities. This reinforced Perrier-Jouët as a status brand (Haig 2004).

The dinner was a reinterpretation of the 1911 Perrier-Jouët Centenary dinner by chefs Jean-Louis Nomicos and Alain Ducasse and the Belle Époque cuvées were served, including the 1998 magnum. The artist who designed the commemorative case also unveiled a diptych sculpture, which he said was in the 'spirit of Perrier-Jouët continuity'. The longevity of the champagne house was thus emphasised, as well as its cultural heritage.

The focus on the artisan qualities of the product gives Perrier-Jouët a certain gravitas and the events to mark its two-hundredth anniversary were in keeping with the brand image that the company has been carefully cultivating. This is an example of a successful campaign that can be built upon by the company in subsequent years, with the age of the product adding to its lustre and desirability as a luxury product. It taps into a desire for distinction and refinement linked to appreciation for art:

> To appropriate a work of art is to assert oneself as the exclusive possessor of the object and of the authentic taste for that object, which is thereby converted into the reified negation of all those who are unworthy of possessing it.
>
> (Bourdieu 1984: 280)

The brand and its commemorative events, reinforce identity – in this case the consumer as aesthete and connoisseur (Bourdieu 1984).

Product branding and commemorative events

Many product commemorations are conceived as an element in a branding or public relations campaign or strategy. Broom (2009: 330) argues that 'special events occupy a special place in public relations practice, because they mix elements of both action and communication'. Their flamboyance holds our attention, creating the right environment to deliver the brand message (Broom 2009; Levine 2003). The most popular form of promotional event is the new product launch, which can create brand awareness and build market share (Frost and Laing 2011; Theaker 2008). In the case of product commemorations, however, the brand has already been established and the company has a long history and established record to work with.

Sometimes product commemorations hit the headlines purely for their novelty value: 'the unusual, bizarre, deviant and offbeat', and the message is framed as such for the media (Broom 2009: 334). Links to celebrities or people of influence might also be a way to get a message across, as this makes the story potentially newsworthy (Broom 2009). There is normally no conflict or dissonance involved as a media hook in product commemorations, unlike say dark commemorations, but this does not diminish their interest to a broad audience. It is compelling enough that we look at these events with fondness; a type of longing for the past that eludes us.

In nearly all cases, as this chapter illustrates, product commemorations involve *iconic brands*. These brands represent powerful myths 'that their consumers use to address identity desires and anxieties' (Holt 2004: 2). These brand stories embody ideas or values that our culture deems to be important, or which help us to express our real selves, or at least who we would like to be (Holt 2004). We buy into the myth that if we drink Perrier-Jouët champagne, we are elegant and sophisticated, or if we buy Lego for our children, we are a good parent, and re-live the comfort and reassurance of childhood. Commemorative events reinforce these narratives.

Iconic brands, through their mythic dimensions, create 'tight emotional connections' with consumers (Holt 2004: 9). We saw in this chapter how fans of *Star Wars* and the Beatles approached anniversaries connected with their passion with almost religious fervour. Haig (2004) compares the top 100 global brands to 'mini-religions', with their omnipresence and power to inspire devotion. This brand loyalty is often manifested as a *social network* (Holt 2004), in that the consumers build and maintain links and relationships with each other through clubs and societies, online blogs or discussion groups or attending events such as commemorations. Some consumers are *insiders*, who act as *gatekeepers* (Holt 2004) for the myth associated with the brand. They influence others, who become brand followers (Holt 2004). It can be argued that these devoted fans start to *co-author* or *co-create* marketing, by contributing to its development and iconic status (Holt 2004). Commemorative events may play a part in the process, by allowing consumers to collectively celebrate their enthusiasms and construct shared identities.

10 The legacy of commemorative events

We – writers, painters, sculptors, architects, empassioned lovers of Paris's beauty ... we have come to protest ... in the name of French good taste, in the name of art, in the name of history, against the construction in the very heart of our beloved capital of this useless and monstrous Eiffel Tower ... for the next twenty years we'll see spreading out across our city like an ink stain ... the foul shadow of this foul and bolt-encrusted pile of sheet metal.

(Petition des Artistes, 14 February 1887, quoted in Mathieu 1997: 62)

The Eiffel Tower is one of the most enduring and recognisable destination images in the world. The first glimpse is breath-taking, perhaps the natural reaction when viewing an icon that one has only seen in books or on television, like the Parthenon, the Pyramids at Giza and the Taj Mahal. But there is something different about the Eiffel Tower. Unlike these other products of human ingenuity, the tower is the essence of *modernity*. It was made of cast and wrought-iron, not traditional stone or brick, and was not adorned with carvings, paintings or precious stones. Its soaring simplicity is the height of Paris chic. Or so we think today. When it was first built for the Exposition Universelle of 1889, it met with ridicule and outrage. A petition against its erection was signed by well-known writers, composers and artists, including writers Guy de Maupassant and *fils* Dumas and composer Charles Gounod, and referred to 'the deflowering of Paris' (Loyrette 1985: 174). Significantly, all identified as conservatives. By the time they presented the petition, plans for construction of the tower were well underway and there was no turning back (Harvie 2004; Loyrette 1985). De Maupassant hated the tower so much that he attributed his penchant for frequent dining in its Jules Verne Restaurant to his desire to be in the one place where he could not see the monument (Ayers 2004; Barthes 1979). It is difficult to believe that such a well-loved building, which Barthes (1979: 3) describes as 'a universal symbol of Paris', and whose image has found its way onto a myriad of souvenirs, including the ubiquitous T-shirts, fridge magnets and key chains, could have attracted such vitriol or come so close to being demolished.

The Eiffel Tower was the winning design in a competition for a symbol of the 1889 Exposition Universelle staged to commemorate the centenary of the French

Revolution. The organisers wanted a design that would 'stun public imagination' (Ayers 2004: 139). Announcing a competition was a common strategy used for Parisian international exhibitions and led to some architectural masterpieces. Competitions were staged to build two buildings for the 1900 Universal Exhibition – the art nouveau Grand Palais, with its elegant glass roof and statues, and the exquisite Petit Palais (Johnston 2007). The former is still used for temporary exhibitions, while the latter, used in 1900 for a retrospective of French art, is now the Musée des Beaux-Arts de la Ville de Paris. The competitive process for the 1889 Exposition was somewhat of a farce, with a deadline of only two weeks for submissions to be filed. The French government had essentially already picked their favourite – the Eiffel Tower. At 300 m high, it was 131 m taller than its nearest world rival, the Washington Monument (Ayers 2004). It remained the tallest monument in the world until the Chrysler Building, an art deco jewel in New York, briefly claimed the record in 1930; ceding it a year later to the Empire State Building (Harvie 2004). This was the era of big buildings that made political statements about national and cultural identities.

The tower had sets of lifts to take visitors to various stages, allowing spectacular views across the city. The technology behind lifts was only new and delayed the opening of the tower to the public for a few weeks. Visitors could also patronise several restaurants within the tower and attend shows at its theatre. The *Figaro* had its own outlet and produced special issues of the newspaper as a souvenir. A commemorative booklet was also available – *Souvenir de mon ascension à la Tour Eiffel* (Loyrette 1985). The tower was thus specifically designed to be seen, ascended and remembered. It was the complete tourist experience. It was a profitable business, recouping around 6.5 million francs during the exposition, just 1 million francs short of the construction costs (Loyrette 1985). This shortfall was made up shortly after the exposition, although patronage did drop off thereafter (Loyrette 1985). Nevertheless, the Tower was now part of the Parisian landscape, and there appears to have been a grudging acceptance of its presence, even from most of the signatories of the petition (Harvie 2004; Loyrette 1985).

Constructed over a period of two years, using the techniques and skills amassed by the Eiffel company through its commissions such as the Pest railway station in Budapest and the Maria Pia railway bridge in Porto, Portugal (Loyrette 1985), the tower became their most high-profile commission and brought them enduring fame. In the case of Gustave Eiffel, it also made his fortune, although his company did assume a large part of the financial risk of the project (Harvie 2004). He gained a prominent celebrity status, galvanised by the insults hurled at what he saw as a work of art, perfection in its exquisite precision and technological sophistication. His response to the petition argued that beauty need not be incompatible with feats of engineering design, or a focus on form and function:

> Do not the laws of natural forces always conform to the secret laws of nature? The first principle of the aesthetics of architecture is that the essential lines of a monument should be determined by their perfect appropriateness to their end.
>
> (quoted in Bergdoll 2003)

Placed in the Champ de Mars, which had been used for commemorative events of the French Revolution since the 1780s (Ozuf 1976), the tower was thus both revolutionary and a symbol of revolution. The choice of the Champ de Mars as the centrepiece of an exhibition was repeated in 1900, but thereafter avenues were built off it, and it was lined with grand classical-style apartments and houses, destined for high Parisian society, which mocks the revolutionary heritage and the sentiment behind the 1889 event. The Exposition Universelle was viewed by the republican left as 'an instrument for solidifying their vision of a progressive, secular state' (Bergdoll 2003: 8). However, it was also intended to bring economic benefits, providing an opportunity to showcase France's industrial might and technological innovation, particularly in the engineering sphere (Johnston 2007). The famous petition opposing the tower was in part a reaction against its revolutionary links, but also against its industrial symbolism. It represented a new age for France that not everyone was happy about, although the general populace were supportive of the tower and eager to make the ascent as soon as it was open (Harvie 2004; Johnston 2007).

The tower is both an object to be gazed upon and a lookout, providing a panorama of Paris, yet it is essentially 'an empty monument' (Barthes 1979: 7). This perceived lack of practical value, coupled with a radical design for the times, was nearly its undoing. It finally found a functional *raison d'être* in the lead-up to World War One, when it was used for radio and telegraphic transmissions (Bergdoll 2003). The artistic community of Paris by this stage had taken it to its hearts, as the symbol of liberation from the old rules and conventions. One of the most provocative acts of the German occupation of Paris in World War Two was to install a banner on the first level containing the words *Deutschland siegt auf allen Fronten* – Germany is victorious on all fronts (Bergdoll 2003). This struck at the hearts of the French, who now regarded the tower as quintessentially Parisian.

A commemorative event may provide an excuse or impetus for the public funding of a permanent structure that becomes a lasting focal point of remembering. This built legacy may bring with it intangible meanings, often connected with identity and heritage. Alternatively, the link with the original commemoration might be lost with the passage of time. The Eiffel Tower is arguably an example of the latter. The initial negative reaction to the tower and its subsequent turbulent history might be the reason why its connection to such a famous commemorative event has been forgotten. Few see it as the legacy of celebrations to mark the French Revolution. Tellingly, today there is no interpretation at the base of the tower that tells this story to visitors.

The focus in this chapter is the *built legacy* of commemorative events. We examine different types as examples, but are not aiming to produce a comprehensive typology of commemorative legacy. Instead, we focus on exploring the reasons why some sort of built legacy is a common phenomenon accompanying commemorative events and its importance for society.

Legacy and collective memory

The creation of a commemorative legacy is both an act of remembrance and of *forgetting* (Connerton 2009). Sometimes this is deliberate, in cases where the past is too painful to carry around with us: 'In effect, the initial impulse to memorialize events like the Holocaust may actually spring from an opposite and equal desire to forget them' (Young 1993: 5). In other instances, the desire to forget has political motives. Governments may wish to preserve a certain discourse and suppress or subordinate others, resulting in a commemoration that recognises only official interpretations of history or sanctioned memories (Mayo 1988; Urry 2000; see also Chapter 2). This might avoid an interpretation which casts a government's actions in a harsh light, such as the decision to wage war on another country (Middleton and Edwards 1990).

The Vietnam Veterans Memorial was a delayed commemorative legacy, dedicated seven years after the last American died in what was regarded as a morally dubious war, ending in ignominious defeat (Wagner-Pacifici and Schwartz 1991). It had sprung from a desire to honour the commitment and sacrifice of the soldiers, many of whom were conscripted, while at the same time wishing to play down the political debacle and taint of the Vietnam War. The US government realised that it could not continue to turn its back on the commemoration, but chose a legacy that was deliberately minimalist, in keeping with a problematic and conflicted political narrative. In response to public outcry, the winning design was modified to include a flag and statue – traditional hallmarks of a war memorial (Wagner-Pacifici and Schwartz 1991).

In extreme cases, the built legacy may be removed, in an attempt by the state to erase memories. Throughout history, a conquering power or change of ruler often saw obliteration of a society's monuments as a necessary step to destroying that society (Lefebvre 1991; Lowenthal 1998). An example of this occurred after the fall of the Soviet Union, when many monuments to Stalin and Lenin were toppled (Donohoe 2002; Lowenthal 1998). This is a different phenomenon from the stated intention to remove a monument once its usefulness has passed. This was often the case with the legacies of international exhibitions in the nineteenth century. Many of these creations were designed to be only temporary, though they might have become tourist attractions in their own right or developed a new function.

Another example of a political decision to not provide a memorial is the lack of any built legacy to mark the spot in Paris where Princess Diana's car crashed (Best, 2013). A poignant hand-made sign, observed in 2011, makes the point – 'where is the official memorial for Diana?' (see Figure 10.1). Both the French and British governments are keen to avoid creating an official pilgrimage site, or dredging up memories that they find embarrassing. The former wife of the heir to the British throne died in a speeding car driven by a man who was allegedly drunk, without wearing a seatbelt, pursued by paparazzi, and without official security. How could this have happened on both countries' watch? The British government preferred more prosaic memorials, such as a memorial fountain and children's playground in Kensington Gardens.

Figure 10.1 Hand-made sign placed in the Place de l'Alma, Paris. Photo by J. Laing.

Despite these efforts, it is not always possible to prescribe a meaning to a monument or memorial, or to prevent the creation of a memorial. They can 'take on lives of their own, often stubbornly resistant to the state's original intentions' (Young 1993: 3). In Princess Diana's case, people have built their own memorial in the form of letters, pictures, flowers and toys left in the Place de l'Alma, near the entrance to the tunnel where the crash took place. Their overwhelming need to mark the tragedy cannot be denied.

Why do we place such store in physical markers of the past and why is their annihilation seen as a precondition to forgetting historical events? Surely our memories survive the removal of a physical legacy? Four arguments have been advanced for the importance of a tangible legacy linked to a commemoration:

1 Legacies help us to *structure* our memories, which are 'often organised around objects and particular spaces' (Urry 2000: 137).
2 A legacy might assist in *constructing public space*, which is often marked by forms of commemorative legacy (Donohoe 2002). The development of precincts and quarters might be anchored by a commemorative monument or memorial. The cityscapes of many world capitals, including Paris, New York and London, are dominated by large-scale monuments and statues (Olsen 1986).
3 The legacy might become a form of relic, icon, shrine or pilgrimage site, giving individuals something tangible to visit or around which to build a ritual process (Lowenthal 1985; Schwartz 1982; Turner and Turner 1978). Visitors to the Vietnam Veterans Memorial leave flowers, flags and military

items beside the wall, often beside the name of a loved one (Wagner-Pacifici and Schwartz 1991). The same occurs at the site of Princess Diana's car crash. Nora (1989) calls these *lieux de mémoire* or places of memory. For this reason, we mark grave sites with plaques or headstones. Where these are not available, we invent them and treat them as deeply poignant, such as the Tomb of the Unknown Warrior in Westminster Abbey.

4   Built legacy may also divest us of the *burden* of remembering, by acting as a prompt to memory or allowing us to forget without guilt (Radley 1990; Young 1993).

While our focus in this chapter is on examples of *built legacy*, it is important to bear in mind that technological innovation is enabling preservation and restoration of heritage through new forms of media, which may be linked to a commemorative event. Anniversaries often provide the momentum and sometimes the funding to make these projects happen. They might reach or at least be perceived as attracting a broader audience than a temporary exhibition or tour. One cogent example relevant to commemorative legacy is the provision of open access to collections, works of art and artefacts through electronic media. The celebrations for the 2012 Dickens bicentenary involved digitising his journalistic works and providing open access to the public through the web, while the Queen's Diamond Jubilee, also held in 2012, was similarly a catalyst for a project that resulted in the journals of Queen Victoria being available online.

Monuments

The terms *monument* and *memorial* are often used interchangeably in a commemorative context. Donohoe (2002) however argues that not all memorials are monuments. A monument reminds us of *something*, whereas the hallmark of a memorial is its ability to facilitate *mindfulness*. The sheer spatial size of monuments means that they often dominate the landscape or streetscape. Olsen (1986: 9) argues that this is deliberate, in that monuments are designed to evoke awe, wonder and 'jolt the individual out of [their] mundane concerns … Any evidence of restraint, understatement, or, worst of all, parsimony, will subvert its intention'. The Gateway to India in Mumbai, built to commemorate the visit of King George V and Queen Mary, Emperor and Empress of India, in 1911, was a statement of British imperial power, symbolised by its extravagant architectural style and size. Rather than evoking an Indian style, its roots are in the triumphal arches of Ancient Rome, reimagined by twentieth-century imperial authorities. When British rule ended, it became its epitaph, and symbolised a new modern era for India. It cannot be overlooked, even in the bustle and jangle of a chaotic city.

Monuments marking a commemorative event might take various forms, including statues, columns or buildings. The Washington Monument was first mooted in 1832, the centenary of President Washington's birth. Commemorative columns include Nelson's Column in Trafalgar Square, in memory of the death of Lord Nelson at the Battle of Trafalgar in 1805, and the Colonne de Juillet or July Column in the Place de la Bastille in Paris, which commemorates the 1830 Revolution. The July Column was built on the spot where the Bastille Prison was stormed in 1789, and the remains of revolutionaries who died in the uprising are entombed in the monument. It is therefore a favourite starting point for demonstrations and political meetings, in recognition of the area's tumultuous past and France's identity as a long-standing democracy.

A statue of Shakespeare was donated and erected in Stratford-upon-Avon for his bicentenary. It was seen as a much-needed shrine, given his bust in the parish church was constantly being mutilated by enthusiasts wanting a piece as a souvenir (Deelman 1964). A similar desecration of the mulberry tree in Shakespeare's former garden by fans led the then owner, the Reverend Francis Gastrell, to chop it down in frustration (Deelman 1964; Lynch 2007). The actor David Garrick came to the rescue of the town, donating a portrait as well as a statue of the bard, which were to be installed in the Town Hall. The statue was supposed to have been dedicated during the jubilee procession, but the heavy rains defeated this. Instead, it formed the centrepiece of the Ode in the Rotunda, a silent spectator to Garrick's triumph (Deelman 1964). The statue is still on display in a niche in the Stratford town hall, although the Gainsborough painting perished in a fire in 1946 (Dobson 1992).

Utilitarian legacies

Creating a commemorative legacy which has both a practical and a symbolic purpose is popular with governments, who see it as less likely to attract public criticism over funding and a way to get projects done that might otherwise languish. Examples of these utilitarian legacies include roads, bridges and parks. When Princess Diana died, there was a flurry of ideas of how to mark her passing. The official choices of built legacy, the fountain (see Figure 10.2) and playground, were spectacularly matter-of-fact for a woman who inspired the affection of millions and became an icon of her time. They contrast with the mawkish sentimentality of the statue of Diana and the man who died with her, Dodi al Fayed, in Harrods, built by its then owner, Dodi's grieving father. It has no utility other than to point to al Fayed's allegations of cover-ups and corruption.

The Baluarte Bicentennial Bridge in Mexico opened in 2012 for the two-hundredth anniversary of Mexican independence. At 403 metres high, it is currently the world's highest cable-stayed bridge and the second highest bridge in the world overall. Many commemorative structures seek status beyond their connection with a famous person or event, by breaking some other record, particularly for height. This has the effect of aggrandising the feats of the past (Donohoe 2002). The Washington Monument and the Eiffel Tower were respectively the highest man-made structures in the world when they were first built.

The Lincoln memorial highway spans the United States of America, and was conceived in the wake of the great excitement around the centenary of President Abraham Lincoln's birth in 1909, and officially opened in 1913. It thus predates the Lincoln Memorial in Washington. The fact that it could be enlarged when

Figure 10.2 Diana Memorial Fountain, Kensington Gardens. Photo by J. Laing.

required, as opposed to a static statue or memorial, was seen as symbolic of the growth in admiration and respect for the man, which peaked during the centennial celebrations (Schwartz 1990). It was America's first large highway, and thus ushered in the age of the automobile and the road trip.

Memorial parks have been built on the site of atrocities and battlegrounds, perhaps as a way of bringing beauty and a sense of peace engendered by nature to a site that is a shameful and ugly remnant of the past. They might also act as a tribute to the victims. Many towns in Australia have war memorial parks. These public spaces played an important role after World War One, when many families lacked a body to bury and a grave at which to mourn (Panayotov 2012).

Parks might also be dedicated to famous people, and created to mark an important anniversary. The Strawberry Fields memorial site in Central Park, New York, is dedicated to Beatle John Lennon, who was shot outside his nearby home in December 1980. Its theme is peace, illustrated by the title of his famous song, *Imagine*, which adorns the central mosaic, and it is an oasis of tranquillity in a busy city. Strawberry Fields was opened on 9 October 1985, which would have been Lennon's forty-fifth birthday. Fans often gather on the anniversary of his birthday and his death, holding a vigil by candlelight, much like the one that occurs at Gracelands in tribute to Elvis Presley (Rojek 1993).

Venues, museums and attractions

A number of buildings have been retained after a commemoration for use as a venue, exhibition space or museum, which become part of the destination's visitor attractions. The Royal Festival Hall was part of the development of the South Bank for the 1951 Festival of Britain and still stands in its original position. Banham (1976) argues that it would have been built in any event, given the Queen's Hall was destroyed by bombing during the war, but was merely inaugurated at the time of the festival for convenience. An alternative view is that the staging of the event accelerated the construction of the hall at a time when most of the focus was on rebuilding essential services.

Other museums or venues, rather than forming the centrepiece of a commemorative event, are linked to an anniversary as a way of raising funds or interest in the project. An announcement was made of the pending construction of the James Joyce Cultural Centre in Dublin on the hundredth anniversary of James Joyce's birth in 1982. Opened in 1996, and described as the 'home of Bloomsday' on its website (www.jamesjoyce.ie), it provides educational workshops, a lecture series and walking tours, as well as staging permanent and temporary exhibitions. The National September 11 Memorial and Museum in New York is at Ground Zero, the name given to the former site of the World Trade Center. The museum contains an oral history collection, and exhibits artefacts, stories and visual images and footage, as well as providing interpretation relating to the events of 11 September 2001, and the earlier bombing of the World Trade Center in 1993. Its stated aspiration is 'to educate the millions of people expected to visit the World Trade Center each year in hopes of building a better future' (9/11 Memorial 2012). The James Joyce Centre and the National September 11 Museum are legacies that aim to keep memory alive, both for local people and visitors.

In France, three major monuments were built for the bicentenary of the French Revolution in 1989 – the Grande Arche de la Défense, the Bastille Opera House and the Louvre Pyramid. Like the Eiffel Tower at the centenary, all were controversial, with the link to the commemoration seemingly forgotten just a few decades thereafter. The Grande Arche de la Défense was the winning entry in an international competition and is a white hollowed-out cube which resembles a picture-frame. The Danish architect described it as a 'window to the world ... with a view into the future' (Ayers 2004: 314), yet its design was compromised and different materials used, which has been argued to affect its 'symbolic function', much like the Sydney Opera House. As Ayers (2004: 315) acidly notes, to some people 'it seems supremely ironic that a monument to the 20C should consist of a giant void'.

The Opéra Bastille was aimed at providing opera for the masses, at cheaper prices than the opulent and olde-worlde Opéra Garnier (Ayers 2004). Its stark functionality is certainly at odds with the dramatic luxury of the older opera house, and despite its public purpose, it is uninviting and intimidating, with no obvious foyer or entrance point. Ayers (2004: 188) refers to its 'uneasy relationship with the Place de la Bastille', which admittedly is a difficult space in which to situate a monumental building, given its size and history.

The Louvre Pyramid (see Figure 10.3) is the third in the triumvirate of revolutionary monuments. Made of glass panels, it shimmers in the Louvre courtyard, both delicately lovely and unsettling at the same time. Morris (1992: 17) describes it as looking like 'it has been dropped there ready-made from some meticulously

Figure 10.3 Louvre Pyramid in Paris. Photo by W. Frost.

navigated spacecraft'. Widely panned when it was first unveiled, it is now accepted as an integral part of the cityscape. Like the Eiffel Tower, it is symbolic of the Parisian desire to be seen as a contemporary and cutting-edge city, which is not afraid to intersect modernity and antiquity. The city uses monuments as works of art, as well as emblems of power and aspiration (Morris 1992; Olsen 1986).

Permanent exhibitions are another legacy of commemorations. The James Joyce Centre in Dublin is the permanent home to highlights from the National Library of Ireland's landmark James Joyce and Ulysses exhibition, which opened in the Bloomsday centenary year of 2004. The date chosen for the exhibition's opening (one day before Bloomsday) was also auspicious, as Joyce planned a meeting with a friend, Francis Sheehy Skeffington, on the steps of the library the day before the first Bloomsday. The postcard sent by Joyce, inviting Skeffington to the meeting, forms part of the exhibition.

Precincts

A desire to create a lasting tourism legacy in the wake of a commemoration sometimes leads to regeneration of urban spaces, to form a precinct, hub, square or quarter. These precincts might combine retail areas; clusters of heritage buildings; attractive eating areas; museums or venues; and interpretive trails or walks (Frost and Laing 2011; McKercher and du Cros 2002; Waitt 2000). Whether they attract visitors during or after the anniversary might depend on a number of factors, including the geographic proximity of the attractions, their appeal to a wide audience and the overall image and attraction of the destination. One tangible legacy of the 1951 Festival of Britain was the South Bank exhibition site, which is now 'a globally significant centre for the arts and culture' (Festival of Britain 2011: 59). It is home to not just the Royal Festival Hall, but also the Hayward Gallery, the Purcell Room and Queen Elizabeth Hall and is now joined by other cultural attractions in the near vicinity, including the re-creation of Shakespeare's Globe Theatre and the London Film Museum, as well as the London Eye, built for the Millennium celebrations. The precinct is thronged by tourists, not just at weekends, and has a vibrant bustle through regular street events and buskers.

Melbourne was the first capital of Australia and Federation Square was built in honour of the centenary of Federation in 2001. While this commemoration was not aimed at tourists, the square was an attempt to build a tourist hub in the city centre (Frost 2012). The failure of an earlier City Square served as a warning that not all precincts are embraced by locals and visitors. Federation Square however appears to have bucked that trend, with approximately 2 million visitors in 2009/2010, although three-quarters of these were domestic visitors (Frost 2012). It is modelled on an Italian piazza (Frost 2012), fringed by cafés, restaurants, the Melbourne Visitor Centre, and several cultural attractions. These include the National Gallery of Victoria and the Australian Centre for the Moving Image. The link to the centenary of Federation is maintained by a permanent free exhibition, the Federation Story. The precinct, with its shards and patchwork effect, was maligned as an eyesore at the time it was opened and voted one of the world's 21 ugliest buildings by the British *Daily Telegraph* (Levy 2012).

The Titanic Quarter in Belfast represents the latest attempt to create a precinct around a commemorative theme – the hundredth anniversary of the building and launch of the *Titanic*. The city has struggled to overcome its image as a bleak place beset by sectarian violence during the troubles, and saw the *Titanic* commemoration as a chance to regenerate itself and present a new narrative for Belfast, based on its industrial, chiefly shipbuilding heritage. The heart of the Titanic Quarter is its new £90 million Titanic Belfast visitor attraction, built in the shape of a star in homage to the White Star Line, and the size of the giant liner. Visitor numbers are hoped to be in the order of 400,000 in the first year of operation (Atkinson 2011), although its ability to sustain long-term tourism growth is yet to be determined. It is an interactive and immersive experience, involving video, audio, touchscreen displays, simulations, a ride through the shipyards and a recreation of life on board for the passengers and crew (Atkinson 2011). Walking tours operate throughout the precinct, to places associated with the *Titanic*, and there are *Titanic*-themed boat tours and visits to the docks. Other developments with tourism potential within the 75-hectare precinct include accommodation and a film studio. Regular events connected to the *Titanic* will also be a feature of the quarter, including the annual Titanic Belfast Festival, which may encourage visitors to the precinct, as well as providing colour and excitement.

Trails

Walking or cycling trails are another way to mark a commemoration. Australia built a walking trail in 1988 to commemorate its bicentenary, which runs from

Cooktown in Queensland to Healesville in Victoria. The new Titanic Quarter in Belfast has a Titanic Trail, with a self-guided commentary, described as an 'interactive treasure trail' (www.titanic-quarter.com). Some trails or walks commemorate a famous *journey* and invite re-enactments. An example is the Lewis and Clark Commemorative Trail, which runs from Jefferson's home at Monticello to St Louis. Fifteen bronze plaques have been placed at strategic points along the trail, to mark the bicentenary of the expedition made by the two explorers to find a westward route through to the Pacific Ocean. Smaller trails were also inaugurated at the time of the bicentennial commemoration, such as the Lewis and Clark Discovery Trail between Ilwaco and Long Beach in Washington State. Canada similarly designated a heritage trail to commemorate the bicentenary of Alexander Mackenzie's expedition to forge a path to the Canadian Pacific Coast.

Other trails have a darker edge and commemorate shameful or contested journeys. A commemorative trail in Ballymurphy, Belfast, marks the site of the killing of 11 civilians by the British Army in 1971 (Wing 2010). It has been created by the families, and is a way for these individuals to tell their version of the story. It gives the marginalised a voice, and the victims an identity. The trail acts as a space for the families to publicise their fight for justice, as well as a series of shrines for their own personal acts of remembrance. The trail originally consisted of crosses, which were replaced with plaques and murals. Wing (2010) argues that the mainstream view of commemorations, that they must be aimed at conflict resolution and achieve consensus, is challenged in the Ballymurphy example. The trail contests the official government narrative, but may be seen as part of the reconciliation process: 'it validates the experiences of victims, provides a framework for articulating what happened, and helps to set the stage for rectifying the past and planning for a peaceful and just future' (Wing 2010: 35).

Replicas

Commissioning replicas of something famous from the past to celebrate an anniversary is a tangible legacy. These replicas often help to revive and encourage artisanal skills, which might otherwise have been lost or forgotten, and provide spectacle through re-enacting past achievements. The 1951 Festival of Britain included a life-sized replica of Cook's *Endeavour* in the Dome of Discovery (Festival of Britain 2011). Australia went one step further during its bicentenary, building a replica of the *Endeavour* that was capable of sailing around the world (see Figure 10.4). Many people applied to sail as crew and were able to experience first-hand what it might have been like to travel on an eighteenth-century vessel. HMS *Endeavour* is now on permanent display at the National Maritime Museum in Sydney. Another mooted replica of a vessel in connection with a commemoration has been announced by Australian billionaire Clive Palmer, who wants to build a replica of the *Titanic*. It hit the headlines in a year when the *Titanic* was uppermost in people's minds, thanks to the high-

Figure 10.4 Replica of the *Endeavour* docked in Melbourne. Photo by J. Laing.

profile centenary. The idea was mostly condemned as preposterous and a form of grand-standing, given Palmer's political pretensions. It reminded some of the magnate Alan Bond's announcement of his gift to the nation – a replica of the *Endeavour* – in honour of the 1988 bicentenary, an offer which later had to be withdrawn when he encountered financial difficulties.

The Parthenon in Nashville was constructed for the Tennessee Centennial Exposition of 1897, which celebrated the state's entry into the union. It is a replica of the Parthenon in Athens, built to scale, and a nod to Nashville's nickname as the 'Athens of the South'. It was hardly authentic, unlike the *Endeavour* replicas, which were at least housed in the country they helped to explore, but that was not their point. The Nashville Parthenon allowed people to see close-up what they were unlikely to be able to visit in its original setting and was treated as a *marvel*, demonstrating American and more particularly local ingenuity. It was originally designed to be demolished after the exposition, but remained in place due to the high cost of its removal and strong public support for its retention. The Parthenon had to be rebuilt from concrete in the 1920s, replacing the fragile original structure, which demonstrated the high level of regard for the monument. It is now a museum dedicated to American art, and the site has been named Centennial Park, in recognition of its origins.

Restorations

Funding for restoration and conservation of heritage is often scarce. A commemoration may provide a rationale for the project to get off the ground and help with resources, through access to a commemorative fund or pool of money, or funds or in-kind support donated by volunteers and supporters. St Paul's Cathedral in London recently celebrated its three-hundredth anniversary, and showed off its newly white facade after 15 years of restoration work, which cost an estimated £40 million (Hill 2001). The eight-hundredth anniversary of Reims Cathedral was marked by the commissioning of new stained-glass windows by a German artist. This choice of artist was motivated by a spirit of reconciliation, given that the cathedral was largely destroyed by German bombs during World War One. This legacy thus has symbolic as well as practical value for the world-heritage listed cathedral and the city.

The Royal Exhibition Building in Melbourne is the last remaining venue of the great nineteenth-century exhibitions (Frost 2012). The others were only designed to be temporary structures, or were destroyed, such as the Crystal Palace in London, burnt down in 1936. Its restoration was made possible by funding under the auspices of the Centenary of Federation in 2001, which contributed to its successful bid for world heritage listing in 2004. It maintains a role as a stunningly impressive site for exhibitions such as art fairs and fashion expos, and hosts regular heritage tours for visitors.

Also in Melbourne is Cook's Cottage, the oldest European building on the continent and a successful tourist attraction. It was acquired and shipped from Yorkshire for the centenary of Melbourne in 1934. At the time it was run-down and facing demolition. Its owner offered it for sale for £300 on condition it did not leave Britain. Russell Grimwade, a wealthy industrialist stepped in with an offer for £800, arguing that it would remain in the British Empire. That it was reconstructed in Melbourne rather than Sydney was a result of one-upmanship, Grimwade getting in just before the 1938 hundred-and-fiftieth anniversary of Sydney.

Charles Dickens stipulated that there was to be no statue to him erected in Britain (Steger 2012). Sydney however has a statue of Dickens in Centennial Park, which was restored in time for his two-hundredth birthday celebrations (Maddox 2012). It was also deemed timely to give his museum in London a face-lift, including updating the interpretation given to the collection of artefacts and personal objects on display. The closure of the museum for this purpose over most of the course of the two-hundredth birthday year was however a case of curious timing. Presumably the publicity of the Dickens commemoration would have boosted interest in visiting the museum, resulting in disappointment and lost revenue in the wake of the closure.

Not all restoration or conservation involves built heritage. A community project in Portsmouth, Dickens' birthplace, involved teaching local residents and groups how to use the city archives; in the process enabling them to explore some of the themes inherent in Dickens' novels. Some of this research will eventually contribute to an exhibition on Dickens at the City Museum during his anniversary year. The archives received a grant of £36,000 in 2012 for conservation purposes, which represented a large jump in their usual annual budget of £1,000 – '36 years worth of conservation in one go!' (Dickens Community Archive Project 2011).

Temporary legacies and lost opportunities

The temporary legacies of commemorations are an alternative history that haunt us. The Eiffel Tower so nearly joined their ranks. Some were ahead of their time and their value unrecognised once the commemoration was finished. Take the Skylon, the thin ellipse-like structure that became the symbol of the Festival of Britain. It was proudly proclaimed as purposeless, but paradoxically became a stimulus for creativity: 'This site was created for dreams, for that great intangible useless necessity called Art, as the makers of the Skylon put it' (Festival of Britain 2011: 13). It was unfortunately a reminder of the previous government's role in staging the festival, and thus a political liability for the new Conservative government (Festival of Britain 2011). The Skylon was dismantled and scrapped for metal, and the South Bank Centre flagpole was built on the site where it stood. A commemorative ring has been placed close to the original site (Festival of Britain 2011).

Many structures built for these great exhibitions were designed to be temporary. The Palais des Machines, built of steel for the 1889 event and considered to be 'a celebration of industrialisation' (Johnston 2007: 98), did not survive beyond 1909. Eiffel was determined that the Eiffel Tower would not suffer the same fate. He had negotiated a 20-year license over the tower, during which time he lobbied to keep it as a permanent monument for Paris. It is now unthinkable that it could have been removed, given its iconic status and popularity with visitors. Similarly, the White City was a beautiful and extensive feature of Chicago's 1893 Columbian Exposition, but it was only made of plaster rendered to look like stone and was quickly demolished (Rydell 1984).

Souvenirs and collections

Souvenirs are essentially examples of personal rather than public legacies of commemorative events, although there is a tendency for them to be exhibited as collections, particularly stamps and coins. Some find their way into museum collections, as 'material aspects of myths' (Radley 1990: 52). Souvenirs purchased to remember a trip or to give to friends and relatives back home are part of the tourist experience. In the case of a commemoration, they help to shape and maintain memory of the anniversary, as well as the event itself (Radley 1990).

These souvenirs usually contain a date, as a way to record the anniversary, and are only available for a limited time, to capitalise on interest generated in the lead-up to and during the commemoration. They may represent something which is readily available, but packaged up and promoted specifically for the commemoration, usually with special features. The Jane Austen House Museum produced a commemorative reproduction of the uncorrected copy of the first edition of *Sense and Sensibility* in 2011, to mark the two-hundredth anniversary of its publication. All 500 copies came with a presentation box, a copy of the Austen family seal, a quill pen, a foreword written by Professor Kathryn Sutherland of Oxford University, and a certificate of authenticity.

Commemorative souvenirs are often associated with royal events, such as anniversaries connected with great victories or the accession to the throne. Smith (1996) refers to the myriad of souvenirs which were released to mark Queen Victoria's Diamond Jubilee in 1897, which she argues formed an integral part of the spectacle. Spectators bought special flags and wore red, white and blue clothing. Plates, mugs, spoons and other commemorative crockery and pottery bore Victoria's visage, both as a young monarch of 18 and an elderly widow, as well as her insignia. This showed the queen as a symbol of longevity, as well as a sober and virtuous wife and mother who served her nation amidst personal tragedy. These types of events helped to make souvenirs valuable commodities (Smith 1996). In turn, the existence of souvenirs signified that the event was worthy of being remembered, thus 'bestowing meaning onto the diamond jubilee itself' (Smith 1996: 342). These commemorative souvenirs were based on but also shaped national myths surrounding the sovereign, and by extension the identity of the populace. They allowed ordinary people to engage with the event by bringing a part of it into their homes (Smith 1996).

Their appeal spans the ages. Shakespeare's jubilee spawned collectables made of the ubiquitous mulberry tree, or at least its twin (Deelman 1964). Many people visiting the 1951 Festival of Britain wanted to collect souvenirs, and they were not disappointed. Their range included teapots, ties, books, games, glasses, and pens, as well as luxury foodstuffs such as tins of tea and lollies. These things were not generally available in the shops at that time. Even metal containers such as biscuit tins were rare in this post-war period (Warren 1976). About 3.5 million souvenir guides were sold, which is another popular form of collectable, priced to be affordable by the masses.

Some souvenirs are produced by governments or under their auspices or imprimatur; anxious to mark the occasion with something tangible, meet public demand, and perhaps raise funds to offset the cost of the commemoration. They may license a logo or image and maintain control over what it is applied to and in what circumstances. The Dickens' two-hundredth birthday anniversary saw the production of a new £2 uncirculated and collectable coin by the Royal Mint (RRP £8.50), featuring a portrait of the author's face that was composed of the titles of some of his works. The Queen's Diamond Jubilee was also noteworthy for the number of official souvenirs produced; everything from tea-towels to commemorative plates was available for purchase from the Jubilee website (www.2012queensdiamondjubilee.com). Also sold on stands and shops across London, they were juxtaposed with less decorous offerings, including Union Jack thongs and boxer shorts and bobble-head versions of the Queen waving. Even the Queen herself laughed, during a jubilee engagement at the Fortnum & Mason department store in London, at a commemorative tin of biscuits that played the national anthem (Herald Sun 2012).

Some commemorative souvenirs have clear fund-raising purposes, and organisers may be keen to distance themselves from charges of over-commercialising these occasions. The Dickens centenary celebrations in 1912 saw a series of penny stamps issued by the Dickens Centenary Testimonial Committee, aimed at helping his 'necessitous dependents' once sales exceeded 10 million. While the media criticised this scheme, it was defended by the committee, who saw this as a debt owed to Dickens for the pleasure he had given readers over the years (John 2010a). The commodification of a commemoration was thus parcelled up as a 'financial and moral obligation' (John 2010a: 159). For the hundred-and-fiftieth anniversary of the Melbourne Zoo in 2012, organisers placed 50 painted elephant sculptures around the city. Towards the end of the commemoration, these were auctioned off to raise funds.

Memorials

Memorials can include plaques, statues, fountains, headstones and natural features such as trees, parks and gardens. They serve to make us *reflect* (Donohoe 2002) and may relate to difficult subjects or events. They are thus seen as appropriate forms of legacy for commemorations relating to wars, acts of terrorism or atrocities, and inevitably have a political dimension (Mayo 1988). An 11 September memorial garden has been built in Grosvenor Square in London, in memory of those who died in the attacks on the World Trade Center in New York. It was opened on the second anniversary of the tragedy, and partly borders the United States Embassy. White roses were planted there, echoing the white roses that the families of British victims laid down in front of Westminster Abbey at the memorial service in 2001.

Memorial plaques are generally small, and only visible from close-range. They are thus a more low-key way to mark an anniversary, which might be seen as more appropriate in some circumstances. The five-hundredth anniversary of the arrival of Charles VII in Reims, accompanied by Joan of Arc, is marked by a plaque, perhaps symbolic of the weight given to this historic event by modern generations. Joan's story is perhaps less relevant or passionately remembered in a deeply secular society like France. Some plaques have strong political motives, like the one that graces the hill near Mawson's huts in Antarctica. According to Day (2012: 13), this plaque 'was just the latest piece of political theatre to be staged in Antarctica', and was more about securing territory than celebrating scientific achievement.

Other memorial plaques are the result of the efforts of interested groups or individuals who make it their personal mission to safeguard memory. A series of ten bronze commemorative plaques were unveiled in Gallipoli in 1990, the seventy-fifth anniversary of the ANZAC landings. They were the result of a campaign waged by an Australian dentist, Dr Ross Bastian, who felt that there was a lack of information on the battlefield to mark Australian involvement and casualties. He raised the money privately, as his efforts to secure government funding proved fruitless. This is perhaps surprising, given official interest in maintaining the commemoration of Gallipoli, particularly in connection with the centenary in 2015.

Memorials to those who have fallen in combat and to other victims of tragedy proliferate 50 to 75 years afterward, precisely to replace those who are no longer around to tell the tale. As eyewitnesses to victimhood pass away, we generate a host of surrogate reminders, lest our descendants forget or disown what Auschwitz and Hiroshima, Masada and Port Arthur have meant to our ancestors and ourselves. As Connerton (2009: 27) argues: 'Many memorials are, admittedly, powerful memory places. Yet their effect is more ambiguous than this statement might imply. For the desire to memorialise is precipitated by a fear, a threat, of cultural amnesia'. While the 'Bloody Sunday' marches have been discontinued in Ireland, political and social memory surrounding the tragedy is kept alive by a memorial in Londonderry, which has become known as the 'Martyrs' Memorial' (Conway 2009).

These memorials may provide a site or shrine for events, chiefly services of remembrance. London holds an annual Remembrance Day service on November 11 at the Cenotaph. The Delhi Memorial (India Gate) resembles the French Arc de Triomphe, and commemorates those of the Indian Army who lost their lives in World War One and Third Anglo-Afghan War. It contains the Tomb of the Unknown Soldier and is the site of a parade and ceremony on Republic Day (26 January).

Memorials, like all commemorative legacies, have the potential to be controversial, perhaps more so due to their often difficult subject-matter. Calls by family members of the outlaw Ned Kelly to create a public memorial, now that his remains have been found, have been met with outrage by the descendants of the policemen who were killed, and there is now a dispute between the family and a developer over who has the right to Ned's remains. The place and type of memorial is also subject to contestation. The Lincoln Memorial in Washington is an acknowledgement of the sacralisation of Lincoln, both through his deeds and the tragic manner of his death, which was fuelled by the centennial of his birth in 1909 (Schwartz 1990). The memorial had to be built in a specific location, which would not overshadow, yet would be grandiose enough for a memorial of this importance (Schwartz 1990). Its design had to be heroic, as befits a man raised to the status of a god in the hearts and minds of many Americans (Schwartz 1990).

The winning design for the Vietnam Veterans Memorial was equally deliberate in its imagery and symbolism – two walls, containing the names of those Americans who lost their lives in Vietnam. The addition of the flag and the statue of three soldiers was made in response to public criticism that the memorial was unpatriotic and glossed over the unpopularity of the war itself. The focus on the individuals was seen as obscuring the collective cause of their deaths (Wagner-Pacifici and Schwartz 1991). This structure needed to conform to what we expect of a memorial, demonstrating its powerful symbolic status and the significance and meaning of commemorative legacy in our lives.

11 Why we need commemorative events

They shall not grow old, as we that are left grow old
Age shall not weary them, nor the years condemn
At the going down of the sun and in the morning
We will remember them.

(*For the Fallen*, Laurence Binyon 1914)

It's almost mythical, as when the twin towers came down. I remember thinking then that this was what it must have felt like on the *Titanic*, that this meant that the world was not a safe place any more.

(Actor Linus Roache, reflecting on his role in the television series *Titanic*, quoted in Bunbury 2012: 3)

Remembrance Day, Armistice Day, the eleventh hour, of the eleventh Day, of the eleventh month, all commemorate the end of the war to end all wars. Occurring nearly a century ago, that war is beyond the memory of nearly all of us. It was the beginning of the break-up of the great colonial empires. Over half the world's present countries did not exist at the time. And it was not the war to end all wars. Today, many of the countries are still engaged in military conflicts. How does Remembrance Day, approaching its centenary, fit into our modern world?

As with many commemorative events, the meaning and relevance of Remembrance Day evolves, ebbing and flowing over time, even if the rituals remain static. It is a salutary example of many of the issues relating to commemorative events and what they say about societies. For us, two incidents from Remembrance Day in 2011 illustrate the dynamic nature of commemorative events.

The first involved a major supermarket chain. One of us entered this on 11 November for some routine shopping. A few minutes before 11am, a young employee came over the public address system, announcing that there would soon be a minute's silence. Most loudspeaker announcements are stilted, faltering and clumsy as they stumble over a script and are invariably hard to follow. This one was quite different. Confident, yet solemn, his message was clear and simple. Staff and customers will remember the sacrifice of the armed services. At 11am, while standing in the checkout queue, a minute's silence was observed. All work, all shopping ceased – silence. Perhaps a hundred people came together in the ceremony. For the customers, their participation was unexpected and unplanned. New customers entering the store joined in. No one spoke and no one asked what was happening.

The last two decades has seen a great increase in interest and involvement in War Remembrance Days (Frost *et al.* 2008; Scates 2006). We live in an age of uncertainty and conflict – War in Iraq and Afghanistan, 9/11, terrorist bombings in London, Madrid and Bali, renewed threats of nuclear weapons. These give War Remembrance Days new meanings. The young supermarket employee made no mention of World War One. He was male, perhaps late teens or early twenties, the common age range for young men to be sent off to war. Remembrance Day 2011 was very much about how the sacrifices of armed services personnel is happening now. And, perhaps many of us were also thinking, in the future.

The second incident had occurred the day before and provides a contrasting perspective. We were attending a university seminar on heritage studies. Drinks were being served by a young graduate student press-ganged for the occasion. Standing at the bar, a colleague asked him why he was wearing a red poppy in his lapel. She had seen quite a few people with them and wondered what their significance was. This innocent enquiry reminded us that in a multicultural society there are many who had no knowledge of (or felt no connection to) the traditions and ceremonies of Remembrance Day. It was a salutary reminder of diversity. While it is tempting to think of communal events reinforcing shared memories and identities, it is important to also understand that this sharing is not universal.

The concept of a period of silence is relatively new. It was suggested by journalist Edward Honey in 1919 and adopted for Remembrance Day later that year as two minutes' silence (Nicolson 2009). Before then, commemorations of war tended to focus on victory, as in the nineteenth-century Arc de Triomphe in Paris. World War One saw a change in the nature of war, particularly with mass casualties from attacks on entrenched positions. The high mortality rate among soldiers – both volunteers and conscripts – forced societies to develop new rituals and institutions to remember and reflect.

In this concluding chapter, our aim is to look forward. Commemorative events exist in three time zones. They remember the past, they occur in the present and they contemplate the future. Each individual commemorative event provokes a set of memories and meanings. While we may think of these events as creating and reinforcing collective memories and identities, we also must realise that these are highly contested. Different stakeholders interpret commemorative events differently. Some use them to promote their view, even to impose it upon others, often tied up in the rhetoric of nationalism and authority. Others struggle to maintain an alternative perspective. Others want to forget, and some are indifferent. Over time, this mixed basket of meanings varies, influenced by changes in society, culture and international relations. Some commemorative events fade away, others (like Remembrance Day) are revived, though often with new meanings.

Any attempt to develop a fixed set of reasons why societies value commemorative events is likely to be contested. Good. It is one of the weaknesses of events studies that it has not greatly engaged in debates over the meanings of events. The topic of commemorative events is a good one to utilise to try and redress that imbalance. Accordingly, in this chapter we aim to focus on a few aspects of why commemorative events are relevant to and valued by societies. Throughout this book we have considered key concepts of reconciliation, closure, ritual, festivity, power, conflict, heritage and identities. In this final chapter, we are interested in relating these concepts to changes in meanings and future trends, examining this through a series of key questions. In formulating this series of fundamental concepts and questions, we are conscious of the boundaries we set ourselves. Our aim is not to explain all, but rather to stimulate an ongoing global debate about the meanings of commemorative events in particular and events in general.

An increasing incidence of commemorative events?

It is tempting to postulate that the incidence and importance of commemorative events is increasing in the modern world. In a number of seminar and conference presentations on commemorative events, we have fielded this question from colleagues, who typically cite a growing research literature on memory and commemorations (including Connerton 2009; Gillis 1994; Nora 1989; Scates 2006). Table 11.1 lists a range of commemorative events which occurred in 2011 and 2012. This was the period in which we were writing this book and at times it seemed that each week brought a new commemorative event. Many of these gained detailed media coverage. Does this extensive range of events signify that modern society now has a greater need of commemoration? Did the ills of modernity, such as increasing conflict, alienation and uncertainty, encourage us to increasingly engage in events, rituals and ceremonies which remembered and reflected upon the past?

This may be so, but we are not completely convinced. Strong interest in commemorative events dates back well into history. The Romans developed a calendar which allowed them to celebrate both individual birthdays and the anniversaries of major events (Feeney 2008). Under the pressure of the Counter-Reformation, Elizabethan and Stuart England developed a range of political commemorative events (Cressy 1989). The eighteenth century saw the celebration of Shakespeare's bicentenary (see Chapter 8). Nineteenth-century USA embraced commemorations, which had particular links to World Fairs (McDonald and Méthot 2006). Australians commemorated the 50th anniversary of Federation in 1951 with more gusto than they marked its centenary more recently (Gapps 2009).

The clear evidence is that commemorative events have been with us for a long time. Even their form and the degree of media coverage have changed relatively little. Their longevity points to their important role in satisfying basic human needs. Considering our list of commemorative events from 2011 and 2012, it is striking that there are similar patterns stretching back into history. There are major anniversaries of nationhood, independence days for new countries, anniversaries of battles and wars and commemorations of national heroes ranging from explorers to writers. There are dark commemorative events and light-hearted

Table 11.1 Selected commemorative events in 2011 and 2012

Bicentenary of Mexican Independence

Centenary of the sinking of the *Titanic*

Bicentenary of the birth of Charles Dickens

60th Anniversary (Diamond Jubilee) of the accession to the throne of Queen Elizabeth II

60th Anniversary of the Festival of Britain

Centenary of the establishment of New Delhi as capital of India

Centenary of Roald Amundsen's expedition reaching the South Pole

Centenary of the death of Captain Robert Scott and members of his expedition in Antarctica

Centenary of Mawson Expedition to Antarctica

150th Anniversary of Burke and Wills' expedition to Central Australia

150th Anniversary of a number of American Civil War battles

Bicentenary of Napoleon's Invasion of Russia and his defeat

10th Anniversary of 9/11

70th Anniversary of Pearl Harbour, the Bombing of Darwin, the Fall of Singapore and other World War Two events

1st Anniversary of the Libyan Revolution and other Arab Spring events

30th Anniversary of the Falklands War

1st Anniversary of the Japanese earthquake and tsunami

1st Anniversary of the Christchurch earthquake in New Zealand

150th Anniversary of the Otago gold rush in New Zealand

10th Anniversary of independence for East Timor

80th Anniversary of the opening of the Sydney Harbour Bridge

Centenary of the Calgary Stampede

Launch of 6 April as Waltzing Matilda Day, commemorating first performance of the song on that day in 1895

Centenary of the birth of North Korean leader Kim Il Sung

Centenary of the birth of French photographer Robert Doisneau

1st Anniversary of Norway Massacre

'Strummer of Love' festival, commemorating 10th Anniversary of the death of Joe Strummer, lead singer of the Clash

350th Anniversary of Punch and Judy

50th Anniversary of the death of Marilyn Monroe

60th Anniversary of publication of first James Bond novel and 50th Anniversary of first James Bond film

150th Anniversary of Melbourne Zoo

ones. Commemorations with a strong official imprint are characterised by parades, flag-raisings and solid monuments. Cultural icons, such as James Bond, Marilyn Monroe, Robert Doisneau and the *Titanic* are marked with gallery and museum exhibitions. Some are aimed at local and regional communities, whereas others aspire to attracting tourists. As a group, they form a microcosm of the types and patterns of commemorative events explored throughout this book.

Is there a place for festivity within commemorative events?

While commemorative events emphasise memory and reflection, this may paradoxically be either through solemn ceremony or the use of humour and music. As Falassi (1987) noted, most events have a strong ritual pattern. From at least medieval times these have included rituals of *inversion*, which turn society and its conventions on their head, encouraging mayhem and poking fun at what is usually very serious. Perhaps fantasy and humour are needed to deal with darkness, as in the cases of Halloween, El Día de los Muertos (day of the dead) and the tradition of funeral wakes (Santino 1994). Certainly many commemorative events have elements of the carnivalesque.

This raises issues of how much is too much. When does festivity cross the line into disrespect? Any answer is dependent on the subjectivity of the stakeholder. With varying cultures, traditions, values and level of engagement, judgements may vary widely and be quite conflicting.

In the case of ANZAC Day, commemorated annually on 25 April, there is a long history of debate about appropriate behaviour (Seal, 2004). The most contentious activities undertaken by veterans are drinking and gambling. Given that it is an official public holiday and that it begins with a dawn service, there are arguments about how early it is appropriate to allow the sale of alcohol. Even more problematic has been the gambling game of two-up. In the past, when many forms of gambling were illegal, the authorities tended to turn a 'blind eye' to this, for this one day of the year.

This tolerance has been unevenly codified. In Victoria, two up is only legal on ANZAC Day and may only be played at Returned and Services League (RSL) premises. In New South Wales, it may also be played on Victory in the Pacific Day (15 August) and Remembrance Day (11 November). In Queensland, it is still officially banned.

In recent years, ANZAC Day commemorations at Gallipoli have become much bigger and attracted crowds of predominantly young people. Many of these are backpackers, who include this event as part of a longer stay in Europe. A large number of general tour companies, including the Fanatics and Contiki, either run specific ANZAC tours or incorporate the event in their agendas. Concerns about appropriate behaviour centre on camping out on the battlefield for the dawn service, leading to drinking and a general party atmosphere. The organisers of the ninetieth anniversary in 2005 came in for special criticism for playing pop music videos on a big screen to a crowd of 20,000. The playing of the Bee Gees' 'Staying Alive', particularly raised the ire of critics (Frost *et al.* 2008; Scates 2006).

2012 saw the seventieth anniversary of bombing of Darwin. For the first time, the anniversary was declared a national day of observance. There was a memorial service at the Darwin cenotaph. Survivors were in attendance and interviews with them featured heavily in the media. A re-enactment of the attack featured fly-pasts of planes and modern-day servicemen firing anti-aircraft guns. A new museum was opened. This was the 'Defence of Darwin Experience', which included the immersive 'Bombing of Darwin experience', featuring computer-generated animation reconstructions of the attack. There was a 'black-tie ball', hosted by the Mayor of Darwin. And there was a fashion show.

For the seventieth anniversary, the city of Darwin organised a programme of creative and artistic projects that would remember and reflect upon the attack. One of these artistic projects was a fashion show – 'A minute's warning'. This was designed by Matilda Alegria, a 22-year-old Charles Darwin University fashion-degree graduate.

Alegria's designs were described in an article in the *Age* newspaper as:

> Its pale silk bodice grips … tightly around the ribs and rises in four jagged shards cut to jut sharply away from her body. "That's the ship, the USS Peary," Alegria explains seriously. "It took several direct hits in the air raids, so it's breaking up, it's disappearing beneath the waves" … "The historic detail was very important to me," she says. "I wanted to emphasise that". Somewhere under the billowing skirts of her USS Peary gown, for example, a tiny "266", the number originally painted on the vessel that sank after five direct hits, is secreted between layers of silk. The collection also includes a mini frocklet with stiffened pink and grey silk "flames" leaping from its bodice and shoulders. Another features an exaggerated bell skirt and circular bodice sculpted with boning and red silk to resemble a hybrid of the Japanese flag and a bomber's propeller.
>
> (Breen Burns 2012: 3)

Such an approach at a commemorative event has strong potential to upset some stakeholders. In this case, the media certainly tried to beat up controversy. However, intriguingly this fashion show had the support of key players in the anniversary. In particular, the main veterans group – the Returned and Services League (RSL) – endorsed it. According to RSL spokesperson John Lusk, the Darwin veterans were at first surprised by the proposal. However, as they thought about it, Lusk argues they began to see the merit of this different approach aimed at a younger generation:

> Here is a young person with a completely new idea to show what happened in Darwin. There was no suggestion of her trying to make a mockery and I'm glad that negativity came and went … Some of us oldies could never imagine anything like it. But, we thought, she's showing that terrible time in a different light and a way that will attract a younger person – what the hell, we'll give her a go.
>
> (quoted in Breen Burns 2012: 3)

Can commemorative events change attitudes?

Commemorative events may have negative or positive effects on how different groups within societies interact. On the negative side, commemorative events may reinforce the power of elites and disenfranchise minority groups. They may stir up old wounds and foment prejudice. On the positive side they may be a force for reconciliation, potentially changing attitudes and forging mutual understandings.

A striking example of how commemorative events may change attitudes and encourage tolerance is provided by Robert M. Utley, a senior official and historian with the US National Parks Service. Utley provided an extraordinarily frank foreword to a book on commemorating American battlefields by Linenthal (1991).

Utley recounts his involvement in the centenary of the Battle of Little Bighorn (held in 1976, the year of the US bicentenary). For Utley, this National Park property was:

> the sacred space that stirred the greatest contention ... demands and complaints of the Indian activists, on the one hand, and the Custer loyalists, on the other, cascaded onto my desk in Washington. The entire episode climaxed with painful directness during the centennial ceremonies at the battlefield in 1976, when I contested the speaker's platform with red power champion Russell Means. My speech, which followed Means's incendiary rhetoric, was a plea to ... refrain from perverting history, the battlefield, and the anniversary in the service of modern political and social agendas, however valid the claims.
>
> (Utley 1991: ix)

Here, the National Parks Service official is presenting a common view of how heritage should be interpreted. It is one constantly repeated around the world. Utley and the National Parks Service claim an *orthodox* position and they present themselves as objective and historical. In contrast, Means and other Native Americans are *heretical*, they are 'incendiary', 'perverting history' in 'the service of modern political and social agendas'. Of course, Utley is a member of the dominate elite, Means from a dispossessed minority challenging their hegemony.

Utley justified his position with a very clear statement of the mission of a historian working for the National Parks Service. The two most important objectives were caring for the historic resources and interpreting these for visitors. Beyond that was a contested area:

> A third purpose sometimes intruded, although we tended to resist it. This was commemoration: to memorialize the achievements and sacrifices of the people who acted out the events we were interpreting. Memorialization took many forms, but too often, we thought, it involved homage that approached worship. This we felt to be unhistorical. We favoured education over veneration. We wanted to tell it and show it as it was, as dispassionately and objectively as possible.
>
> (Utley 1991: x)

Having set out the orthodox view of interpretation, Utley then surprisingly revealed that he had modified his views. Academic studies like Linenthal's:

> Suggest our insensitivity to a robust current in American thought. Commemoration has always been a powerful motive, perhaps the most powerful, for preserving historic places ... The custodians of historic places may frown on excesses of commemoration, but this is not likely to change the public's instinct to look on these places as shrines ... The shrine aspect of historic sites ... makes them ideal arenas for ... the struggle over symbolic possession.
>
> (Utley 1991: x)

Reflecting on the case studies in Linenthal's work and his own involvement in commemorative conflicts, Utley went even further:

> First, such struggles are inevitable and should be anticipated. They can even be viewed as healthy symptoms of democracy, demonstrating the depth of public feeling about the nation and its heritage, promoting public discourse on fundamental issues. Second, in such struggles no single point of view should be allowed to prevail. The orthodox and the heretical should have equal access.
>
> (Utley 1991: x)

Can commemorative events help us to forgive and forget? Should they?

The example of Little Bighorn highlights that commemorative events may promote an agenda of understanding and reconciliation between contesting stakeholders. While a worthy objective, it is important to understand that this is not always achievable. Commemorative events may leave some stakeholders still marginalised and seeking revenge. Others may be angry that the rituals of reconciliation are covering up continuing injustices. For example, nineteenth-century Black activist Frederick Douglass was a staunch critic of American Civil War commemorative events. A former slave, Douglass felt that their emphasis on soldiers doing their duty obfuscated the larger issues of racism and slavery (Blight 1989). Similarly, it was announced that the commemorative Bloody Sunday Marches in Northern Ireland would cease, as a UK government enquiry had found that the shooting of protesters in 1972 was unprovoked and illegal (Conway 2009). However, now the march looks set to continue, primarily to exert pressure that criminal charges be laid. Such examples perhaps demonstrate that remembering and reflecting may not lead to closure.

A curious example of reconciliation is the bicentenary of the 1812 war between Britain and the USA. In 2012, Prime Minister David Cameron met with President Barack Obama in Washington. At their press conference, they both referred to this war. Their comments were jokey, perfect fodder for the media contingent.

Lurking behind their quips was a sense of amazement that two such strong allies could ever have been in conflict with each other. The War of Independence is one thing worth commemorating with ceremony, but the 1812 war is seemingly just an historical oddity. For both these leaders it only merits mentioning for the contrast it creates with their long-standing relationship today.

At the tourist town of Niagara-on-the-Lake in Canada, the bicentenary of the 1812 war is a major series of events (see www.visit1812.com and www.1812niagaraonthelake.ca, we are grateful to Ed Booker for bringing this event to our attention). Activities include a son et lumière show, exhibitions, walking tours and re-enactments. It will be interesting to see who it attracts, probably Canadians for whom the war ensured that they would not be subsumed by the USA. However, it is being staged in a well-established destination and the planning is directed towards tourism.

Is there a place for cultural commemorations in an increasingly globalised world?

In an increasingly globalised world, there is a tendency for commemorative events to be staged anywhere in the world where there is interest. The recent bicentenaries of Darwin and Dickens are good examples. In various parts of the world, there were a wide array of events, including exhibitions, conferences, debates, talks and theatrical performances. As figures of global importance, they generated widespread interest.

However, not all cultural commemorative events become global phenomena. Interest may be limited to small pockets of individuals, such as residents of a place associated with a famous person or historical event, or a fan club, association or society. The centenary of *The Wonderful Wizard of Oz* had the advantage of leveraging off not just a well-known and beloved book, but an equally successful film (Littlefield 1964; Nathanson 1991). Nevertheless, commemorative events surrounding this important anniversary were largely confined to the United States. Interestingly, Kansas, the setting for the book, appeared to ignore the event, perhaps because of its unflattering description of the state as 'dreary and gray'. The Library of Congress in Washington staged an exhibition, 'The Wizard of Oz: an American fairytale', which included film memorabilia and costumes, as well as retail products associated with the story, such as toys and games. This was probably the most high-profile event associated with the anniversary. The International Wizard of Oz Club celebrated the centennial with a conference at the University of Indiana in Bloomington in September 2000. The choice of location was motivated by its Lilly Library's extensive Oz collection (Bloomington is also where Baum's niece Dorothy– who provided the name of his fictional heroine – is buried). The university library created its own exhibition, titled 'We're off to see the wizard, the wonderful wizard of Oz, 1900–2000', while the town of Bloomington staged a film festival, 'A tribute to L. Frank Baum' and events at the public library and local county museum, including a Silver Slipper fashion show and a Toto look-alike contest. The North American settings and small scale of the events to mark the anniversary of the book are a noticeable contrast to the film's seventieth anniversary celebrations in 2009, which were spread out over the course of a year and took place in various places around the world. The film was seen as global property, while the book was largely considered to be an American icon and treated as such through its commemorative events. It may also be that the reputation of author L. Frank Baum is at odds with his creation. Writing at the end of the nineteenth century, Baum was an advocate of genocide for Native Americans. Clearly organisers of commemorative events would be worried about such matters coming to the fore, leaving it safer to focus on the later Hollywood movie.

Cultural anniversaries that transcend their country of origin and are replicated across the world might be the result of multiple countries seeking to claim an association, however tenuous, with the giants of cultural history. The two-hundredth anniversary of the birth of Hungarian composer Franz Liszt in 2011 was not centred on a single destination. The town of Bayreuth where he is buried is otherwise famous for its Wagner Festival (Wagner was Liszt's son-in-law), and staged 150 events for the Liszt anniversary under the theme *'Desire for Liszt'*. The Liszt celebrations in Budapest, including an exhibition 'The faces of Liszt' at the Palace of Arts, coincided with Hungary's presidency of the Council of the European Union, giving it a platform to demonstrate its heritage and links with other European countries. Events were also staged in Paris and Weimar, where Liszt had lived and worked. Many countries celebrate Bloomsday (MacCabe 2004; Spangler 2002). This can be attributed, in part, to the movement of the Irish across the globe seeking relief from poverty and famine (Spangler 2002), but is also a consequence of the high regard held for Joyce, as 'one of the great masters of English and the supreme figure of modernism in our language' (Craven 2012: 19), which Priestley (1960: 424) goes so far as to call 'the Joyce cult'.

Some cultural commemorations have little resonance outside their home countries, but have important significance in affirming the cultural dimensions of national identity. An example is the Australian Ballet, which has embarked on a tour to New York, to celebrate its fiftieth anniversary, showcasing an avant-garde version of *Swan Lake* choreographed by Graeme Murphy, as well as some more modern works, including a joint production with indigenous dancers from the Bangarra Dance Theatre. The choice of repertoire is deliberate, which Schofield (2012: 18) describes as a 'metaphor for the company', showing that Australian dance is cutting-edge and culturally diverse. This plays a part in creating a more complex image of the nation, interestingly juxtaposed with an Olympics year. While the tour takes place overseas, the message is directed internally, promoting Australia as a country nurturing creativity and the arts and demonstrating that Australians can match those nations that have been most identified with ballet through their history (France, Russia) in what is acknowledged to be a technically demanding art form.

Parochial interest in cultural commemorative events is supported by the view of a past *golden age*. Such an idea is common to many cultures and dates back to the ancient Greeks (Lane Fox 2009). In many nations, this golden age is heavily mythologised, constructed as a time when society, customs and morals were far better than in the modern world. By gazing backwards at this past, we may be provided with an antidote for the ills of modernity. Our society, as this view sees it, would be much improved if we could return to a simpler, more stable and ordered world. This modern obsession is often linked with snobbery, the valorisation of past social values and even political fundamentalism (Laing and Frost 2012). Cultural commemorative events often trade on this appeal of returning to the past, utilising subjective memories to critique the present.

Accordingly, commemorative events of great figures in literature, music and the arts dwell on their superiority to the present. Even popular culture anniversaries feature this rhetoric; *Sergeant Pepper's* and *Star Wars* are lauded as being far better than anything produced today, despite all our modern technical advances. An interesting example of this attitude popped up in a recent Australian newspaper. The television columnist noted that it was the twentieth anniversary of *The Late Show*, a short-lived, but much loved comedy sketch show. His fond reminisces were tempered by an argument that television comedy had gone backwards from this golden past:

> I do wonder whether it could happen again, a show as wild and ballsy as it was. Would anyone these days be willing to give a timeslot to a bunch of talented young comedians and give them their heads? ... But, they'll never be another *Late Show*. Those two years will stand forever, lightening in a bottle, a milestone that lit up the lives of all who saw it.
>
> (Pobjie 2012: 47)

A research agenda for commemorative events?

The range of ongoing issues regarding commemorative events leads us to put forward a possible research agenda. This is only tentative and is not intended to be prescriptive. Our intention is to simply provide some pointers for future directions. Accordingly, we propose ten key areas requiring further research:

1 Why do some commemorative events fade away, while others are resilient? In some cases, commemorative events have even reappeared after a long hiatus.
2 Are commemorative events just a Western construct with little relevance to other cultures, or is globalisation spreading these rituals and institutions around the world?
3 The tourism nexus needs to be explored further. What are the success factors for attracting tourists via commemorative events?
4 Why has there been a decline of commemorative exhibitions? Are they likely to reappear?
5 What is the role and influence of the media on planning and staging? Will this change with the evolution of new media?
6 Is there a shift to more cultural and commercial commemorations? If so, what is driving this change?

7   Are commemorative events just a medium to reinforce elites? How can they be a force to challenge the status quo and empower marginalised groups?

8   Are there questions of the appropriateness of commemorative event structures and formats? What is causing the shift in emphasis from speeches, parades and flag-raising to pop concerts and fashion shows?

9   Why are re-enactments so popular? What is the appeal of this deep immersion in the past?

10   We need to understand more about the ritual structures of events in general, including how they are used in commemorative events.

Some final words

In this book, our aim was to move beyond individual case studies, towards a more in-depth, thematic examination of commemorative events and their role in society. While covering a wide range of case studies, we are conscious that there are many more examples worthy of consideration. Ours is a subjective selection, very much based on our background and interests. Nonetheless, we feel we have succeeded in identifying the key issues. Hopefully, we will also stimulate other researchers to keep delving into this fascinating area.

In closing, we highlight five major factors which are vital to better understanding commemorative events. First, commemorative events are an important category of events. There has been a tendency to ignore them in typologies and that needs to be redressed. Second, while sometimes being similar in form to other events, commemorations have a special and distinctive function. Their primary role is to encourage society to remember something from the past and how that influences the present and shapes the future. Third, many commemorative events are irregular. Major anniversaries, such as centenaries, are so widely spaced apart in time that this has major implications for their organisation. In essence, they need to be reinvented each time. Fourth, commemorative events are about the heritage and identity of specific communities and societies. They may be of significant value to these groups, but of little interest to others. This disconnection affects the tourism potential of commemorative events and must be considered in planning and bids for funding. Fifth, different stakeholder views of heritage and identity mean that commemorative events may encourage conflict. For some organisers, this may be disruptive and undesirable. However, it must also be understood that conflict may be good for societies. Debate and controversy, arguments about the past and the future, pluralism and provocation – these are all necessary for a healthy community – and commemorative events can help in stimulating these.

References

9/11 Memorial (2012) *National September 11 Memorial and Museum*, The Museum Exhibition Design, www.911memorial.org/museum-exhibition-design-0 (accessed 1 August 2012).

Addley, E. and McDonald, H. (2012) 'Will Titanic Belfast do for the city what the Guggenheim did for Bilbao?' *The Guardian*, 23 March.

Allwood, J. (1977) *The Great Exhibitions*, London: Studio Vista.

Allred, R. (2004) 'Catharsis, revision and re-enactment: Negotiating the meaning of the American Civil War', *Journal of American Culture*, 19(4), 1–13.

Anderson, B. (1983) *Imagined Communities: Reflections on the Origins and Spread of Nationalism*, London and New York: Verso, 2006 edn.

Anderson, B. (1996) 'Report on the sesquicentennial of the Bear Flag Revolt celebration, June 14–15, 1996', *California Historian*, 43(1), p. 10.

Atkinson, D. (2011) 'Titanic Belfast Exhibition to relaunch the capital', *The Telegraph*, 22 December.

Ayers, A. (2004) *The Architecture of Paris*, Stuttgart and London: Edition Axel Menges.

Bakir, A. and Baxter, S. G. (2011) 'Touristic fun: Motivational factors for visiting Legoland Windsor theme park', *Journal of Hospitality Marketing & Management*, 20(3–4), 407–24.

Banham, M. (1976) 'Introduction', in M. Banham and B. Hillier (eds.), *A Tonic to the Nation: The Festival of Britain 1951* (pp. 70–2), London: Thames and Hudson.

Barthes, R. (1979) *The Eiffel Tower and Other Mythologies,* First U.S. edn, New York: Hill and Wang.

Batchelder, A., Rusden, A., Webster, R. and Williams, K. (2002) *The Centenary Test*, Melbourne: Melbourne Cricket Club Library.

BBC News (2007) 'Bands mark Sgt Pepper anniversary', www.news.bbc.co.uk/go/pr/fr/-/2/hi/entertainment/6711385.stm (accessed 24 February 2012).

BBC News (2009) 'What would a real life Barbie look like?' www.news.bbc.co.uk/2/hi/uk_news/magazine/7920962.stm (accessed 22 February 2012).

Beccaloni, G. and Smith, V. S. (2008) 'Celebrations for Darwin downplay Wallace's role', *Nature*, 451 (28 February), 1050.

Beja, M. (1985) 'Synjoysium: An informal history of the international James Joyce symposia', *James Joyce Quarterly*, 22(2), 113–29.

Belk, R. and Costa, J. A. (1998) 'The mountain man myth: a contemporary consuming fantasy', *The Journal of Consumer Research*, 25(3), 218–40.

Bell, D. (2008) 'Destination drinking: Towards a research agenda on alcotourism', *Drugs: Education, Prevention and Policy*, 15(3), 291–304.

Bennett, T. (1992) 'The shaping of things to come: Expo 88', in T. Bennett, P. Buckridge, D. Carter and C. Mercer (eds.), *Celebrating the Nation: A critical study of Australia's Bicentenary* (pp. 123–41), Sydney: Allen and Unwin.

Bennett, T., Buckridge, P., Carter, D. and Mercer, C. (eds.) (1992) *Celebrating the Nation: A critical examination of Australia's Bicentenary*, Sydney: Allen & Unwin.

Bergdoll, B. (2003) *The Eiffel Tower*, New York: Princeton Architectural Press.

Best, G. (2013) 'Dark detours: Celebrity deaths, automobility and place', in L. White and E. Frew (eds.), *Dark Tourism and Place Identity: Marketing, managing and interpreting dark places*, London: Routledge.

Blight, D. W. (1989) 'For something beyond the battlefield: Frederick Douglass and the struggle for the memory of the Civil War', *The Journal of American History*, 75(4), 1156–78.

Bloomberg News (2011) 'Barbie packs her bags as Mattel closes Shanghai dream house', March 7, www.bloomberg.com/news/2011-03-07/barbie-packs-her-bags-as-mattel-closes-shanghai-dream-house.html (accessed 22 February 2012).

Bourdieu, P. (1984) *Distinction: A social critique of the judgement of taste*, Cambridge, MA: Harvard University Press.

Boyer, P. (1996) 'Who's history is it anyway?', in E. Linenthal and T. Engelhardt (eds.), *History Wars: The Enola Gay and other battles for the American past* (pp. 115–39), New York: Henry Holt.

Breen Burns, J. (2012) 'Darwin bombings inspire a woven lesson in history', *The Age*, 18 February, 3.

Broom, G. M. (2009) *Cutlip and Center's Effective Public Relations*, tenth edn, Upper Saddle River, NJ: Prentice Hall.

Brown, S., Kozinets, R.V. and Sherry, J. F. (2003) 'Teaching old brands new tricks: Retro branding and the revival of brand meaning', *Journal of Marketing*, 67, 19–33.

Browne, J. (2008) 'Birthdays to remember', *Nature*, 456, 20 November, 324–5.

Bunbury, S. (2012) 'Thinking of the unsinkable', *The Age*, 12 April, TV section, 3.

Carnegie, E. and McCabe, S, (2008) 'Re-enactment events and tourism: Meaning, authenticity and identity', *Current Issues in Tourism*, 11(4), 349–68.

Carter, R. A. (2000) *Buffalo Bill Cody: The man behind the legend*. New York: Wiley.

Casson, H. (1976) 'Period piece', in M. Banham and B. Hillier (eds.), *A Tonic to the Nation: The Festival of Britain 1951* (pp. 76–81), London: Thames and Hudson.

Cendrowicz, L. (2008) 'Lego celebrates 50 years of building', *Time*, January 28.

Cesarani, D. (2000) 'Seizing the day: Why Britain will benefit from Holocaust Memorial Day', *Patterns of Prejudice*, 34(4), 61–6.

Charters, S. and Pettigrew, S. (2005) 'Is wine consumption an aesthetic experience?', *Journal of Wine Research*, 16(2), 121–36.

Classic & Sports Car (2011) *Classic & Sports Car*, October 2011.

Clydesdale, G. (2006) 'Creativity and competition: The Beatles', *Creativity Research Journal*, 18(2), 129–39.

Cocteau, J. (1936) *Round the World Again in 80 Days*, London and New York: Taurus Parke, 2000 edn.

Collins, A., Hand, C. and Snell, M. C. (2002) 'What makes a blockbuster? Economic analysis of film success in the United Kingdom', *Managerial and Decision Economics*, 23, 343–54.

Conekin, B. E. (2003) *'The Autobiography of a Nation': The 1951 Festival of Britain*, Manchester and New York: Manchester University Press.

Connerton, P. (1989) *How Societies Remember*, Cambridge: Cambridge University Press.

Connerton, P. (2009) *How Modernity Forgets*, Cambridge: Cambridge University Press.

Conway, B. (2009) 'Rethinking difficult pasts: Bloody Sunday (1972) as a case study', *Cultural Sociology*, 3(3), 397–413.

Craik, J. (1992) 'Expo 88: fashions of sight and politics of site', in T. Bennett, P. Buckridge, D. Carter and C. Mercer (eds.), *Celebrating the Nation: A critical study of Australia's Bicentenary* (pp. 142–59), Sydney: Allen and Unwin.

Crang, M. (1996) 'Magic Kingdom or a quixotic quest for authenticity?' *Annals of Tourism Research*, 23 (2), 415–31.

Craven, P. (2012) 'A timeless day in the life of everyman', *The Weekend Australian*, June 16–17, 19.

Cressy, D. (1989) *Bonfires and Bells: National memory and the Protestant calendar in Elizabethan and Stuart England*, Stroud: Sutton, 2004 edn.

Cressy, D. (1994) 'National memory in Early Modern England', in J. R. Gillis (ed.) *Commemorations: The politics of national identity* (pp. 61–73), Princeton: Princeton University Press.

Crisp, J. (1992) 'Past history, present concerns: The Bicentenary of the French Revolution', in T. Bennett, P. Buckridge, D. Carter and C. Mercer (eds.), *Celebrating the Nation: A critical study of Australia's Bicentenary* (pp. 47–65), Sydney: Allen and Unwin.

Crompton, J.L. (2006) 'Economic impact studies: instruments for political shenanigans?' *Journal of Travel Research*, 45(1), 67–82.

Daniels, S. (2006) 'Suburban pastoral: Strawberry Fields forever and Sixties memory', *Cultural Geographies*, 13, 28–54.

Danziger, M. K. (1964) 'Shakespeare in New York', *Shakespeare Quarterly*, 15(4), 419–22.

Darwin, C. (1887) *The Autobiography of Charles Darwin, 1809–1882*, New York: The Norton Library.

Dawkins, R. (2006) *The God Delusion*, London: Bantam Press.

Day, D. (2012) 'Antarctica is no place for politicking', *The Age*, January 19, 13.

Debo, A. (1976) *Geronimo: The man, his time, his place*, Norman and London: University of Oklahoma Press.

Deelman, C. (1964) *The Great Shakespeare Jubilee*, London: Michael Joseph.

Delingpole, J. (2009) 'When Lego lost its head – and how this toy story got its happy ending', *The Daily Mail*, 18 December.

Dickens Community Archive Project (2011) 'A tale of one city', *The Dickens Community Archive Project News*, Issue 1, July 2011.

Dion, D. and Arnould, E. (2011) 'Retail luxury strategy: Assembling charisma through art and magic', *Journal of Retailing*, 87(4), 502–20.

Dittmar, H. and Halliwell, E. (2006) 'Does Barbie make girls want to be thin? The effect of experimental exposure to images of dolls on the body image of 5-to 8-year-old girls', *Developmental Psychology*, 42(2), 283–92.

Dobson, M. (1992) *The Making of the National Poet: Shakespeare, adaptation and authorship, 1660–1769*, Oxford and New York: Oxford University Press.

Domansky, E. (1992) 'Kristallnach, the Holocaust and German unity: The meaning of November 9 as an anniversary in Germany', *History and Memory*, 4(1), 60–94.

Donohoe, J. (2002) 'Dwelling with monuments', *Philosophy & Geography*, 5(2), 235–42.

Donovan, A. and DeBres, K. (2006) 'Foods of freedom: Juneteenth as a culinary tourist attraction', *Tourism Review International*, 9, 379–89.

Douglas-Fairhurst, R. (2011) *Becoming Dickens: The invention of a novelist*, Cambridge, MA and London: Belknap Press.

Dubin, A. (2009) '*A Doll's House*', www.bizbash.com/story_print2.php?id=14819, accessed 22 February 2012.

Edwards, A. W. F. (2011) 'Mathematizing Darwin', *Behavioral Ecology and Sociobiology*, 65, 421–30.

Egan, B. (1976) 'Grotesque to say the least', in M. Banham and B. Hillier (eds.), *A Tonic to the Nation: The Festival of Britain 1951* (pp. 180), London: Thames and Hudson.

Eklund, E. C. (2002) *Steel Town: The Making and Breaking of Port Kembla*, Melbourne: Melbourne University Press.

Elder, C. (2009) 'Colonialism and reenactment television: Imagining and belonging in *Outback House*', in V. Agnew and J. Lamb (eds.) *Settler and Creole Reenactment* (pp. 193–207), Basingstoke: Palgrave Macmillan.

Elliott, M. (2007) *Custerology: The enduring legacy of the Indian wars and George Armstrong Custer*, Chicago, IL and London: University of Chicago Press.

Falassi, A. (1987) 'Festival: definition and morphology', in A. Falassi (ed.), *Time Out of Time: Essays on the Festival* (pp. 1–10), Albuquerque, NM: University of New Mexico Press.

Feaver, W. (1976) 'Festival star', in M. Banham and B. Hillier (eds.), *A Tonic to the Nation: The Festival of Britain 1951* (pp. 40–55), London: Thames and Hudson.

Feeney, D. (2008) *Caesar's Calendar: Ancient time and the beginnings of history*, Berkeley, CA: University of California Press.

Festival of Britain (2011) *Festival of Britain Souvenir Guide*, London: Southbank Centre.

Findling, J. (1994) *Chicago's Great World Fairs*, Manchester and New York: Manchester University Press.

Foote, K. E. (1997) *Shadowed Ground: America's landscapes of violence and tragedy*, Austin, TX: University of Texas Press.

Forty, A. (1976) 'Festival politics', in M. Banham and B. Hillier (eds.), *A Tonic to the Nation: The Festival of Britain 1951* (pp. 26–38), London: Thames and Hudson.

Foulkes, R. (2002) *Performing Shakespeare in an Age of Empire*, Cambridge: Cambridge University Press.

Frew, E. (2012) 'Interpretation of a sensitive heritage site: The Port Arthur Memorial Garden, Tasmania', *International Journal of Heritage Studies*, 18(1), 33–48.

Frew, E. and White, L. (eds.) (2011) *Tourism and National Identities: An international perspective*, London and New York: Routledge.

Frost, W. (2001) 'Golden anniversaries: festival tourism and the 150th Anniversary of the Gold Rushes in California and Victoria', *Pacific Tourism Review*, 5(3/4), 149–58.

Frost, W. (2006) 'Braveheart-ed Ned Kelly: historic films, heritage tourism and destination image', *Tourism Management*, 27(2), 247–254.

Frost, W. (2007) 'Eureka Stockade', in C. Ryan (ed.), *Battlefield Tourism: History, place and identity* (pp. 177–86), Oxford: Elsevier.

Frost, W. (2011) 'Zoos as tourist attractions: Theme parks, protected areas or museums?', in W. Frost (ed.), *Zoos and Tourism: Conservation, Education, Entertainment?* (pp. 121–30), Bristol: Channel View.

Frost, W. (2012) 'Commemorative events and heritage in former capitals: A case study of Melbourne', *Current Issues in Tourism*, 15(1/2), 51–61.

Frost, W. and Hall, C. M. (2009) 'Reinterpreting the creation myth: Yellowstone National Park', in W. Frost and C. M. Hall (eds.), *Tourism and National Parks: International perspectives on development, histories and change* (pp. 16–29), London and New York: Routledge.

Frost, W. and Laing, J. (2011) *Strategic Management of Festivals and Events*, Melbourne: Cengage.

Frost, W., Wheeler, F. and Harvey, M. (2008) 'Commemorative events: Sacrifice, identity and dissonance', in J. Ali-Knight, M. Robertson, A. Fyall and A. Larkins (eds.), *International Perspectives on Festivals and Events: Paradigms of Analysis* (pp. 161–72), London: Academic.

Fuller, L. K. (2004) *National Days/ National Ways: Historical, political and religious celebrations around the world*, Westport, CT: Praeger.

Gapps, S. (2009) '"Blacking up" for the explorers of 1951', in V. Agnew and J. Lamb (eds.) *Settler and Creole Reenactment* (pp. 208–20), Basingstoke: Palgrave Macmillan.

Gapps, S. (2010) 'On being a mobile monument: Historical reenactments and commemoration', in I. McCalman and P. Pickering (eds.) *Historical Reenactment: From realism to affective turn* (pp. 50–62), Basingstoke: Palgrave Macmillan.

Getz, D. (2008) 'Event tourism: Definition, evolution, and research', *Tourism Management*, 29, 403–28.

Gillis, J. R. (1994) 'Memory and identity: The history of a relationship', in J. R. Gillis (ed.), *Commemorations: The politics of national identity* (pp. 3–24), Princeton, NJ: Princeton University Press.

Gold, J. R. and Gold, M. M. (2005) *Cities of Culture: Staging international festivals and the urban Agenda, 1851–2000*, Aldershot: Ashgate.

Goldberg, S. (1999) 'The Enola Gay affair: What evidence counts when we commemorate historical events?', *Osiris*, 14, 176–86.

Greenhalgh, P. (1988) *Ephemeral Vistas: The expositions universelles, great exhibitions and World Fairs, 1851–1939*, Manchester: Manchester University Press.

Guy, K. M. (2007) *When Champagne Became French: Wine and the making of a national identity*, Baltimore, MD and London: John Hopkins University Press.

Haig, M. (2004) *Brand Royalty: How the world's top 100 brands thrive and survive*, London and Sterling, VA: Kogan Page.

Haigh, G. and Frith, D. (2007) *Inside Story: Unlocking Australian cricket's archives*, Melbourne: New Custom & Cricket Australia.

Hall, K. (2004) 'A soldier's body: GI Joe, Hasbro's great American hero, and the symptoms of empire', *Journal of Popular Culture*, 38(1), 34–54.

Han, Y. J., Nunes, J. C. and Drèze, X. (2010) 'Signaling status with luxury goods: The role of brand prominence', *Journal of Marketing*, 74, 15–30.

Harvie, D. I. (2004) *Eiffel: The genius who reinvented himself*, Stroud: Sutton.

Healey, E. (2001) *Emma Darwin: The inspirational wife of a genius*, London: Headline.

Herald Sun (2012) 'Girls' day out', *The Herald Sun*, March 3, 30.

Hewison, R. (1988) 'Great expectations – Hyping heritage', *Tourism Management*, 239–40.

Hill, A. (2011) 'St Paul's Cathedral shines after 15-year restoration', *The Guardian*, June 16.

Hill, J. R. (1984) National festivals, the state and 'Protestant ascendency' in Ireland, 1790-1829. *Irish Historical Studies*, 24(93), 30–51.

Hillier, B. (1976) 'Introduction', in M. Banham and B. Hillier (eds.), *A Tonic to the Nation: The Festival of Britain 1951* (pp. 12–19). London: Thames and Hudson.

Hoctor, M. (2008) 'Mt Kembla Festival has much to dig', *The Illawarra Mercury*, August 4.

Hodgdon, B. (1998) *The Shakespeare Trade: Performances and appropriations*, Philadelphia: University of Pennsylvania Press.

Hoelscher, S. and Alderman, D. H. (2004) 'Memory and place: Geographies of a critical relationship', *Social & Cultural Geography*, 5(3), 347–55.

Hoenselaars, T. and Calvo, C. (2007) 'European Shakespeare on either side of the channel', *Shakespeare*, 3(1), 102–7.

Hoffenberg, P. (2001) *An Empire on Display: English, Indian and Australian exhibitions from the Crystal Palace to the Great War*, Berkeley, CA: University of California Press.

Hogan, M. (1996) 'The Enola Gay controversy: History, memory and the politics of presentation', in M. Hogan (ed.), *Hiroshima in History and Memory* (pp. 200–32), Cambridge: Cambridge University Press.

Holt, D. B. (2004) *How Brands Become Icons: The principles of cultural branding*, Boston, MA: Harvard Business School Press.

Howarth, D. (1977) *1066: The year of the conquest*, London: Penguin, 2002 edn.

Hubbard, P. and Lilley, K. (2000) 'Selling the past: Heritage-tourism and place identity in Stratford-upon-Avon', *Geography*, 85(3), 221–32.

Hunt, S. (2004) 'Acting the part: living history as a serious leisure pursuit', *Leisure Studies*, 23, 4, 387–403.

Hutchinson, J. (1992) 'State festivals, foundation myths and cultural politics in immigrant nations', in T. Bennett, P. Buckridge, D. Carter and C. Mercer (eds.), *Celebrating the Nation: A critical study of Australia's Bicentenary* (pp. 3–25), Sydney: Allen and Unwin.

Huxley, J. (2012) 'Dickens and sons' great, big adventure down under', *The Age*, February 7.

Inglis, I. (2001) 'Nothing you can see that isn't shown: The album covers of the Beatles', *Popular Music*, 20(1), 83–97.

John, J. (2010a) 'Dickens and the heritage industry; or culture and the commodity', in D. Birch and M. Llewellyn (eds.), *Conflict and Difference in Nineteenth-Century Literature* (pp. 157–70), Basingstoke: Palgrave Macmillan.

John, J. (2010b) *Dickens and Mass Culture*, Oxford: Oxford University Press.

Johns, N. and Gyimóthy, S. (2003) 'Postmodern family tourism at Legoland', *Scandinavian Journal of Hospitality and Tourism*, 3(1), 3–23.

Johnston, R. (2007) *Parisian Architecture of the Belle Epoque*, Chichester: Wiley.

Joyce, J. (1922) *Ulysses*, London: The Bodley Head, 1966 edn.

Julien, O. (2008) 'Their production will be second to none: An introduction to Sergeant Pepper', in O. Julien (ed.), *Sgt. Pepper and the Beatles: It was forty years ago today* (pp. 1–9), Aldershot and Burlington, VT: Ashgate.

Kaplan, R. M. (2004) 'Bloomsday 100: The making of a literary legend', *Australasian Psychiatry*, 12(2), 179–82.

King, A. (2010) 'The Afghan War and "postmodern" memory: Commemoration and the dead of Helmand', *The British Journal of Sociology*, 61(1), 1–25.

Knox, D. (2006) 'The sacralised landscapes of Glencoe: From massacre to mass tourism, and back again', *International Journal of Tourism Research*, 8, 185–97.

Kohl, P. R. (1996) 'A splendid time is guaranteed for all: The Beatles as agents of carnival', *Popular Music and Society*, 20(4), 81–8.

Kolchinsky, E. I. (2010) 'The Charles Darwin Anniversary, 2009', *Paleontological Journal*, 44(12), 1467–70.

Kozinets, R. V. (2001) 'Utopian enterprise: Articulating the meanings of *Star Trek*'s culture of consumption', *Journal of Consumer Research*, 28, 67–88.

Laing, J. and Frost, W. (2012) *Books and Travel: Inspirations, quests and transformation*, Bristol: Channel View.

Lane Fox, R. (2009) *Travelling Heroes: Greeks and their myths in the epic age of Homer*, London: Penguin.

Langford, N. P. (1905) *The Discovery of Yellowstone Park: Journal of the Washburn Expedition to the Yellowstone and Firehole Rivers in the year 1870*, Lincoln, NE: University of Nebraska Press, reprinted 1972.

Laws, C. and Ferguson, R. (2009) 'Where mega meets modest: Community events and the making of Canadian national identity', in E. Frew and L. White (eds.), *Tourism and National Identities: An international perspective* (pp. 121–35), London and New York: Routledge.

Lefebvre, H. (1991) *The Production of Space*, Oxford: Blackwell.

Leigh Fermor, P. (1977) *A Time of Gifts*, London: Penguin.

Lennon, J. J. and Foley, M. (2000) *Dark Tourism: The attraction of death and disaster*, London: Cassel.

Levine, M. (2003) *A Branded World: Adventures in public relations and the creation of superbrands*, Hoboken, NJ: Wiley.

Levy, M. (2012) 'How ugly? Federation Square ranked among worst ever', *The Age*, April 4.

Liburd, J. (2008) 'Tourism and the Hans Christian Andersen bicentenary event in Denmark', in J. Ali-Knight, M. Robertson, A. Fyall and A. Larkins (eds.), *International Perspectives on Festivals and Events: Paradigms of analysis* (pp. 41–52), London: Academic.

Linenthal, E. T. (1983) 'Ritual drama at the Little Big Horn: The persistence and transformation of a national symbol', *Journal of the American Academy of Religion*, 51(2), 267–81.

Linenthal, E. T. (1991) *Sacred Ground: Americans and their battlefields*, Urbana and Chicago, IL: University of Illinois Press.

Littlefield, H. M. (1964) 'The Wizard of Oz: Parable on populism', *American Quarterly*, 16(1), 47–58.

Logan, W. and Reeves, K. (2009) 'Introduction: Remembering places of pain and shame', in W. Logan and K. Reeves (eds.), *Places of Pain and Shame: Dealing with 'difficult' heritage* (pp. 1–14), London: Routledge.

Lowenthal, D. (1985) *The Past is a Foreign Country*, Cambridge: Cambridge University Press.

Lowenthal, D. (1998) *The Heritage Crusade and the Spoils of History*, Cambridge: Cambridge University Press.

Lowenthal, D. (2003) 'Tragic traces on the Rhodian shore', *Historic Environment*, 17(1), 3–7.

Loyrette, H. (1985) *Gustave Eiffel*, New York: Rizzoli.

Lucie-Smith, E. (1976) 'On not visiting the Festival of Britain', in M. Banham and B. Hillier (eds.), *A Tonic to the Nation: The Festival of Britain 1951* (p. 189), London: Thames and Hudson.

Lynch, J. (2007) *Becoming Shakespeare*, London: Constable.

MacCabe, C. (2004) 'Bloomsday 2004', *Critical Quarterly*, 46(3), 79–81.

MacDonald, S. (2006) 'Undesirable heritage: Fascist material culture and historical consciousness in Nuremberg', *International Journal of Heritage Studies*, 12(1), 9–28.

Macrone, M. (1993) *Brush Up Your Shakespeare!* New York: Cader.

Maddox, G. (2012) 'It was the best of times', *The Age*, Traveller, February 18, 3.

Magalaner, M. (1953) 'The anti-semitic Limerick incidents and Joyce's Bloomsday', *PMLA*, 68(5), 1219–23.

Maitland, R. and B.W. Ritchie (eds.) (2009) *City Tourism: National capital perspectives*. Wallingford: CABI.

Månsson, M. (2011) 'Media convergence: Tourist attractions in the making', *Tourism Review International*, 15(3), 227–41.

Matei, S. (2004) 'The Romanian Way: from nationalism to privatism', in L. K. Fuller (ed.), *National Days/National Ways: Historical, political and religious celebrations around the world* (pp. 183–96), Westport, CT: Praeger.

Mathieu, C. (1996) 'Exposition Universelle 1889', in P. Green (ed.), *Paris in the Late 19th Century*, Canberra: National Gallery of Australia.

Mayo, J. M. (1988) 'War memorials as political memory', *Geographical Review*, 78(1), 62–75.

McClatchie, S. (2008) 'Götterdämmerung, *Führerdämmerung?' The Opera Quarterly*, 23(2–3), 184–98.

McDonald, T. and Méthot, M. (2006) 'That impulse that bids a people to honour its past: The nature and purpose of centennial celebrations', *International Journal of Heritage Studies* 12 (4), 307–20.

McKercher, B. and du Cros, H. (2002) *Cultural Tourism: The partnership between tourism and cultural heritage management*, New York: Haworth.

McKercher, R. and Ho, P. (2006) 'Assessing the tourism potential of smaller cultural and heritage attractions', *Journal of Sustainable Tourism*, 14(5), 473–88.

McKercher, R., Mei, W. S. and Tse, S. M. (2006) 'Are short duration cultural festivals tourist attractions?' *Journal of Sustainable Tourism* 14(1), 55–66.

Mendelsohn, D. (2012) 'Unsinkable: why we can't let go of the Titanic', *New Yorker*, April, online version www.newyorker.com, 1–12.

Middleton, D. and Edwards, D. (1990) 'Introduction', in D. Middleton and D. Edwards (eds.), *Collective Remembering* (pp. 1–22), London: Sage.

Morris, J. (1992) *Locations*, Oxford and New York: Oxford University Press.

Murray, S. (2005) 'Brand loyalties: Rethinking content within global corporate media', *Media Culture Society*, 27(3), 415–35.

Musa, M. and Oyeleye, A. (2004) 'Nationalism, mass media, and the crisis of national identity in Nigeria', in L. K. Fuller (ed.), *National Days/National Ways: Historical, political and religious celebrations around the world* (pp. 159–76), Westport, CT: Praeger.

Nalçaoglu, H. (2004) 'Nation and celebration: An iconology of the Republic of Turkey', in L. K. Fuller (ed.), *National Days/National Ways: Historical, political and religious celebrations around the world* (pp. 261–84), Westport, CT: Praeger.

Nash, R. (1970) 'The American invention of national parks', *American Quarterly*, 22(3), 726–35.

Nathanson, P. (1991) *Over the Rainbow: The Wizard of Oz as a secular myth of America*, Albany, NY: State University of New York.

National Audit Office (2000) *The Millennium Dome*, London: The Stationery Office.

Nicolson, J. (2009) *The Great Silence: 1918–1920 – Living in the Shadow of the Great War*, London: John Murray.

Nora, P. (1989) 'Between memory and history: *Les lieux de mémoire*', *Representations*, 26, 7–24.

Nora, P. (1996) 'General introduction: Between memory and history', in P. Nora (ed.), *The Realms of Memory: Rethinking the French past* (Vol. 1: Conflicts and Divisions) (pp. 1–20), New York: Columbia University Press.

Norman, P. (2008) *John Lennon: The life*, London: HarperCollins.

O'Connor, J. (1998) 'Questioning our self-congratulations', *Studies: An Irish Quarterly Review*, 87(347), 245–51.

Olsen, D. J. (1986) *The City as a Work of Art: London, Paris, Vienna*, New Haven, CT and London: Yale University.

Orpana, S. (2010) 'Simulacra of social desire: Reflection on collecting and the 'lost toy' archive', *SPECS Journal of Art and Culture*, 3(1), Article 50, http://scholarship.rollins. edu/specs/vol3/iss1/50 (accessed 21 February 2012).

Ozouf, M. (1976) *Festivals and the French Revolution*. Cambridge, MA: Harvard University Press, 1991 edn.

Panayotov, J. (2012) 'Memorial parks to remember the Anzacs', *The Brisbane Times*, April 24.

Paradis, T. (2002) 'The political economy of theme development in small urban places: The case of Roswell, New Mexico', *Tourism Geographies*, 4(1), 22–43.

Pearson, M. and Mullins, P. R. (1999) 'Domesticating Barbie: An archaeology of Barbie material culture and domestic ideology', *International Journal of Historical Archaeology*, 3(4), 225–59.

Pederson, E. L. and Markee, N. L. (1991) 'Fashion dolls: Representations of ideals of beauty', *Perceptual and Motor Skills*, 73, 93–4.

Peers, J. (2004) *The Fashion Doll: From Bébé Jumeau to Barbie*, Oxford and New York: Berg.

Philbrick, N. (2010) *The Last Stand: Custer, Sitting Bull and the Battle of the Little Big Horn*. London: Bodley Head.

Pickett, C. (1998) 'Car fetish', in C. Pickett (ed.) *Cars and Culture: Our driving passions* (pp. 22–41), Sydney: HarperCollins.

Plouviez, C. (1976) 'A minor mannerism in art history', in M. Banham and B. Hillier (eds.), *A Tonic to the Nation: The Festival of Britain 1951* (pp. 165–6), London: Thames and Hudson.

Pobjie, B. (2012) 'Here's to a champagne moment', *The Age*, Life & Style section, 28 July, 47.

Presse News Leipzig (2012) 'Richard Wagner – the most famous Leipzig-born composer', *Presse11/017/05.31*, www.richard-wagner-leipzig.de/en/News_Press/Richard_Wagner_ press_release (accessed 30 April 2012).

Priestley, J. B. (1960) *Literature and Western Man*, Melbourne: Penguin, 1969 edn.

Radley, A. (1990) 'Artefacts, memory and a sense of place', in D. Middleton and D. Edwards (eds.), *Collective Remembering* (pp. 46–59), London: Sage.

Ray, N., McCain, G., Davis, D. and Melin, T. (2006) 'Lewis and Clark and the Corps of Discovery: Re-enactment event tourism as authentic heritage travel', *Leisure Studies*, 25(4), 437–54.

Reijnders, S. (2011) *Places of the Imagination: Media, tourism, culture*, Farnham and Burlington, VT: Ashgate.

Richards, G. and Palmer, R. (2010) *Eventful Cities: Cultural management and urban revitalisation*, Oxford and Burlington, VT: Butterworth-Heinemann.

Riley, T. (1987) 'For the Beatles: Notes on their achievement', *Popular Music*, 6(3), 257–71.

Rivera, L. A. (2008) 'Managing "spoiled" national identity: War, tourism and memory in Croatia', *American Sociological Review*, 73(4), 613–34.

Robertson, D. and Hjuler, P. (2009) 'Innovating a turnaround at LEGO', *Harvard Business Review*, September, 20–1.

Roesch, S. (2009) *The Experiences of Film Location Tourists*, Bristol: Channel View.

Rojek, C. (1993) *Ways of Escape: Modern transformations in leisure and travel*, London: Macmillan.

Rogers, A. (1999) *Barbie Culture*, London and Thousand Oaks CA: Sage.

Russell, A. (1976) 'A broadcasting marathon', in M. Banham and B. Hillier (eds.), *A Tonic to the Nation: The Festival of Britain 1951* (pp. 166–8). London: Thames and Hudson.

Ryan, C. and Cave, J. (2007) 'Cambridge Armistice Day celebrations: making a carnival of war and the reality of play', in C. Ryan (ed.), *Battlefield Tourism: History, place and identity* (pp. 177–86), Oxford: Elsevier.

Rydell, R. W. (1984) *All the World's a Fair: Visions of Empire of American International Expositions, 1876–1916*, Chicago, IL and London: University of Chicago Press.

Rydell, R. W. (1993) *World of Fairs: The century-of-progress expositions*, Chicago, IL and London: University of Chicago Press.

St Onge, T. (1991) 'Canada's 125th Anniversary: an example of public participation', *Journal of Applied Recreation Research,* 16(1): 53–60.

Saito, H. (2006) 'Reiterated commemoration: Hiroshima as national trauma', *Sociological Theory*, 24(4), 353–76.

Santino, J. (1994) 'Introduction: Festivals of death and life', in J. Santino (ed.), *Halloween and Other Festivals of Death and Life* (pp. xi– xxviii), Knoxville, TN: University of Tennessee Press.

Sauter, W. (2009) 'Bloomsday: James Joyce celebrated as theatrical event', *Culture Unbound: Journal of Current Cultural Research*, 1, 469–85.

Scates, B. (2006) *Return to Gallipoli: Walking the battlefields of the Great War*, Cambridge: Cambridge University Press.

Schofield, L. (2012) 'Pointe of order', *Qantas: The Australian Way*, June, 36–42.

Schullery, P. and Whittlesey, L. (2003) *Myth and History in the Creation of Yellowstone National Park*, Lincoln, NE: University of Nebraska Press.

Schwartz, A. (2010) '… Just as it would have been in 1861: Stuttering colonial beginnings in ABC's outback house', in I. McCalman and P. Pickering (eds.) *Historical Reenactment: From realism to affective turn* (pp. 18–38), Basingstoke: Palgrave Macmillan.

Schwartz, B. (1982) 'The social context of commemoration: A study in collective memory', *Social Forces*, 61(2), 374–402.

Schwartz, B. (1990) 'The reconstruction of Abraham Lincoln', in D. Middleton and D. Edwards (eds.), *Collective Remembering* (pp. 81–107), London: Sage.

Schwoeffermann, C. (1994) 'Bonfire Night in Brigus, Newfoundland', in J. Santino (ed.), *Halloween and Other Festivals of Death and Life* (pp. 62–81), Knoxville, TN: University of Tennessee Press.

Scott, D. (2012) 'Last wave on Titanic trail', *The Age*, April 14, 11.

Seal, G. (2004) *Inventing ANZAC: the digger and national mythology*, Brisbane: University of Queensland Press.

Seaton, A. V. (1996) 'Guided by the dark: From thanatopsis to thanatourism', *International Journal of Heritage Studies*, 2(4), 234–44.

Seaton, A. V. (1999) 'War and thanatourism: Waterloo 1815–1914', *Annals of Tourism Research*, 26(1), 130–58.

Shapin, S. (2010) 'The Darwin show', *London Review of Books*, 32(1), 3–9.

Sharpe, J. A. (2005) *Remember, Remember: A cultural history of Guy Fawkes Day*, Cambridge, MA: Harvard University Press.

Shefrin, E. (2004) 'Lord of the Rings, Star Wars and participatory fandom: Mapping new congruencies between the Internet and media entertainment culture', *Critical Studies in Media Communication*, 21(3), 261–81.

Shone, A. and Parry, B. (2010) *Successful Event Management*, Andover: Cengage.

Sider, G. and Smith, G. (1997) 'Introduction', in G. Sider and G. Smith (eds.), *Between History and Histories: The Making of Silences and Commemorations* (pp. 3–28), Toronto: University of Toronto Press.

Smith, A. D. (1991) *National Identity*, London: Penguin.

Smith, T. (1996) 'Almost pathetic ... but also very glorious: The consumer spectacle of the Diamond Jubilee', *Histoire Sociale/Social History*, 29(58), 333–56.

Smocovitis, V. B. (1999) 'The 1959 Darwin centennial celebration in America', *Osiris*, 14, 274–323.

Spangler, M. (2002) 'A fadograph of a yestern scene: Performances promising authenticity in Dublin's Bloomsday', *Text and Performance Quarterly*, 22(2), 120–37.

Spillman, L. (1997) *Nation and Commemoration: Creating national identities in the United States and Australia*, Cambridge: Cambridge University Press.

Stanton, C. (1997) 'Being the elephant: The American Civil War reenacted'. Unpublished MA thesis, Vermont College of Norwich University, USA.

Stebbins, R .A. (1992) *Amateurs, Professionals, and Serious Leisure*, Montreal and Kingston: McGill-Queen's University Press.

Steger, J. (2012) 'Surprise: Callow does Dickens', *The Age*, 23 August 2012, 22.

Stephen, A. (1998) 'Trafficking in cars and women', in C. Pickett (ed.) *Cars and Culture: Our driving passions* (pp. 104–11), Sydney: HarperCollins.

Stern, T. (2004) *Making Shakespeare: From stage to page*, London and New York: Routledge.

Stokes, R. (2007) 'Relationships and networks for shaping events tourism: an Australian study', *Event Management*, 10, 145–58.

Stone, P. R. (2006) 'A dark tourism spectrum: Towards a typology of death and macabre related tourist sites, attractions and exhibitions', *Tourism*, 54(2), 145–60.

Stone, P. and Sharpley, R. (2008) 'Consuming dark tourism: A thanatological perspective', *Annals of Tourism Research*, 35(2), 574–95.

Stott, R. (2012) *Darwin's Ghosts: In search of the first evolutionists*, London: Bloomsbury.

Strange, C. and Kempa, M. (2003) 'Shades of dark tourism: Alcatraz and Robben Island', *Annals of Tourism Research*, 30(2), 386–405.

Strong, R. (1976) 'Prologue: Utopia limited', in M. Banham and B. Hillier (eds.), *A Tonic to the Nation: The Festival of Britain 1951* (pp. 6–9), London: Thames and Hudson.

Takebe, Y. (2010) 'Yokohama's anniversary snafu sparks suits over losses', *The Japan Times Online*, 14 May, www.searchjapantimes.co.

Taylor, G. (1989) *Reinventing Shakespeare: A cultural history, from the Restoration to the present*, New York: Weidenfeld & Nicolson.

Theaker, A. (2008) *The Public Relations Handbook*, (third edn, Abingdon and New York: Routledge,

Tiffin, J. (1999) 'Digitally remythicised: Star Wars, modern popular mythology, and madame and Eve', *Journal of Literary Studies*, 15(1–2), 66–80.

Timothy, D. and Boyd, S. (2004) *Heritage Tourism*, Harlow: Prentice Hall.

Toffoletti, K. (2007) *Cyborgs and Barbie Dolls: Feminism, popular culture and the posthuman body*, London and New York: I. B. Tauris.

Tomalin, C. (2011) *Charles Dickens: A life*, London: Viking.

Tunbridge, J. E. and Ashworth, G. J. (1996) *Dissonant Heritage: The management of the past as a resource in conflict*, Chichester: Wiley.

Turner, F. J. (1894) 'The significance of the frontier in American history', in R. W. Etulain (ed.) *Does the Frontier Experience Make America Exceptional?* (pp. 18–43), Boston and New York: Bedford/St Martin's, 1999.

Turner, R. (1989) 'The play of history: Civil War reenactments and their use of the past', *Folklore Forum*, 22(1/2), 54–61.

Turner, R. (1990) 'Bloodless battles: The Civil War reenacted', *TDR*, 34(4), 123–36.

Turner, V. and Turner, E. (1978) *Image and Pilgrimage in Christian Culture*, New York: Columbia University Press.

Urde, M., Greyser, S. and Balmer, J. M.T . (2007) 'Corporate brands with a heritage', *Brand Management*, 15(1), 4–19.

Urry, J. (2000) *Sociology Beyond Societies: Mobilities for the twenty-first century*, London and New York: Routledge.

Utley, R. M. (1991) 'Foreword', in E. T. Linenthal *Sacred Ground: Americans and their battlefields* (pp. ix–xi), Urbana and Chicago, IL: University of Illinois Press.

Vaget, H. R. (2001) 'Poisoned arrows: Wagner, Hitler, und kein Ende', *Journal of the American Musicological Society*, 54(3), 661–77.

Varaste, C. (2001) 'Top knot', *Barbie Bazaar*, February, 40–5.

Vaux, C. (1865) 'Letter to Frederick Law Olmstead', in V. P. Ranney (ed.) *The Papers of Frederick Law Olmstead: Volume V The California frontier 1863–1865* (pp. 383–90), Baltimore, MD: John Hopkins University Press, 1990.

Wagner-Pacifici, R. and Schwartz, B. (1991) 'The Vietnam Veterans Memorial: Commemorating a difficult past', *American Journal of Sociology*, 97(2), 376–420.

Waitt, G. (2000) 'Consuming heritage: Perceived historical authenticity', *Annals of Tourism Research*, 27(4), 835–62.

Walsh, K. (1992) *The Representation of the Past: Museums and heritage in the postmodern world*, London: Routledge.

Walsh, M. (2011) 'The most beautiful car ever made, E-type at 50: A tribute to an icon', *Classic & Sports Car* magazine, October 11, 4–11.

Walvin, J. (2010) 'What should we do about slavery? Slavery, abolition and public history', in I. McCalman and P. Pickering (eds.) *Historical Reenactment: From realism to affective turn* (pp. 63–78), Basingstoke: Palgrave Macmillan.

Warren, D. E. (1976) 'Souvenirs were snapped up for use', in M. Banham and B. Hillier (eds.), *A Tonic to the Nation: The Festival of Britain 1951* (pp. 188–9), London: Thames and Hudson.

Watson, N. (2006) *The Literary Tourist,* Basingstoke and New York: Palgrave Macmillan.

Weiermair, K. (1998) 'The effect of environmental context and management on the performance characteristics of cultural events: the case of the 700 Year Tyrol exhibition in Stams and Meran', *Festival Management & Event Tourism*, 5 (1/2): 85–92.

Wells, J. (2011) 'Marketing Australia in the 1930s', *The National Library Magazine*, December, 24–27.

Wheeler, F., Laing, J., Frost, L., Reeves, K. and Frost, W. (2011) 'Outlaw nations: tourism, the frontier and national identities', in E. Frew and L. White (eds), *Tourism and National Identities: An International Perspective* (pp. 151–163). London and New York: Routledge.

White, L. K. (2004) 'The Bicentenary of Australia: Celebration of a nation', in L. K. Fuller (ed.), *National Days/National Ways: Historical, political and religious celebrations around the world* (pp. 25–40), Westport, CT: Praeger.

White, R. (1997) 'When Frederick Jackson Turner and Buffalo Bill Cody Both Played Chicago in 1893', in R. W. Etulain (ed.) *Does the Frontier Experience Make America Exceptional?* (pp. 46–57), Boston and New York: Bedford/St Martin's, 1999.

Whitmarsh, A. (2001) 'We will remember them: Memory and commemoration in war museums', *Journal of Conservation and Museum Studies*, 7, http://www.ucl.ac.uk/~ycrnw3c/JCMS/issue7/0111Whitm.pdf

Wienberg, C. (2008) 'Lego marks 50th anniversary with reintroduced building bricks', *Bloomberg*, January 28, http://www.bloomberg.com/apps/news?pid=21070001&sid=a RTBxPQelakk (accessed February 22 2012).

Willard, P., Lade, C. and Frost, W. (2013) 'Darkness beyond memory: The battlefields at Culloden and Little Bighorn', in L. White and E. Frew (eds.), *Dark Tourism and Place Identity: Marketing, managing and interpreting dark places*, London: Routledge.

Williams, D. (2011) 'Jaguar announces celebrations to mark the E-type's 50th anniversary', *The Telegraph*, 25 January.

Williams, N. (2008) 'Building up to the Darwin double', *Current Biology*, 18(5), R182–R183.

Wilmut, R. (1980) *From Fringe to Flying Circus: Celebrating a unique generation of comedy, 1960–1980*, London: Methuen.

Wing, L. (2010) 'Dealing with the past: Shared and contested narratives in "post-conflict" Northern Ireland', *Museum International*, 62(1/2), 31–6.

Witz, L. (2009) 'History below the water line: the making of Apartheid's last festival', in V. Agnew and J. Lamb (eds.) *Settler and Creole Reenactment* (pp. 138–55), Basingstoke: Palgrave Macmillan.

Young, J. E. (1993) *The Texture of Memory: Holocaust memorials and meaning*, New Haven, CT and London: Yale University Press.

Ziakas, V. (2010) 'Understanding an event portfolio: The uncovering of interrelationships, synergies, and leveraging opportunities', *Journal of Policy Research in Tourism, Leisure & Events*, 2(2): 144–64.

Index

9/11 *see* September 11

Alamo, The 37
Alexander, Steve 90, 93–4
American Civil War 7, 21, 25, 32, 37,
    40–4, 78–9, 81, 91–3, 96, 162, 166
American War of Independence 81, 167
Andersen, Hans Christian 7, 13, 25,
    48–9, 51
Anschluss 12, 34
ANZAC Day 7, 13, 35, 38, 163
apartheid 88
Arab Spring 18, 162
Armistice Day *see* Remembrance Day
Australian Bicentennial Authority 10,
    29, 49, 75
autoethnography 98

Ballet, Australian 168
Ballymurphy 152
Baluarte Bicentennial Bridge 147
Barbie 125, 127–30
Bastille Day 17–18, 22, 24, 37
battles 7, 9, 12–13, 22, 24, 37, 40–1,
    43–4, 48, 54–5, 78, 81–2, 87–93,
    97–106, 162, 165–7
Bear Flag Revolt 28–9
Beatles, The 8, 125, 130–3, 140, 148,
    169
Berlin Wall 24–5
Black Saturday 35–6
Bloody Sunday 30, 40, 158, 166
Bloomsday 7–8, 52, 85, 121–3, 149–50,
    168
Bonfire Night *see* Guy Fawkes Night
Bosworth, Battle of 44
Boyne, Battle of the 9, 39
Britain, Battle of 24–5, 81
Buckland Riot 38–9

Buffalo Bill's Wild West Show 44, 72
Bull Run, Battle of 7
Bureau de Expositions 63

Castle Hill, Battle of 81
Centenary Test 14, 84
champagne 134, 137–40
Cocteau, Jean 2, 94
Cody, William 71–2
Columbus, Christopher 25, 28, 64–6, 69
Cook's Cottage 154
Crownation Day 27
Crystal Palace *see* Great Exhibition
Culloden, Battle of 41

Darwin, Bombing of 8, 162, 164
Darwin, Charles 7, 25, 51, 117–20, 167
Dawkins, Richard 118–19
Day of the Dead 34, 163
Declaration of Independence 82
destination marketing 46–61
Diana, Princess 38, 144–8
Dias Bartolomeu 11, 13, 25, 84, 88
diaspora 51
Dickens, Charles 51, 86, 115–17, 146,
    154–7, 162, 167
Disney, Walt 74–5
Douglass, Frederick 43, 166
Dr Who 97, 115

economic impact 50–4, 60
Eiffel Tower 22–4, 67, 75, 141–3, 147,
    155
English Civil War 27
English Heritage 44, 81, 91, 100–1,
    103–4
Enola Gay 36, 43,
ethnic cleansing 45
Eureka Stockade 13, 39, 43, 93

events portfolio 46–8
exhibitions, international 51, 62–77, 141–3, 161
Expo Y 150 55–6

Falassi, A. 3–5, 86–7, 98, 105–7, 163
Federation, Australian 13, 23, 30, 49, 84, 89, 151, 154, 161
Federation Square 36, 130, 151
Festival of Britain 65, 74, 112–15, 149–52, 155–6, 162
First Fleet 10, 18, 25
Flynn, Errol 7, 89, 105
Fourth of July *see* Independence Day
French Revolution 15, 21–4, 26, 64, 82, 141–3, 147, 149–50

Gallipoli 7, 24–5, 38, 157, 163
Geronimo 70–1
Gettysburg, Battle of 7, 12, 44, 78–9, 91–2, 96
Glorious Revolution 12
Gold Rushes 7, 13, 25, 38–9, 49, 51–2, 83, 162
Great Depression 73–4
Great Exhibition 65, 67, 112
Guy Fawkes Night 3–6, 9, 13, 27–8, 34, 48, 106–7

Halloween 3, 5, 34–5, 40, 163
Hastings, Battle of 7, 37, 48, 54–5, 81, 87, 91, 97–106
Hiroshima Day 7, 29, 32, 37
Holocaust, The 38–9, 41–3
House of Terror 45

Independence Day 2, 6, 13, 17–18, 20–1, 23, 26, 37, 53, 67, 91
Isandlawana, Battle of 81

Jaguar, E-Type 134–7
Joyce, James 8, 52, 85, 121–3, 149–50, 168
Juneteenth 32, 39–40

Kelly, Ned 13, 54–5, 83, 94, 158
Kokoda 38
Kristallnacht 41–2

Late Show, The 169
Lego 126–7
Lewis and Clark 13, 47, 51, 64, 69, 84, 152
Lincoln Memorial Highway 147–8

Liszt, Franz 168
Little Bighorn, Battle of 7, 13, 22, 37, 44, 54–5, 81, 88–90, 93–4, 165–6
living history 78–80, 92
Louisiana Purchase 64, 69–70

Man From Snowy River 54, 85, 94
Manifest Destiny 69
Medicine Crow, Joseph 89–90
Merlin 99–101, 104
Millennium Dome 56
Monster Meeting, The 83, 93
Mountain Men Rendezvous 94–5
Mount Kembla 40

Nashville Parthenon 153
Natale di Roma 6, 17
National Parks Service, US 10, 44, 89–92, 165–6
New Delhi 19, 57, 158, 162
Northern Territory 57

Perrier-Jouët 137–40
Petra 57
Pol Pot 41
Port Arthur 33
Presley, Elvis 8, 32–3, 148
Punch and Judy 9, 162

re-enactments 7, 9–11, 36–7, 40–1, 43–4, 51, 78–106, 170
Reims Cathedral 7, 154
Remembrance Day 7, 13, 35, 37, 39, 159–60
replicas 152–3
ritual inversion 3, 5, 86–7, 105, 107, 163
Robinson, Tony 79, 83
Roswell 7, 13, 46, 53–4
Royal Exhibition Building 154

September 11 32, 36, 43, 149, 157, 160, 162
serious leisure 80, 94–5
Shakespeare, William 109–12, 147, 151, 156, 161
slavery, abolition of 13, 32, 36–9
souvenirs 155–7
Spanish Armada, Defeat of 9, 12–13, 24–5, 27
Star Wars 127, 131, 133, 140, 169
stolen generation 7, 30, 45
St Paul's Cathedral 154
Strummer, Joe 38, 162

Talyllyn Heritage Railway 2
thalidomide 44–5
Titanic 8, 25, 38, 42, 57–61, 151–3, 159,
   162
tombstone 37, 54–5, 83
Tour de France 2–3
tourism 15, 20, 31–2, 38, 46–61, 66,
   75–6, 99, 121–2, 167, 169
Turner, Frederick Jackson 71–2

Verne, Jules 2, 62, 94, 141
Veterans Day *see* Remembrance Day
Vietnam Veterans Memorial 144–6, 158

Vinegar Hill, Battle of 13

Wagner, Richard 120–1, 168
Wallace, Alfred Russel 118–19
War of 1812 166–7
Waterloo, Battle of 7, 24, 44, 81
Wilder, Laura Ingalls 82
Wizard of Oz 131, 167–8
world's fairs *see* exhibitions
World Trade Center *see* September 11

Yellowstone National Park 10, 21, 72, 91
Yokohama 55–6, 65, 75